Steve Reeves

Legends Never Die

By
Deborah Reeves Stewart

Copyright © 2014 Deborah Reeves Stewart

All rights reserved

ISBN: 1503006166

ISBN 13: 978-1503006164

FOREWORD

The life of Steve Reeves had three major parts:

First there was Steve Reeves the ultimate, and in my opinion, incomparable world class bodybuilder. He won all the National and International bodybuilding titles without using steroids, artificial enhancers or unethical practices. Steve was hard-working and innovative. His sharp mind and determination mixed workouts with nutrition to create a magnificent male body.

Next there was Steve Reeves the actor who filled our movie theater screens with sensational, larger than life portrayals. He played the lead in fifteen movies including *Hercules, The Thief of Baghdad, Duel of the Titans, Son of Spartacus,* and *Goliath and the Barbarians.* His personal favorite was *Long Ride from Hell* - his only Western

Last there was Steve Reeves the rancher, horse breeder and author. Steve was never deluded about being a great actor. He made movies in order to build a nest egg which enabled him to own and enjoy a couple of ranches back home in the Western United States. Ranching was always his first love and passion. This Steve Reeves was mostly out of the limelight. He spent his time hard at work digging post holes and breeding gaited Morgan horses. This book is about my life with Steve Reeves, the rancher, during the last seven years of his life. It is written from the perspective of a woman who was (and will always be) deeply, madly in love with Steve Reeves

I am writing these memories down now due to concerns that dementia, the disease which has devastated my mother's mind, may be germinating in me. It is a case of "before I forget what I can still remember." I have relied heavily on my personal journals to bring focus to that which the passage of time, my series of small strokes and what might be dementia, has fogged. I do not want the memory of my Stephen (Steve Reeves to millions of fans) to dissolve and become forever lost. He was such a remarkable man. Once I knew him, I would never be the same.

Steve Reeves was more than just an actor with a powerful physique. He was quite brilliant. He would examine a machine, tool or product and then explain how he would change this part or that aspect to improve its function. He used a complex combination of his natural creativity with his work experience and logic to improve the workings or the designs of many things. Experiencing first hand his ability to improve on everything that arrived on the ranch (from a brand-new Featherlite horse trailer to halters and toilet roll holders) made me wish his fans could realize how much more there was to their Steve Reeves. His face, his physique, his movies and his voice were only a small part of the total man. Add to those attributes, among other things, his expert knowledge of physical training and nutrition. His work ethic was unsurpassed and his determination to improve the Morgan horse breed was tragically interrupted.

ACKNOWLEDGMENTS

I would like to personally acknowledge all those who helped Stephen enjoy life on a regular basis. Those people include, first and foremost, Dave Morris, then George and Tuesday Coates, and also George Helmer.

I would also like to acknowledge those who understood that my decision to separate from Stephen just weeks before he died was not made lightly and therefore did not condemn or turn their backs on me: Dave Morris, Russ and Jean Warner, Angie Angiuano, Linda Locklear, Malcom Wyatt, Milton Moore Jr., and the various members of my family.

I need to acknowledge those who encouraged me to write this memoir: my loving husband, Gene Preston Stewart, who passed from this life on January 20, 2014, just shy of fourteen years of blissful marriage; my children, Lynx and Naomi; and my sister-in-law, Joanne, and my brother, Pete. I owe a special thanks to my son's friend, Nanie, who read the first hundred pages of the initial draft of this book and gave me a thumbs-up. I want to thank my old friend, Steven Taylor, who was the first person I ever knew that was a fan of Steve Reeves. He also supported my efforts to share Stephen's and my story. A very special thanks and nod of appreciation needs to be given to my attorney and good friend, Earl W. Husted, who worked tirelessly as my editor and assisted me in preparing and having the book finally published.

Last but certainly not least, I thank God for not giving up on this sometimes dense and headstrong woman.

DEDICATION

I dedicate this book to the God who loves us all, rich and poor, great and small, every flawed one of us. I also dedicate this book to spouses and life partners who endeavor to put their loved one's needs and wants before their own, which is more often than not a difficult path to follow.

Table of Contents

CHAPTER 1 MR. REEVES AND I MEET 7

CHAPTER 2 1993 - A BEGINNING 9

CHAPTER 3 STEVE OFFERS US A PLACE TO STAY 11

CHAPTER 4 OUR RELATIONSHIP CROSSES THAT MAGIC LINE 14

CHAPTER 5 A LITTLE BACKGROUND ON MY PAST 16

CHAPTER 6 LIFE SETTLES INTO A ROUTINE 18

CHAPTER 7 EURO TRIP - FRENCH PRO EVENT 23

CHAPTER 8 BACK HOME AND THEN OFF TO OREGON 25

CHAPTER 9 GRAND OPENING OF GOLD'S GYM IN HAWAII 27

CHAPTER 10 OUR FIRST HOLLYWOOD COLLECTORS SHOW 29

CHAPTER 11 ROUTINE 31

CHAPTER 12 WHAT IF 32

CHAPTER 13 FIRST NOVEMBER AND A DAY IN THE LIFE 33

CHAPTER 14 OUR FIRST DECEMBER TOGETHER 35

CHAPTER 15 NEW YEAR - 1994 38

CHAPTER 16 TENTH ANNUAL AMERICAN CINEMA AWARDS 40

CHAPTER 17 VALENTINE'S DAY, FAN MAIL, MARRIAGE ISSUES 43

CHAPTER 18 TRIP TO LONDON 46

CHAPTER 19 BACK HOME: SEX AND MARRIAGE, ALMOST 48

CHAPTER 20 BREAK UP AND MAKE UP 53

CHAPTER 21 WESTERN FILM CARAVAN IN KNOXVILLE, TENNESSEE 55

CHAPTER 22 LIFE GETS BACK TO "NORMAL" 57

CHAPTER 23 DRIVING TRIP TO MONTANA AND BACK AGAIN 60

CHAPTER 24 BACK HOME 64

CHAPTER 25 GOLD'S GYM EVENT IN OAKLAND 65

CHAPTER 26 BIRTHDAY PARTIES, THE BEST SEX AND A HIGH SCHOOL REUNION 66

CHAPTER 27 MUSCLE BEACH CELEBRATION ACCEPTED AND LONDON DECLINED 71

CHAPTER 28 NEW SCHOOL YEAR; A BLACK HOLE AND NAOMI'S BIRTHDAY 72

CHAPTER 29 JACK LALANNE'S BIRTHDAY PARTY 74

CHAPTER 30 GEORGE HELMER; CARROW'S PRIME RIB DINNER 76

CHAPTER 31 TRIP TO THE EAST COAST 78

CHAPTER 32 OUR SECOND NOVEMBER TOGETHER	81
CHAPTER 33 ACADEMY OF BODYBUILDING AWARDS	85
CHAPTER 34 DECEMBER AND THE SO CAL MOTION PICTURE COUNCIL AWARDS	88
CHAPTER 35 1995 BEGINS	92
CHAPTER 36 "SO-CALLED WIFE"; FAILURE TO LAUNCH	93
CHAPTER 37 VALENTINE'S DAY PROPOSAL	96
CHAPTER 38 RANCHITA PLANS; NO MORE TIERA DEL SOL	98
CHAPTER 39 ANOTHER HOLLYWOOD COLLECTORS SHOW	100
CHAPTER 40 TRIP TO AUSTIN, TEXAS	102
CHAPTER 41 CRITICISMS; DOZER WORK OUT AT RANCHITA	104
CHAPTER 42 STEPHEN'S LAST WILL AND TESTAMENT	105
CHAPTER 43 SOLO TRIP TO ROME	107
CHAPTER 44 NICKNAMES AND IRRITATIONS	108
CHAPTER 45 ONE PROHIBITED SEXUAL FAVOR; SOLO TRIP TO VEGAS	110
CHAPTER 46 TRIPS TO WYOMING AND WASHINGTON STATE	112
CHAPTER 47 PALM SPRINGS; NEW BOOK; RAIN	115
CHAPTER 48 A MISERABLE THANKSGIVING; FAILURE TO LAUNCH, AGAIN	117
CHAPTER 49 NEW YORK EVENT	119
CHAPTER 50 VISIONS OF A DREAM LIFE; YEAR END	121
CHAPTER 51 1996 BEGINS; I MAKE A PROPOSAL	122
CHAPTER 52 VALENTINE'S DAY; BIRTHDAYS; POEMS	123
CHAPTER 53 STEPHEN FULFILLS A PROMISE	126
CHAPTER 54 FUN BREEDING ZEE TO HOPE	127
CHAPTER 55 SOLO TRIP TO MONTANA	128
CHAPTER 56 FRECKLES	129
CHAPTER 57 SIXTH ANNUAL MONTANA GAITED HORSE CELEBRATION	131
CHAPTER 58 ANOTHER WHAT IF	133
CHAPTER 59 THE 50TH ANNIVERSARY OF THE MR. AMERICA CONTEST	134
CHAPTER 60 GLIMPSES OF THE FUTURE; LOSS OF A FAVORITE HORSE	136
CHAPTER 61 WILDFIRE	138
CHAPTER 62 ACAD. OF CINEMA AWARDS; WORLD BODYBUILDING CHAMPIONSHIP	141
CHAPTER 63 A CHRISTMAS SEPARATION	144
CHAPTER 64 1997 BEGINS	146
CHAPTER 65 CONCERN FOR THE FUTURE; A DISPUTED FULL BODY MASSAGE	148

CHAPTER 66 A LITTLE THAW; A BIT OF HEALING	150
CHAPTER 67 ZEE THROWS HERCULES; THE WOUND THAT NEVER WOULD HEAL	152
CHAPTER 68 FIRST WARNING SIGN; CHANGE AND UPGRADES	155
CHAPTER 69 YEAR END	157
CHAPTER 70 1998 BEGINS	158
CHAPTER 71 PASSING ON HIS TRAITS; ANOTHER WARNING SIGN	159
CHAPTER 72 A PICTURE WINDOW FLASH	161
CHAPTER 73 RESTORED PICTURES OF SANDRA; PEPPER TREE NEAR DISASTER	163
CHAPTER 74 FIFTIETH ANNIVERSARY OF THE MR. UNIVERSE CONTEST	165
CHAPTER 75 RETURN TO RANCH ROUTINE; TRAILRIDE; THIRD WARNING SIGN	167
CHAPTER 76 JACUMBA HOT SPRINGS; WORKING OUT	169
CHAPTER 77 CHRISTMAS; YEAR END	171
CHAPTER 78 1999 BEGINS; THE HISTORY BEHIND THE RANCH	172
CHAPTER 79 BROKEN DREAM	174
CHAPTER 80 MORE WARNING SIGNS; SPRING CLEAN-UP	175
CHAPTER 81 INSTRUCTIONS TO MY SUCCESSOR	178
CHAPTER 82 DUNE AND THUNDER; ABSCESS WARNING SIGN	181
CHAPTER 83 TRIP TO MONTANA	183
CHAPTER 84 LIFE ON THE RANCH CONTINUES; WALKER GETS HIS HEAD STUCK	184
CHAPTER 85 A MISUNDERSTANDING OF INTENTION	186
CHAPTER 86 CAPITOL REEF TRAIL RIDE	187
CHAPTER 87 A NEW RENTER AT THE RANCH; THANKSGIVING	189
CHAPTER 88 STEVE REEVES SNEAKS OFF TO VISIT SANDRA	192
CHAPTER 89 YEAR END	195
CHAPTER 90 2000 BEGINS	196
CHAPTER 91 MORE MUSINGS; MORE WARNING SIGNS	197
CHAPTER 92 STEPHEN'S ERROR IN JUDGMENT	199
CHAPTER 93 MY HEALTH ISSUES WORSEN	201
CHAPTER 94 A NEW ARRANGEMENT BETWEEN US	202
CHAPTER 95 THE THORN IN THE SIDE OF HERCULES	203
CHAPTER 96 GENE	204
CHAPTER 97 STEPHEN'S MEDICAL CRISIS BEGINS	205
CHAPTER 98 A MARRIAGE OF NECESSITY	207
CHAPTER 99 STEPHEN'S HEART SOFTENS	209

CHAPTER 100 STEPHEN'S PROGNOSIS	211
CHAPTER 101 STEPHEN'S SURGERY	214
CHAPTER 102 THE PASSING OF A LEGEND	216
CHAPTER 103 MEMORIAL SERVICE	218
CHAPTER 104 THE BATTLE OVER THE ESTATE BEGINS	220
CHAPTER 105 THE WHEREABOUTS OF STEPHEN'S ASHES AND MONTY	222
CHAPTER 106 POST DEATH GRIEF AND AN EPIPHANY	224
CHAPTER 107 EPILOGUE	226
APPENDIX	228

CHAPTER 1
MR. REEVES AND I MEET

I first met Steve ("Hercules") Reeves in 1973 when I was twenty-one years old. My significant other, Larry, and I were living and working as counselors at Ahern Ranches, an organization set up to house, treat and educate disabled boys in Valley Center, California. Someone mentioned in passing that a retired movie star named Steve Reeves owned and lived on the neighboring ranch. I did not think much about it until one day when I observed a handsome stranger riding a very impressive Morgan stallion along the road in front of where I was busy tending my garden. The handsome stranger paused briefly to pass the time of day. He introduced himself as Steve Reeves.

After that chance meeting I occasionally observed Mr. Reeves driving by in his pickup truck on his way into town, sometimes alone and sometimes with his wife, Aline. Other times I saw him riding by on one of his beautiful Morgan horses. On one occasion Mr. Reeves stopped to inquire whether any of the boys living at Ahern Ranches might be allowed to earn some pocket money by mucking out horse stalls and doing other odd chores on his ranch. After checking with the manager of the program I called the telephone number Mr. Reeves had given me. When Aline answered the phone I explained to her who I was, what Mr. Reeves had requested and asked her to let him know that his kind offer had been declined.

A short time later Larry and I married and then moved to Oregon so my husband could finish college. Although we were blessed during that time with two children, Lynx and Naomi, our relationship was rocky at best. Many, many years later, in May of 1987, we returned to north San Diego County in California. We leased a place in Escondido to serve as a rehabilitation home for boys coming out of juvenile hall. Our family moved into a home we rented in Valley Center which happened to be on the northern border of the Reeves ranch. Despite our return to California and the opening of our new business Larry's and my relationship continued to be strained. The possibility of divorce was all too real. A few times a week I enjoyed taking a brisk walk around the neighborhood. I started this exercise program while living in Oregon and enjoyed it even more in the rural town of Valley Center. Every now and then I would come across Mr. Reeves doing one of his famous Power Walks. I would say, "Morning!" as he passed by me. He would either grunt or say nothing at all. I must have really made an impression on him back in 1973.

In October of 1992, I told Larry I wanted a divorce. He begged me to reconsider and promised, if given a second chance, that he would be a better man. The changes I expected Larry to make (and which he agreed to) involved mostly behavior issues: irrational bouts of accusations, threats to kill me, rage at the drop of a hat and violent outbursts at other people (strangers and friends alike). It also involved his smoking pot and drinking too much Wild Turkey. We agreed to a three month trial period and took the time to put my expectations down in writing. The clock was ticking.

Southern California experienced a really wet winter that year. There was flooding in low areas and erosion damage on all the hills. In mid-December, after another night of heavy rain, we woke up with no running water in the house. I called Tom Curran, who was an excellent landlord, about our lack of water. He commiserated but said he could not come out until the next day. It was left up to me to investigate our water problem as Larry had to go to work. I back tracked our water source which I knew ran along the east side of our driveway on the Reeves ranch. Right next to the ranch's rental house on the southwest corner of the ranch property I came across the problem. The land had eroded overnight and fell away from the district water pipe which caused the pipe to crack. I knew my landlord Tom could not come that day and that Larry was on his way to work. Since the water line was on the Reeves property and hoping that pipe also supplied water to the Reeves rental home, I decided to call Mr. Reeves to see if a hired hand could look into it, maybe even dig out the pipe and repair it while I went to work. When I called, Mr. Reeves answered the phone. I had read in 1989 that his wife had died. I introduced myself and stated the problem with the broken pipe and asked if his hired man could turn off the water and figure out if the needed repair was my landlord's responsibility or his. He indicated he would get right on it and for me to call him back when I got off work.

When I called him after work, Mr. Reeves explained that the pipe broke at a point past where his property's water supply branched off. Although the repair work would be the responsibility of my landlord, as a courtesy Mr. Reeves had his worker turn the water off for us. That brief conversation was our first interaction since 1974 (which by the way he had no memory of). After the water pipe incident if I came across Mr. Reeves on one of my morning walks he would smile and answer back to me, "Morning!" Thereafter I found myself comfortable referring to him as "Steve" rather than as "Mr. Reeves".

Stephen on Torrey

CHAPTER 2
1993 - A BEGINNING

The level of stress in my home was at an all-time high. The three month trial period that Larry and I had agreed to back in October was almost over and, as a result, tensions increased and life with my husband became severely strained. As I walked past the rental house on the Reeves ranch one morning, Steve came down the front steps. He stopped and asked me how my dogs and I were doing. I thought at first that he was just being neighborly but his questions became more personal. He was curious about my place of birth, where I grew up and how long I had lived in Valley Center. I could sense his more than neighborly interest in me and I was flattered. I knew next to nothing about him except that he had once been a bodybuilder and then an actor. I knew he owned a really nice ranch that featured Morgan horses. I could hear a flock of chickens and also the cooing of non-native doves when I passed by his property. I surmised from the doves that Steve must have a sentimental side. It is not profitable to be feeding and caring for animals that do not produce - and doves never produce.

On January 18, I told Larry we needed to talk. The conversation was short and sad. He admitted that he had done nothing to address the items on the list which we had prepared three months ago. As far as I was concerned the marriage was over. I moved into Naomi's room with her.

One morning, as I returned from walking our kids to the bus stop, I heard Steve call out to me. He was saddling a horse in front of his barn. He called out, "Hey, do you ride?" As I had been lost in thought about the ending of my marriage I responded somewhat brusquely, "No." Then he asked, "Do you want to learn?" I snapped back at him, "NO!" As soon as the terse and insensitive response was out of my mouth I regretted it. He seemed to shrug it off. Well I hoped so because I did not dare look in his direction. By the time I returned home I had decided to write him a brief apology. I was ashamed of my behavior and felt the need to explain that I was dealing with some serious family issues and was deep in thought at the time. After I wrote the apology to Steve he called and asked a lot of questions about my marriage and the impending divorce. He asked if I would like to have lunch with him. I did. We enjoyed sharing a meal and chatted until it was time for me to walk to the bus stop to meet Naomi. I talked to Steve about my children and how it had been decided that my son Lynx would live with his dad while Naomi would live with me.

Having this beginning of a new relationship was made more intriguing because of Steve's life and history. Who was I to have caught his attention? I was just a regular person who grew up in the small coastal town in San Diego County known as Leucadia. When Steve asked me to lunch and later to take walks with him I was both surprised and excited. Steve and I did not do exciting, romantic things together in those early days. Once he let me tag along on a business appointment. Another time we drove to a one hundred and fifty acre ranch in Boulevard, California that he had purchased and later subdivided. He showed me the part he still held title to and asked my opinion on it as a possible place to build a weekend home, a sort of get away.

Those hours spent with Steve seemed like heaven compared to the endless barrage of wild accusations and threats at home. During one of our conversations, Steve found out that my all-time favorite personal retreat was in an area located in Ranchita, California. I had discovered Old Mine Road in this tiny back country community a year or so before. It reminded me of my aunt's ranch in Campo, California, which was a favorite childhood memory. Imagine my surprise when Steve revealed that he had purchased a five acre parcel of land on Old Mine Road a little more than a year earlier, long before our relationship had started. These stolen hours were not entirely guilt free. Although Larry and I were finished as a married couple I felt guilty about enjoying myself while we were in the midst of working out the details of how to end the marriage.

I came home one day in March and discovered that Larry had moved out. My car and all the furniture were gone and the place was trashed. Naomi and I were living in an empty house with two cats, two parakeets, a six month old German Shepherd and one nearly featherless cockatiel we named Mr. Shivers. We continued to stay in her room although now we both slept on the floor. I spent that night trying to figure out what I needed to do and how to accomplish anything without a car to drive.

CHAPTER 3
STEVE OFFERS US A PLACE TO STAY

I had made arrangements to stay for a while at the home of my dear friend, Linda Locklear, in Valley Center. Unfortunately Larry had nixed that plan by threatening Linda and making it impossible for me to endanger her by staying there. The next day Steve rode his horse by our place and saw the boxes I had packed and the heaps of trash in the cans outside. He stopped his ride long enough to inquire if what he had heard from his hired hand, Juan, was true. Juan told him Larry was loco and not finished with me. So I broke down and shared some of my very personal problems with Steve. It all seemed unreal. After he asked a lot of questions and expressed his sympathy he mounted his horse and rode away. The next day the phone quit working and the electricity went out. I will admit that I was afraid. I had no place to live and a soon to be ex-husband I felt ill equipped to battle.

Naomi and I spent two nights in the dark. Darkness comes early in March, even in Southern California, but it feels extra early and extra dark when you are sitting in an empty home in the dark with your twelve year old daughter. At first I thought that Larry just did not pay the bills but later discovered that he had both services terminated. Naomi went to school as usual but we were getting short on food and I only had about $70 to my name. The nearest food store was about seven miles away and I was carless. The next morning, as I was walking back from dropping Naomi off at the school bus stop, I noticed a pile of cigarette butts outside the front gateway. Someone had been there in the dark watching the house - watching us. It made the hair on my back and arms stand up. Later, when I was out back of the house, I heard someone drive up. I was on edge. I thought briefly about hiding but it was Steve not Larry. My relief showed on my face. He apologized for not coming by the day before and then said, "I've made a decision. You and your daughter will come live at the ranch with me. I don't think you are safe and you can't stay here anyway - you don't even have a car." I showed him the place where someone stood smoking the night before. He took charge of the situation. He asked me if Larry had a gun. When I responded in the affirmative he then said, "The walls of my adobe ranch home are two feet thick and with Juan and I there you two will be safe. We'll put what you've packed in my truck right now and head to my place."

My relief made me dizzy. My gratitude nearly undid me - or maybe it did undo me because I think I was crying as I thanked him over and over. I knew that while it was daytime Larry would be busy at the group home. So we loaded what was ready into his truck and he drove away, I went back into the rental home to finish packing and cleaning. Naomi and I had just been rescued; we were going to be safe. I was only uncertain on one point - what to do with all the animals? As I was walking to meet Naomi at the bus stop a few hours later, Steve was working with a horse south of his barn. He had to have been inspired because he called out to me, "Bring your zoo with you. There is room for another dog and the cats can catch mice in the barn. I haven't had a cat on the place for a long time."

I cannot adequately think of words to describe all that I was feeling. It was a rare euphoria I guess. I was happy handing control over to Steve. I had been tied in knots inside for so long. I knew I was vulnerable but part of me shrugged it off. Naomi and I would have food, a house to call home, at least for now, and protection offered by this kind, kind man. Privately I swore before God that Mr. Steve Reeves would never regret his offer. I promised myself that I would make him happy about our presence in his home, may be even in his life. A woman can aspire and work tirelessly to fulfill such a promise.

Naomi and I settled in a room at the far end of the house from Steve's room. The house felt huge. In the swirling state of mind I was in (or was it my heart?), I became easily confused in that house during those first few days. There was a queen sized bed in our room and the carpet was bright turquoise with green bits in the shag. The room was a corner room and had large windows along two walls and mirrored closet doors on another. I think we were sort of stunned at the good turn our lives had taken.

I do not remember what I made for dinner that first evening. I have been a pretty good cook most of my life so I was not actually worried. I knew I would have to learn Steve's favorites, his preferences and I was eager to learn. Naomi was trying not to make too much noise as we knew Steve was not accustomed to children at all. A home with so many bare walls and tile floors did seem to accentuate noise. No matter how perfect Naomi tried to be it was obvious having a woman and her daughter in his home full time had to be a major adjustment.

Steve and I began spending every waking hour together. We voraciously devoured information about each other. Steve did not mind filling me in on all of his accomplishments and his personal history. He was a sixty-seven year old man with considerable experience. He had seen a lot of the world. We talked nearly non-stop about everything from our personal histories (his was really impressive) to religious beliefs, to dream house locations, to horses. We sat together in the evenings watching television but mostly talking through the programs. Not being a big Steve Reeves fan I was not familiar with much of his bodybuilding or movie past. I vaguely remember seeing a few of his movies when I was growing up and a high school friend, Steven Taylor, had a large photo of Steve Reeves as a bodybuilder on the wall of his bedroom.

When Naomi and I moved to the ranch only Steve and Juan were living there. Steve lived in the adobe ranch house while Juan stayed in what was referred to as the groom's quarters. About a week after we moved in, Juan told Steve he wanted to go home to Mexico. Apparently he had continued to work for Steve after Aline died because he did not want Steve to be alone. With our arrival on the ranch he felt he could go home. Steve was surprised but it occurred to him that Juan was aware that Steve had no immediate family and might have been hoping to inherit a large part of Steve's estate when he died. With Naomi and me in the picture perhaps he felt his chance of inheriting anything was slim to none. At any rate, all the ranch work that had kept two men busy full time now fell on the shoulders of one man, Steve. Naomi helped out to some extent as did Lynx when he visited, but naturally it fell to me to help lift some of the burden.

Steve took me on a short trip to dine at Casa de Zorro in the desert town of Borrego Springs. I remember I wore a fetching little white with black polka dot halter dress. I was looking as good as I get. We went in his vintage Jaguar that had custom plates that read SR JAG3. Steve wore gray slacks and V-neck red sweater. He looked very handsome. I was happy yet nervous and I do not even remember what I ate. While we were sitting across the table from each other, Steve leaned forward as if he wanted to whisper something so I leaned forward to catch what he was about to say. With deft quickness he slipped his hand into my dress, lightly tweaked one nipple and then just as quick pulled his hand out. I gasped - more from the fear of being busted by fellow diners or staff than from the surprise of his actions, but no one seemed to have noticed. Steve's eyes twinkled with mischief and he was grinning from ear to ear.

There was a band playing out on the patio by the pool, so once we were finished with our meal we headed out there. Steve found a chaise lounge for us to relax on. I sat there wrapped in Steve's arms, without a care in the world, listening to the music and daydreamed of someday being married to Steve. All was right in my world. The day before Steve showed me a drawing of a house and garden scene with a sign out front that said Mr. and Mrs. Reeves. As he showed me the drawing he asked me, "How would you like to be Mrs.

Reeves? Some day that could be you and me." It was almost a proposal but not quite. Still, his intention seemed pretty clear. I count that day as among my favorites.

In getting to know each other I did a lot more listening than talking. I learned how his father, Lester Dell Reeves, died when Steve was about twenty-two months old. His father was harvesting hay with a crew of men. The cut and dried hay was being loaded onto a conveyor belt that took the hay up and dropped it into a huge trailer. Pitchforks were used to load the hay from the ground onto the conveyor belt. One of the men on the far side of the harvesting rig accidentally got his pitchfork stuck in the conveyor belt. When the pitchfork reached the top of the conveyor belt it was launched through the air and stabbed Steve's father in the stomach. He was rushed into town but the local doctor, in a drunken stupor, gave Lester coffee to drink and he bled out and died. The townspeople wanted to hang that doctor for allowing Lester to die. Steve loved that part of the story because it indicated just how much his father was loved.

CHAPTER 4
OUR RELATIONSHIP CROSSES THAT MAGIC LINE

One afternoon I was sitting in a chair in the living room. We had been doing our usual getting to know each other talk when he left the living room briefly. When he returned he paused behind my chair then slipped his hand down my scoop necked top. I was both surprised and aroused. He took me by the hand and led me down the hall and around the bend where I had yet to venture. I was not expecting the master bedroom to be as plain and simple as it was. His bed was just a simple mattress and box spring sitting on a metal frame. No headboard, no footboard and no bedspread - just a sheet and a light blanket. There was a large, dark, solid wood dresser and two matching bedside tables with a lamp on each. The walls were white with one Smoke Tree desert scene painting he purchased at a Holiday Inn painting sale. Other than that the walls were bare. The drapes over the large sliding glass door and the one window were from another era as was the royal blue shag carpet. Steve taught me to refer to the curtains as drapes. I thought a cloth or fabric window covering could be called either curtains or drapes. Steve told me he would not buy curtains for his home - only drapes. So drapes they were.

We got to know each other on a very intimate basis. Once we began that part of our relationship it became a huge part of us. Steve had been a widower for almost four years and had gone on only one date before we met and started our relationship. His pent up sexuality came on like a runaway stallion who just found an open mare on his range. We spent a lot of time each day enjoying each other. I asked if anyone, his mother, girlfriends, wives or anyone, had ever called him Stephen. He frowned and said no. Then I asked if he would mind if I did as I had always liked it over Steve. He said he would really like that.

Stephen shared with me his devastation at never having fathered a child or raised a family. This loss was probably his greatest regret. He had been married first in 1955 to the young and beautiful Sandra Smith. He talked about how he arranged to take a few days leave of absence from his acting career in New York City in order to travel to Southern California to marry his Sandra. Shortly after the marriage ceremony he had to fly back to New York. He and Sandra decided to delay parenthood until he got on his feet. He said Sandra was a dancer with great legs and he was crazy about her. He told me they had made plans to run a gym and that he would work at his acting too. Their plan was to work hard, save money and then buy land in Brazil and raise horses. At one point they moved to Miami and he did own a gym but something went wrong with their relationship. Shortly thereafter they divorced. Stephen felt a lot of regret about losing Sandra. I could hear it in his voice and see it in his beautiful eyes as he shared those memories. His voice always softened when he spoke of Sandra.

When Stephen spoke of his second wife, Aline, which he did a lot of course as they shared some thirty years before she died, his voice was entirely different. We went once to her graveside and he told me he had gone there every month since her death. While we were there he spoke to her in the way a lot of people do. He told her he was moving on now and that he was not coming back. Aline could speak seven languages. I speak English and know a phrase here and there in Spanish but that is about it so far as languages are concerned. She had her juris doctorate degree and practiced law. I have a two year Associate's degree in general education. Aline was Stephen's agent when he was acting in Europe. She was also what is known as a "procurer" in the movie industry. She would find out what a studio needed for an upcoming production and then with her language skills, her legal background and her unmatched network of connections she would fulfill those needs. Her duties could entail procuring anything from a ship, to a herd of cattle or permission to use a certain castle for scenes. She had been part of the Polish aristocracy, a princess of sorts, whose family had been forced to leave their homeland and run for their lives as a result of a change in regime. She had been a political prisoner of war in Poland just after World War II. She and some of her surviving family later escaped to England. For a long time I felt that I would never measure up to Aline.

CHAPTER 5
A LITTLE BACKGROUND ON MY PAST

I was born in San Diego California on June 14, 1951, to an English war bride, Audrey (Jane to her friends) and George (Gene to his friends) Engelhorn. I grew up with an older brother, David, and a younger brother, Peter. We moved to the coastal town of Leucadia, California when I was eight years old. My father was a fine man who taught school. He was quiet, unassuming, had a high moral character and a wonderful sense of humor. He never had much money but he created his dream houses out of balsa wood and little handmade furnishings and gardens. One was an A-frame cabin and the other a futuristic home under a climate controlling clear dome. My mother was the perfect partner for my father. She was often found dancing with her broom and leaping around the living room when music was playing. She scrimped and saved as best she could, sewing shirts for dad and dresses for me when I was young. I remember her baking. I remember her painting with oils and I remember her laughing.

When I was twelve years old my father took my friend Michael and me to the beach across the street from our home. Unlike most beaches in southern California, this beach was isolated and rarely used due to the difficulty involved in scrambling down a forbidding cliff in order to reach the water. A few local surfers had learned the trick of getting down the cliff's face as had some of the residents who lived close by. Michael and I went in for a dip while my dad lay on his towel reading his favorite book. At one point Michael, who was a good swimmer, went further out and coaxed me to join him. Our family rule was simple: without an adult with me I could not go into the water past my waist. I hesitated briefly then succumbed to Michael's taunts. No sooner had I broken the rule then I slipped into a deep hole in the ocean floor. I came up sputtering with kelp entangled around one leg. I was trying to kick it off when I realized I could not touch the bottom. It was a struggle to stay on the surface because I was not much of a swimmer. To make matters worse I was quickly being pulled farther out into the ocean. Michael's face was full of fear for me. I panicked and screamed for my daddy! My dad heard my screams and immediately came to my aid. My dad put his arm around me and started swimming towards the shore. However, we were caught in a rip current and were both being sucked farther and farther out to sea. We were ignorant about riptides back then and fought against the current until even my father was exhausted. I remember my dad speaking strange words to me. He said, "Your mother will be okay. We have insurance." I did not understand. Twelve year old me was irritated because we were fighting for our lives and all my dad was thinking about was mom.

A moment later I could not find him on the surface, I went underwater and saw my daddy with his eyes open, sort of drifting down. As I watched, the contents of his stomach came out of his mouth and I died inside. I fought my way to the surface, gulped air and went back down to retrieve my daddy. In my youthful innocence all I was thinking is you cannot have a funeral if you do not have a body. I was able to bring his body back to the surface but all I could do was hold on to his wrist, tread water and catch a gulp of air when I could. It seemed so hopeless and I was so tired. Michael, in the meantime, had made it back to shore. Realizing that we were in trouble he climbed back up the cliff and went to call for help.

Sometime later I became aware that I could hear waves crashing. I turned my head, looked and realized I could see the beach. A surge of strength came back into me as I fought to move us toward the shore. A few minutes later I saw a local surfer, Richard Zinneger, running through the surf toward us. I was dazed but I knew who he was and thought maybe I was going to live after all. God brought me full circle. When Richard grabbed me I accidentally dropped my daddy's wrist. I panicked and screamed, "My dad, we have to get my dad!" Richard assumed my dad was drowned and still somewhere out in the ocean. He said regretfully, "He's gone." I struggled from his grasp and said, "No! he's right there in that wave - I just dropped his hand!" Then he saw my dad's arm flip up as a wave came in and he dove for him. As soon as I saw Richard had my dad's body I turned and stumbled for the beach.

It is believed that we were in the water for about an hour. Richard and another man attempted to revive my dad to no avail. I am not sure whether Richard was at the beach by some coincidence (as it was one of his preferred places to surf) or if he got the word somehow. I remember that paramedics arrived and that my mother came and watched them try to save her husband. She was thirty-four years old at the time and my dad was thirty-eight. Later, as we climbed back up the cliff to the road, I heard a hair-raising wail that turned into a long, high pitched scream. It was my very civilized English mother emitting a primal call. I will never forget it.

CHAPTER 6
LIFE SETTLES INTO A ROUTINE

As Stephen and I grew closer I was full of high hopes that even though we did not see eye to eye on some things he might find he could not help but love me. I believe great love is often conceived with a decision. I concentrated on his good qualities and heck there were tons of them. I decided to devote my time, thoughts, prayers, imagination and affection to making Stephen happy and safe. Sure seemed like a good goal. And so it began.

Naomi was such a charming child. She was bright, funny, loved animals and was always polite around adults. She was Stephen's first experience with children in his household. At first he was puzzled by her because he did not realize that she was already what he called "a real person". I am not entirely sure what he meant by that but I felt certain that he would come to love her in time. How could he not? Typical mom!

The first problem in our relationship evolved around the fact that everything belonged to Stephen and we were entirely dependent on his generosity. That included personal effects in his home which he said we could not begin to understand the value of. So we lived in fear we might break, scratch or chip something we could never afford to fix or replace. While sweeping the dining room floor one day Naomi's broom handle hit a silver pitcher and knocked it off the silver cart and onto the Italian tile floor. The impact did not chip the Italian tile but did break a fancy leg off of the pitcher. I quickly found some superglue and reattached the little leg to the pitcher just as Stephen came back in from the barn. As soon as Stephen went back outside I got out the Yellow Pages. I made a few calls before I found a silversmith that could repair the pitcher. Then I started to save a little bit of the grocery money every week until I had enough to pay for the repairs. Once I had everything taken care of I explained to Stephen what happened and showed him the pitcher. He asked why I had not brought the matter to his attention earlier. He said, "It's not like I am some sort of a tyrant." When he saw the look on my face, he continued, "Well, not that much of a tyrant." As a term of endearment I often thereafter referred to Stephen as "my dearest Lord Tyrant" or "my Lord Tyrant", depending on my mood and the circumstances.

When Naomi and I became part of the ranch household we also became part of the ranch staff as I have said. My mornings began as early as 4:30 a.m. so that there was time for personal hygiene and ranch chores before starting an exercise program with Stephen. We always commenced a Power Walk when it was just starting to get light regardless of the time of year. Afterwards we headed to the ranch's gym where I usually worked out for forty-five minutes, five days a week. Stephen continued his work out after I was gone. He established for me a customized workout program to sculpt and strengthen my body. He varied his own workout depending on the day of the week. Some were leg days. Other days he concentrated on torso, arms and shoulders, but he worked all parts of his body to some degree every workout. He modified my workout program as my body developed.

After my workout I would feed Daisy (our goat), Stephen's two white doves, Mr. Shivers, my parakeets and the chickens. After that I collected eggs and picked oranges for juice. Stephen would head out to a custom built rack located near the pool, against one wall of the house. He would place custom created wrist wraps on each hand then suspend himself from the hand bars. His own weight would stretch his muscles, ligaments and the tendons of his shoulders. He did this rather painful routine in order to improve the range of motion and limberness in his left shoulder. During production of one of his movies in Europe some thirty years ago he crashed at high speed while doing a chariot scene and severely injured his shoulder. Although he had surgery and had consulted with many specialists, he was still trying to rehabilitate that painful shoulder. After his stretch he put on a weight belt and entered into the unheated pool to do water exercises. He did these exercises year round come rain or shine.

After I was done with my chores and juicing, I would usually eat breakfast while waiting for Stephen. Like clockwork he would dry off, come into the kitchen and make his Power Drink which he consumed five days a week unless we were traveling. His Power Drink included, among other ingredients, fresh squeezed orange juice, a banana, wheat germ, Knox gelatin, bee pollen and raw eggs. He was a big believer in supplements. He regularly took high potency B complex, zinc, kelp, calcium and ginkgo biloba. He also took lysine to help him better absorb the protein in the Knox gelatin. In my mind, my chores on the ranch had two primary purposes; first, to help offset what we cost Stephen; and, second, to render assistance to Stephen where Juan's absence left a void. To be honest, in my heart of hearts I was hoping that Stephen would learn to love me. In addition to my ranch chores I also did all the wifely housework sort of duties such as darning his wool socks (which he always called stockings!) while we watched his favorite programs on television such as *Lawrence Welk*, *JAG* or *Dr. Quinn Medicine Woman*. Stephen occasionally took over the kitchen from me and cooked for us which was real nice. I also handled the office related work such as correspondence and answering the phone. Outdoors I helped with the horses, cleaned Daisy's pen and the chicken coop, and cared for the landscaping and the gardens.

As a horse breeder and rancher Stephen's responsibilities seemed endless. We did however take a siesta after lunch almost every day. Our nap was such a luxury to me. I appreciated all the blessings living with Stephen bestowed on us but my favorite was having the time and the luxury to take a long, restful nap right in the middle of the workday. Stephen developed the habit of taking siestas while he was in Spain and Italy during his movie years. And boy was I grateful!

Running a ranch requires a wide variety of skills and experience. Stephen handled the feeding, training, grooming, doctoring, cleaning up after and breeding his beautiful Morgan horses. He was often found working on his Miley horse trailer, or the ranch fences, or the orange and avocado groves. He also was in charge of irrigating the pastures which was a labor intensive effort because the water lines had to regularly be disconnected, moved and reconnected in order to cover the entire area. I was beside him for much of his work and I learned a lot. We led a good, busy, hard-working life.

Stephen introduced me to hot spring spas in Southern California. The ones that we went to early on were Agua Caliente and Murrieta Hot Springs. Later we went to Glen Ivy and the hot springs in Jacumba. Stephen also began teaching me to ride a horse. I had only ridden bareback before that. He instructed me on proper posture, how to keep my heels down and out, how to hold the reins properly and how to guide my mount with pressure from my legs. I learned that he had become a Master Horseman under the tutelage of masters in Spain and Portugal. I was always discovering new talents and learned skills that were part of who this complete man had become. Movies and body building were what he was famous for but there was so much more to Steve Reeves.

His desire to keep his body in great shape led to excellence in the bedroom as well. We participated in amorous contact three or four times a day. We culminated each intimate contact by bringing Stephen to a climax when and if he elected to take it that far. At first he opted to climax only a few times a week but he later increased his routine to once a day. Mind you, the man was sixty-seven years old when we started out! I just could not believe it. Being Stephen he set up a schedule of sorts for sexual encounters. He preferred a lot of visual and oral stimulation. The general schedule started with oral stimulation every morning which we called a wake-up episode. We came back after our workout fairly often for another short interlude. Our next appointment was at the beginning of our afternoon siesta and our final amorous contact would be at bedtime. We referred to our sexual contacts as interludes, episodes, sessions etc. Stephen enjoyed exercising that part of his anatomy since it had been fairly dormant after Aline died. Porn had kept him from being completely inactive but he was concerned about the effects of sexual inactivity for extended periods of time. I was happy to do my part in his sexual study.

At the end of April I could see that Stephen was trying to be really giving and parent-like toward Lynx. One time he had Lynx help him move the television and VCR from our room to Lynx's room because Lynx's friend Eric Woods was coming to spend the night. Stephen then made a joke about our honeymoon being over and our marriage begun. I must say that sounded real nice to me. A day or so later though, while in the midst of one of our sexual interludes, Stephen criticized me so harshly that I quit what I was doing, jumped off the bed, grabbed my clothes and said between clenched teeth, "Suck your own damn cock!" I went outside and began raking out the dove enclosure. Sometime later Stephen came out to where I was working and apologized. He said he had been looking everywhere for me - the closets, the rooms, the barn and even the horse trailer (what funny places he thought I might be). I would like to share a few odd tidbits about Stephen and his habits that I learned during my time with him:

> 1. He did not leave the lid off the toothpaste but he did always keep two toothbrushes. The blue one he used in the morning and the red one he used right before going to bed for the night.
>
> 2. He insisted on always starting with a dry toothbrush - no water - he hated soggy toothbrushes. He also never rinsed his mouth out with water after brushing his teeth. He just spit out the residue when he was done brushing.
>
> 3. When we would return from a trip into town Stephen would often step over by the lime tree next to the garage to relieve himself. Mr. Shivers, who was in a nearby bird cage, would let out a distinct wolf whistle. We joked that it was at the sight of Stephen's magnificent manhood.
>
> 4. Stephen recycled empty food cans by using them for measuring horse and chicken feed. He used empty horse feed bags and saw dust bags as trash bags. He stored all of his business files in Milk Bone Biscuit boxes.

I think it can safely be said that Stephen and I brought out the adventurous sexual side in each other. We were not afraid to experiment or to do daring acts in unusual places or at unusual times. We lost our inhibitions and some might say our common sense in that regard. We had a grand time having unexpected interludes full of fun and passion. However, outside of sex I found that Stephen had most tasks, methods and directions down to a rigid science. It seemed he had come up with a working formula for pretty much everything he did. At the age of forty-one I was still quite happy to try out different methods of doing things or different ways to get from point A to point B. I found Stephen's penchant for having a fixed system for doing a task to be aggravating at times. He knew the best way to do anything and everything. He insisted that everyone around him do things exactly how he had everything worked out. He was brilliant and he saw no reason to waste time doing things in less than the most economical fashion. I understood his perspective but being an adult I had my own way of accomplishing many daily tasks. We clashed sometimes when he acted as if his way was the only way. I held my tongue a million or more times in order to keep the peace. You can imagine that my children were annoyed at his insistence that they do everything his way. I will admit that Stephen more often than not had the best way already figured out. But it was hard to always accept that fact at face value and express gratitude for his superior knowledge.

Life moved on and we were about to host our first foreign visitor, Giuseppe Alletto, from Italy, and his New Yorker nephew, John, who came along to interpret. Giuseppe is the president of the Italian Steve Reeves Fan Club. He was really excited to be visiting with Stephen and spending an afternoon in his home. He was a charming man who would later become a friend of mine. His nephew did a great job of interpreting and took many photos and videos of their visit. We spent time talking in the house as well as giving them a tour of the ranch. Stephen learned to speak Italian quite well during his movie making days in Italy. But that was a long time ago. Since retiring to his ranch he had largely dealt with migrant workers and other Spanish-speaking locals. So although Stephen understood some of Giuseppe's dialogue, communicating in Italian was difficult at best. He found himself occasionally speaking Spanish while trying to ask a question or answer one from Giuseppe. All in all I think it was a very good visit and Stephen seemed pleased.

Near the end of May, Stephen, Lynx, Naomi and I went to my brother David's home for dinner. It was our first visit as a couple to any of my extended family. I have to admit I was a bit tense at first. David's wife, Joanne, made enchiladas, rice and salad, and provided chips with salsa. Everything was really good but we all liked the enchiladas in particular. Joanne enjoyed getting to know Stephen a little bit. Lynx said he counted one hundred and one leg reps that morning when Stephen was lifting 480 pounds on the press. Everyone could tell Lynx was impressed.

In early June we received word from Josette Rauch that a bodybuilding event was being planned in France and they wanted Stephen to attend as their guest of honor. Stephen indicated he was interested if certain conditions were met. Those conditions included airfare, land transportation in France with a driver who spoke English, all meals and lodging for two. Stephen was trying to get my body into shape for our trip to France. My butt and boobs had shrunk with age and consistent dieting. Trying to tone muscles was our endeavor. So I was giving my workout sessions my total effort and Stephen was my guide.

On June 14, I turned forty-two. I awoke to find a lovely card and a present from Stephen on the counter in our bathroom. I was well aware just how lucky I was. Later in the week Stephen slipped and referred to me as his wife which enveloped me in a wave of pleasure. The next day, while I was making lunch for us, he came through the house feeling hot and sweaty. He stripped off his clothes and jumped into the pool to cool off. I could not help myself. I stripped naked there in the kitchen and, while his back was turned, I joined him in the pool. I liked to see him smile, to feel him smile. We enjoyed our little episodes in the car, truck, theaters, swimming pool, groves and desert. We were grateful that God created sex and we made full use of our imaginations.

We were invited to a birthday party for Tom Lincir aboard the yacht Crystal. I had never been on a yacht until then. There were three main decks on the yacht. We explored each deck and decided upon a rendezvous spot for later interlude use. That evening I met Bob and Madeleine Delmontique, I liked Madeleine a lot, right off. I was also introduced to Vic Boft who had known Stephen quite a while. Later I met Joe Marino, George Eiferman and his charming wife Gerrie who were newlyweds. Actually I think I met George earlier but this event was the first time I really got to talk to him. He was happy to share funny stories about his and Stephen's youthful exploits together. George, like Stephen had been involved in early bodybuilding. Tom, whose birthday we were celebrating, owned a company that made weightlifting equipment. At one point an airplane flew over with a banner that read "Happy Birthday Tom!" It was on this yacht that I finally met Stephen's favorite photographer from his bodybuilding days, Mr. Russ Warner. Sometime later we snuck away to our previously ordained rendezvous spot - a private cabin. When we reappeared about half an hour later Bob Delmontique asked why Stephen was perspiring so much. We just smiled to ourselves.

Back on the ranch we were anticipating the birth of a special foal. Our newest mare called Sugarfoot, a rare single footing or gaited Morgan, was due to give birth soon. It was with real excitement that all of us awaited that event. Stephen had studied the lineage of dozens of possible breeding mares. He spent hours checking and cross-referencing the bloodlines and characteristics of each potential mare. Sugarfoot was the chosen one. On the morning of June 29 I discovered a new colt next to our Sugarfoot as well as two very curious coyotes. I hollered to Naomi to run out and chase off the coyotes while I ran to get Stephen. What a great morning! Before our walk Stephen thoroughly examined the new foal and put bluecoat medication on his umbilical stump to ward off infection. Our habit had always been to say prayers before we slept at night.

This morning one of our prayers had been answered. Stephen named the colt Traveling Man or Traveler for short.

When July arrived I decided that I needed to find a job so I could have an income. It plagued me to always be so needy and I did not like never having money to buy my children things. I began looking for part-time work that would not interfere with my ranch and household responsibilities. I applied at motels for evening desk clerk positions. I checked out evening relief work at care facilities. When I was offered a night position at the Howard Johnson Inn in Escondido I was really pleased but Stephen was not happy. He said he needed me full time at the ranch. He did not want me to be down in Escondido during the evenings or any other time. I was at a loss as to how to handle the situation.

One day that July Stephen and I were speaking of the very unlikely possibility of parenting a child together. He said that I was the only mother he had ever made love to. To him I was sort of a proven mare in this horseman's world. He liked to refer to me affectionately as his Palomino. Good thing I love animals so much. Anyway we were again discussing the subject of parenting a child when I said I would want our child to be just like him (except have my vision as his was his only weak point). Stephen agreed and said he would not mind if our child also had my cheekbones. I felt pleasure at that comment. A few minutes later he said how much he wished he had children with his first wife, Sandra, because she did not have any features he could find fault with. Then, as I lay there with the wind knocked out of me at such thoughtless words, he said, "I wasn't comparing you - it's just that I can't help wishing she had produced my children." He rolled over and started his prayers as I rubbed his back and started mine.

Stephen with Giuseppe Alletto of the
Italian Steve Reeves Fan Club at the Ranch on May 15, 1993

CHAPTER 7
EURO TRIP - FRENCH PRO EVENT

Stephen had been approached by a young man by the name of Chris LeClaire from Massachusetts who wanted to write a book about Stephen's life. I plead Chris' case but Stephen was not initially interested. It seemed so little to ask to have Chris conduct interviews at the house then let him write his book (which Chris said was a dream of his) knowing that at least the facts would be straight. At the time there was just the Milton Moore book, *Steve Reeves One-of-a-Kind*, and Stephen's book entitled *Power Walking*. I felt there was a lot to be said for helping people attain their individual dreams, especially if it cost Stephen next to nothing. How could it hurt?

Stephen was invited to make an appearance at the French Pro International Bodybuilding event which was to be held in Antibes, France during the latter part of July. Since we needed an adult to watch over the ranch in our absence, Stephen decided to kill two birds with one stone. He contacted Chris LeClaire and agreed to go along with Chris' interviews provided Chris would come out and act as caretaker while we were in Europe. Chris agreed to the arrangement and arrived at the ranch on May 9 in order to conduct his first interview and learn the ropes of managing the ranch. Stephen allowed Chris to stay in the groom's quarters. Chris was charming, hard-working and succeeded in learning Stephen's requirements for proper ranch management.

Two months later, on the flight from Atlanta to Nice, France, when the lights were dimmed and the movie *Sommersby* was playing in the cabin, we used our three seats to pretend I was sleeping with my head in his lap. We only had to pause once for a passerby. Membership in the "Mile High Club" occurred in a jetliner over the Atlantic ocean. We eventually landed and were picked up by Josette and Lucienne Rauch and their friend Brigette. They whisked us off to the Villa LaFontaine outside Nice in Mougins. We were settled in a two room suite with very nice antique furniture and two bathrooms. Everyone treated us so warmly. We later met Brigette's fiancé, Raymond, whom we liked equally well. We had not slept for what seemed like forever but tried to enjoy the meals and the village they took us to tour. There was a festival and everyone endeavored to show us a great time. I never saw such beautiful scenery. Josette did a great job translating, Lucienne took a million photos.

Sometime later all eight of us went out for dinner. Stephen's command of the French language was returning to him so conversations at the table became more and more incomprehensible to me. I never saw so many courses of sumptuous foods. I was terrified I might embarrass Stephen by falling asleep at the table. Well after midnight their time we finally returned to the villa. When we got back to our room all I wanted to do was crash on the bed but Stephen wanted to talk, so we talked. Partially due to our complete exhaustion, that night in the Villa Lafontaine Stephen and I had one of the biggest fights we were ever going to have. Stephen attacked my character, my personal life and my motives. I was more than surprised, I was emotionally wounded. When the dust settled, Stephen took two Valium pills and went to sleep. I went outside to the pool where I felt like drowning myself. After an hour of prayer and replaying the words Stephen had spoken, I returned to our room and curled up with a blanket on the floor. I was sick inside. This new side of Stephen painfully reminded me of my ex-husband. Stephen's attack was just done with more eloquent venom. The next day we acted like nothing had happened while Stephen made his appearances and took care of his obligations at the event.

The following morning, we left by train for Switzerland where we stayed at the Hotel de la Paix in Lausanne. Our sixth floor suite had a spectacular view. We had an interlude in the elevator and later in the fancy second floor men's room (which were both "firsts" location-wise). I think Stephen must have been repressed as a young man because he was full of ideas for adventurous liaisons now. After his business was completed we did a few local tourist attractions then boarded a train to Interlochen, Switzerland (which became a favorite scenic area for both of us). We window shopped and Stephen purchased and gave me a beautiful set of heart-shaped charms on hoop earrings. I was delighted and felt that he was quietly trying to apologize. We next traveled to Lausanne then on to Geneva. We almost got busted having a little fun on our way to Geneva by a woman passenger on our train. After Geneva we boarded a return train back to Nice, France where Josette and Lucienne met us. They first took us to a beautiful park and then to the picturesque mountaintop village of Eze which we both later agreed was the best part of our whole trip. Eze was so wonderfully unique. It is definitely my favorite place in France. We met Andre, Brigette and Raymond for lunch. Later that evening, everyone joined us on the Villa Lafontaine's patio for a farewell dinner. I knew I was going to miss our new circle of friends, our French connections. We traveled home the next morning. It is always good to be home.

Deborah and Stephen in Nice, France July 25, 1993

Stephen in Nice, France July 25, 1993

CHAPTER 8
BACK HOME AND
THEN OFF TO OREGON

The day after we returned home Stephen and I had a long, heart-to-heart discussion about our blowout in France. He insisted on going over the painful, regretful portions of my life. Despite his own similar experience, Stephen refused to understand why I stayed with Larry as long as I did. At one point I told him, "I am awfully tired of going over and over my mistakes in life, tired of fighting slanderous accusations. I am not the only one who has ever made a bad decision. Let he who has a clean slate cast the first stone at me - this is the last time I do this!"

The next day felt like a new beginning, or perhaps I just wanted so badly for things to be right between us. My strongest desire was for a peaceful, loving, healthy harmony between Stephen and me. Chris was still at the ranch of course and he even took Lynx and Naomi to the movies while Stephen and I attended a party for Helen Davis at the San Diego Design Center. That was one of those galas with fortune tellers, miniature horses, jugglers, bands doing music from different lands and food from Bavaria, Spain, Greece and Italy.

We had been thinking of going to Montana, which was Stephen's second favorite state, to visit his boyhood haunts, visit his birthplace and visit his uncle Claire. Suddenly Stephen said he could not afford the plane tickets and suggested that we could drive up to Oregon where we could stop by his mother's former ranch and visit Applegate Valley where he once owned a great 360 acre cattle ranch. Eminent domain forced him out so the government could build a dam on his property. I was excited at the prospect either way.

Chris' interviews of Stephen continued but I have to say my Stephen was getting really grumpy about it. He found fault with poor Chris' every effort. I tried various maneuvers to calm him. I gave him a massage, I made him a pie, I made him his very favorite meal from Italy. He loved it all but I do not think he was much more cheerful with Chris and his interviews. That evening we watched the television series *Dr. Quinn Medicine Woman* which we all liked. At bedtime, in the privacy of our lair, I set up candles and incense then started caressing him, beginning with his toes. I know for a fact he felt much better after that. No more grumpy Stephen.

We did end up going to Oregon after visiting his cousin Claudia and her husband Dan in Galt, California. They could not have been more hospitable. I will pray for them forever as their son disappeared years ago and is presumed dead. Along the way we also visited my younger brother, Pete, and his pretty wife Lin in Grants Pass, Oregon. That went well and their choice of Mexican restaurant was excellent. We rented a motel room in Cave Junction. The annual Blackberry Festival was in full swing so we spent some time browsing the various booths and exhibits. Stephen generously purchased a pair of silver disc earrings with copper accents for me, a pair of opal earrings for Naomi and a talon and Onyx pendant for Lynx. I was so grateful.

We went the next day to Takilma where the seventeen acre cattle ranch Stephen had purchased and given to his mother was located. The man who bought it after she died was real happy to see Stephen. I picked wildflowers on her old ranch in case Stephen could not find flowers to buy for her grave. Visiting her grave was part of our plan. I liked her headstone when we finally found it. Later we headed for Eagle Point for lunch with my old friends, Bud and Sheryl Davis. Bud barbecued chicken and Sheryl did veggies and potato salad. Stephen and Bud talked livestock and ranching topics as they both were into horses and cattle. Our last family goal was to find Stephen's cousin, Teddy Lee, and her family in Janesville California. We found their place and were delighted to meet not only Teddy but also her husband, George, her son, Silas, in addition to Teddy's brother, Gordon, and his son. We had a really nice visit, I liked Stephen's people.

Although we enjoyed our trip to Oregon, shortly after we returned home a tension in Stephen developed, and in that tense state he spoke of replacing me with someone new. I was not amused. This would be the first of many times he aired his desire to have someone else in his life. I have to admit that I found this attitude disturbing. My garden gave me an outlet for some of the tension which I held inside. Hard shovel and hoe work always calmed my worries and my anger. You can talk to God any time but somehow He seems closer out in the garden or up in the hills. I was really hurt but the next day we had the most memorable time at a barbeque at George and Tuesday Coates' home. It seemed as if everyone we knew was there: Russ and Jean Warner, Dr. Charles Moss (who was a really special soul) and his wife, Marge, George and Gerrie Eiferman, George Redpath, Henry and Betty Atkins, Betty's father who was ninety-two years old and, saving one of the best for last, Armand Tanny. The company was almost outdone by the ton of food: steaks, BBQ chicken, green salad, potato salad, beans, meatballs in gravy, rolls, fruit salad, two dessert cakes, a fruitcake and gallons of beer and sodas. We came to love George and Tuesday as very good and entirely unique friends.

September came and Chris was still with us. After dinner one evening, Stephen, Naomi, Chris and I went out to work with the horses. Naomi brushed Sugarfoot, Stephen trained Traveler while Chris helped by getting medications (for minor cuts on the colt) and watched Stephen training Traveler. I was wiping fly repellent on Sugar then on Traveler. I think it was good for Stephen to have such a family time after being alone for so long. It was nice for all of us.

CHAPTER 9
GRAND OPENING OF
GOLD'S GYM IN HAWAII

Earlier that year, Stephen was requested by the powers that be at Gold's Gym to attend the grand opening of one of their workout facilities in Honolulu, Hawaii. All expenses paid, of course. So in early September we traveled to Hawaii and checked into the Pacific Beach Hotel on Waikiki Beach (room number 824 for those interested). We were met by Steve D'Amico who was really helpful and friendly. Steve D'Amico and his Elise presented us with a fruit basket, t-shirts and a hat for Stephen. Sometime later, Stephen said he finally had his dream come true: he was in Hawaii with a private masseuse, his love, his sex slave and the best part of the deal - someone else was paying the whole bill! Wow, sure worked for me. At that point in time we still were very positive about this trip to Hawaii.

The next morning after our walk along the Waikiki beachfront, we had breakfast with Steve and Elise then they took us on a personal tour of Oahu. We did the Gold's Gym event which went as good as possible with people crowded around, jousting for autographs and wanting to have Stephen pose for photos with them. For Stephen it felt like a private hell. He became increasingly tense and irritated at everyone touching him. It was hard for this private recluse to be gregarious and friendly when people crowded him. Stephen made appearances for profit. He was not interested in publicity or public displays of admiration. Stephen was by nature a rancher, a horse breeder, a man who preferred quiet hard work in the dirt with his hands. He felt like a fraud accepting ovations.

Stephen's mood took a dive during our last evening in Hawaii. We were invited by our host to be the guests of honor at a luau. As a part of the program, the master-of-ceremony invited all the women at the luau to come up on stage to learn how to hula, I was loathe to go up but thought it inappropriate and unsocial for the companion of the guest of honor to refuse, so I went up. I purposefully stood in the back of the crowd of women on stage but the MC would have none of that. He insisted I come to the front and even introduced me as the wife of the guest of honor, Steve Reeves. When I returned to my seat, Stephen hissed at me through clenched teeth, "No wife of Steve Reeves gets up on a stage with the rest of the women in the audience!" With that he stood up and marched out of the area. He refused to speak a word to me until almost a day later, when we were back home on the ranch.

Deborah, Stephen and Steve D'Amico in Hawaii September of 1993

CHAPTER 10
OUR FIRST HOLLYWOOD COLLECTORS SHOW

On September 25 we drove up to the Beverly Garland Hotel to try out our first Hollywood Collectors Show. The promoter, Ray Courts, was warm and friendly. While we were unsure of exactly what to expect, we were soon put at ease and given a table to set up on. The goal was to place our stacks of photos (8x10 glossies in color and in black and white) out for viewing and sale. On the other side of Stephen sat Gordon Scott who Stephen had known for years and worked with in the movie *Duel of the Titans*. I was on the other side of Stephen. Sitting next to me was the actor Peter Breck (of the hit television series *Big Valley*). I worked as cashier. There were lots of pin-up type girls wearing next to nothing or lace see-through bodysuits. A centerfold from Playboy came by wanting something from Stephen. Although she bent over right in his face all he gave her was an autograph, not even a glance. I think he knew I was watching and was trying not to offend me. I was tickled and grateful for his effort. Thankfully we sold a lot of photos and the tables were set up in a horseshoe shape which helped keep the average fan from crowding the celebrities signing autographs. A photo taken with a fan, however, required going out and around the horseshoe set up. A couple of really scantily clad femme fatales boldly came around the tables and plopped into Stephen's lap for a close cuddly shot. I steeled myself with clenched teeth. Guess it was not as hard on Stephen - that kind of fan crush Stephen seemed to enjoy.

The morning of the second day of the event I dressed in a somewhat shorter skirt. Stephen jokingly said, "Giving the pin-ups competition?" I shot back, "Could I ever compete with them?" He surprised and pleased me by replying, "You don't have to." I smiled at him and said, "That's 'cuz you love me." He grunted his agreement. Cool, huh! We enjoyed socializing with Gordon and Peter as we sold photos and interacted with some really nice fans. Ray Courts put on a fantastic and profitable event.

September 1993 Hollywood Collectors Show.
Stephen and Deborah sitting next to Peter Breck
(of television show Big Valley fame)

CHAPTER 11
ROUTINE

By October my rides on Monty were going much better. Sometimes he decided he was a bloodhound - keeping his nose to the ground and trying to sniff were other horses had walked by. That was difficult to stop but I was more confident now and Stephen seemed pleased with my progress. In the evenings I spent time altering shirts for Stephen. He decided he wanted several long-sleeved shirts made short-sleeved. Another time he asked me to mend a shirt his mother made for him some thirty years before. I think he was well pleased with the results. In the evenings I also sometimes darned his wool socks and was now glad my mother had taught me how.

The ranch work went on of course, day in and day out. Horses are hay burners, require regular shots, need to have their hooves trimmed and their stalls and paddocks mucked out. We almost always bought our grains, wormers and supplements at Terry's Hay and Grain in Valley Center. We always had a farrier by the name of Dave Morris take care of our horses' hooves. Dave Morris was one of Stephen's oldest and best friends. He knew a lot about horses in particular and ranching in general. They talked and laughed out at the barn whenever it was hoof trimming time and I realized Stephen really liked and valued Dave's opinions. At first, I found Dave sort of rough around the edges with his good old boy sort of attitudes and jokes, but he had a heart of gold and was honest through and through. Later he and I became friends and I added Dave and his family to my prayer list.

Another man Stephen valued as a friend was Jim Ford. He was a scuba diving instructor and tour guide. They shared a common interest in bicycling, mostly long distance bicycling. They each had really serious bicycles and spent years biking together across distant deserts and up steep winding mountain roads. To choose to sweat and travel together meant they really liked each other's company. In Stephen's life that was rare. By the winter of 1992 though, Stephen had quit long distance bike rides.

CHAPTER 12
WHAT IF

One rainy day in mid-October, as we snuggled together during nap time, Stephen wistfully said he wished that we had started our relationship twenty-two years ago. Back then he was living in the little white rental home (which sat on the corner of his property) while the adobe ranch home was being built. About that same time my ex and I were living and working at Ahern Ranch next door. He was daydreaming about a "what if" scenario. When my ex and I would fight I would wait until everyone was asleep then go for a cooling-off walk up past the Reeves ranch. I would sit in the middle of a decomposed granite orange grove road and talk to God about my problems. I passed right by Stephen's temporary living quarters in the dark. So twenty-two years later Stephen daydreams about what if we had not just been passing acquaintances but had gotten together as a couple back then. I was surprised at his wistful, romantic musings. It was hard to understand how this man I loved could speak to me so wistfully and lovingly one minute and then hiss at me so venomously the next.

Stephen decided he wanted to lick peanut butter and honey off of me during one of our episodes. About a month earlier he had tried Cool Whip and chocolate syrup. He said it sounded yummy. It occurred to me that perhaps God had not put me together with Stephen when he was younger because He knew I wouldn't be able to keep up with Stephen's appetites. He said he had been dreaming of doing these sexual activities all of his life but that I was the first woman in his life he felt would be game. Maybe he was right about that.

George and Tuesday Coates, as well as my older brother, David, and his lovely wife, Joanne, came for dinner one evening. They brought with them my Aunt Hilda. We all had a great time and George seemed to enjoy getting to know Hilda a little bit. She needed to get out more often. Stephen was an excellent host serving wine, German beer and Martinelli's sparkling apple cider. We talked some politics and then George and my Aunt Hilda (both originally from England) shared some of their "life in the old country" memories. There were a lot of laughs and some real getting to know each other moments, I promised myself next time we would add my mother to the guest list. After our guests were long gone we were playing "what if" as we wound down from our great evening. Stephen said, "What if we got together New Year's Eve instead of later this year? What if you had come to my door New Year's Eve instead of just going for a walk in the dark by yourself that night? What if you came to my door and you came inside?" I said, "You would have thought I was a loose woman if I just showed up at your door and offered myself to you." And he said, "I wouldn't have thought badly of you for that. I think too much of myself to think that." This statement struck me as hilarious. Then he rolled over and we said our individual prayers, I rubbed his back as he fell asleep. Good night God.

CHAPTER 13
FIRST NOVEMBER AND A DAY IN THE LIFE

On November 1, Stephen suddenly says, "If you can run up 'mother f—er hill' without stopping, I'll marry you in June." Stephen was referring to a local, very steep hill with a flat top that he nicknamed "mother f—er hill" because he always had to stop and catch his breath part way up. If he could not do it there was no way I would even make the attempt. Early in our relationship, Stephen had said he could not wait until I was free from Larry so he could, as he put it, "make me his own". My divorce had been final on September 23rd and the fact that he had not asked me to marry him was not lost on me.

Fairly often in the evening before bed Stephen liked me to read to him sexual scenarios from books. I knew he liked reading such scenarios so I decided in late fall to write a secret letter to my Stephen. I had already written two such scenarios at his request. Both were a hit. This time I decided to write a pretend letter from a fan, a really steamy letter. I wrote the letter, dropped it into the mail and waited for it to be delivered. A day or two later it arrived. I did a good job of disguising my handwriting. He thought some hot woman was propositioning him in really explicit and descriptive words, offering him everything and anything he could want or imagine. Boy did he love that letter! I signed the letter in such a way that he could not help but realize it was actually from me. He was excited because now he could play the game openly with me. After that we did a lot of role playing.

Stephen was contracted to do an appearance at a gym in Bozeman, Montana. We flew up and were met by Ileana and Mike Delaney, the gym owners. We found them to be warm and very helpful. They invited us to stay with them in their home. They also offered us their Mercedes so we could do a bit of sightseeing while we were there. We attended their event and Stephen signed the usual photos and posters. Stephen was pleased with the trip for two reasons: it was a financial success and we developed a great friendship with Ileana and Mike.

Of all things we did socially our favorite was barbecues at George and Tuesday's in San Diego. On one such occasion in mid-November we took Naomi (her first time) and also our Rottweiler puppy whom we nicknamed Rommel Rottenweiler Reeves ("Rommel" for short). We found the crowd to be jovial and hungry. Among the guests at the barbeque were Dr. Charles Moss ("Charlie"), Russ and Jean Warner, Edwardo and his wife, Ken and Millie, George Redpath, John and Angela Grimek, Glenn Sunby and his friend Sue. Stephen decided to selectively invite George and Tuesday, Charlie Moss and the Grimeks over for dinner at the ranch the next day. I was a bit uncomfortable at the time but it turned out to be a great idea and everyone had a wonderful time. Stephen later explained to me that he wanted to have the dinner because the Grimeks rarely came to the West Coast plus we really owed George and Tuesday. He invited Charlie Moss because we both were honored to have him consider us his friends. Charlie was a very special man. While finishing up our workout the following day Stephen said something about being the captain of this ship and I said, "Then I am the first mate." He chuckled and said with a wistful smile, "I wish you had been, I really do." Wow, I would hold that remark to my heart for quite a while.

Stephen religiously read my journals at the end of every week. Mostly my journals were just a recording of our day-to-day lives. However, since I knew that Stephen would read them I sometimes left messages for him. The following is an excerpt from one of my journals which covers the events and feelings of one day. Hereafter I will refer to these excerpts as "A Day in the Life".

A DAY IN THE LIFE

November 20, 1993
Saturday
Sunny & Breezy

Well we slept a little hot so we tossed and turned a bit and woke up less rested than some mornings. Got up at 7 a.m. Stephen off to the barn and horses, me to climb the grapefruit tree to harvest some of the upper ripe fruit for Stephen's breakfast drink and skim the pool. Rommel kept me company and chased the fruit I dropped to the ground. When it was time for Stephen to shave and get changed, I headed for Naomi's bathroom to shower. Turns out that while I was showering and putting on my face Stephen got a little sidetracked by reading a few of my old letters to him and viewing his photos of me. Makes me feel awfully tender inside. Then we got back on track, he showered and I vacuumed.

At 9:05 a.m. the reporter and camera person arrived. The reporter, Dale, is the new owner of the paper. Both were nice men it seemed. They stayed a good hour—took some photos in the gym. After they left we took off ourselves. Stephen gave me a choice, the coast or the mountains. I chose the coast this time. So I drove us to La Jolla. We walked on the La Jolla Shores Beach. Then Stephen treated me to a good lunch at La Jolla Pasta Company. We had lasagna. Browsed an antique shop next door and headed for Escondido. Shopped at Lucky's, stopped at Terry's for grain, the video store for Silverado, Country Junction for a shared special order chocolate shake, the post office for mail, then home. After unloading groceries, we unloaded feed, talked to Claire about feeding the horses on Friday, I put Monty away, fed Daisy, put the car way, checked for eggs, returned to the house. Went out to start the row (on the west side) of cactus plants (for fire retardant purposes). I got fifteen in the ground about three feet apart. Someday they will be large mature cacti and if a wildfire should come, just maybe they will help. After this—(lots more to do) I will put in ice plant too.

Stephen's dinner of leftover Beans and Ham was yummy. We used BEANO this time. Later watched *Silverado* then *Dr. Quinn Medicine Woman*. After that we headed for bed and our late night entertainment. I wore black stockings and the purple lace teddy that Stephen bought me at Victoria's Secret. So I gave him a good working over. Poor, poor man!

The End.

In late November, Stephen and I went to test drive two vehicles he was considering as our next major buy: a 1993 Nissan Pathfinder and a 1993 Jeep Grand Cherokee. We left without buying either. Stephen needed more time to consider all their pros and cons before making his decision. That same day we had enjoyed two brief personal warm-ups or encounters before 6 a.m., then another session just before 8 a.m., and a fourth during what turned out to be a short nap. Our plan at that time was for a grand finale at bedtime but we did not make it past 8:45 p.m. We watched some television and then went to bed. Time for prayers and giving thanks for a particularly strong culmination.

Every day I was hoping Stephen would ask me to marry him. When Stephen suggested that we go alone to Arizona for Thanksgiving, I rather thought that he might propose to me while there. I suspected that is why he wanted me alone instead of with family. But I was wrong.

CHAPTER 14
OUR FIRST DECEMBER TOGETHER

Our first December arrived. The days and evenings grew noticeably colder. Back in October, Stephen told me, "We don't turn on the heat until the temperature in the house drops to fifty-five degrees." Likewise, during the summer, Stephen's rule was air conditioning is not turned on until it is eighty-five degrees in the house. Now, finally, it was cold enough for Stephen's rule to allow us to have some heat in the house other than the fireplace in the living room. It felt so good. Building a good hot fire was one of my talents. Stephen would learn that I excel at doing unexpected things. From then on, I was in charge of all things having to do with the fireplace: cleaning it each morning, maintaining the woodpile, preparing the kindling then starting and sustaining the fire. It usually felt good building our fires. Both kinds.

When Naomi and I first moved in to Stephen's home he removed the small table between the two leather recliners in the living room and shoved them side-by-side so we could be more intimate. That winter we snuggled, watched television and enjoyed the snap crackling cheerful fire in the fireplace. Stephen often worked on tack projects such as horse reins and head stalls while watching evening programs. My evening projects included placing our photos into albums, writing in my journals, mending or altering clothes (usually for Stephen but not always) and reading the Bible. It was by agreement that I read the Bible out loud in the evenings. Stephen, on his good days (and there were tons of those), was content to listen. So we snuggled close together in the two recliners (his was a navy blue leather and mine a tan leather) with a good fire raging in the fireplace and did a daily reading. Sometimes he would ask me to continue reading when our allotted time period was up. It turned out he had never read the Bible cover to cover, just little pieces of it here and there. I realize that religion is a sensitive subject but in order to know and appreciate Steve Reeves you need to understand the role it played in his daily life.

For a long time Stephen made a concerted effort to like and interact as a step-father with my son, Lynx. I saw a lot of generosity in him toward both my children at different times. Stephen had no trouble loving Naomi who he called Sky (from her middle name SkyHorse). Stephen had no previous parenting experience and never had brothers or sisters or close family ties with anyone other than his mother (Golden "Goldie" Boyce Reeves Maylone). This lack of parenting skills and close family interactive relationships had a direct bearing on how difficult an instant family must have been for Stephen to cope with. His relationship with his stepfather, Earl, was not one of mutual affection or respect. In describing how he felt about Earl he said to me, "I tolerated him." He was quite disappointed when his mother decided to marry Earl as he really preferred another of his mother's suitors.

By December 3rd, I was well underway writing our Christmas cards in the evenings while sitting side-by-side with Stephen watching movies and enjoying the fire. Stephen had rented *Shalako* and *Cat Ballou*. Since we had a good session during our nap time that afternoon I was pleasantly surprised that he pursued my satisfaction at bedtime. My ultimate pleasure required considerable effort and manual stimulation so I appreciated his gift that night. I fell deeply into sleep after a sort of blurry set of prayers. Sorry God.

Later the next week, when we were about to eat our lunch and say our pre-meal prayers, he said to me, "You haven't given me your hand." Half joking I replied, "You haven't asked for my hand." To that he retorted, "I have to ask a dad, a brother or mother first." Then he just grinned and we said grace.

My children and I found that Stephen viewed receiving gifts, such as at Christmas or birthdays, quite differently than we did. We receive presents more personally, more gratefully I guess - with a loving attitude. December of 1993 was our first holiday season in Stephen's life. Sometime prior to Christmas I purchased a present for Stephen and brought it home. He told me rather brusquely to "Hang onto that receipt in case I don't like it." Boy, what Christmas spirit! Stephen said his Christmas tree must be set up on the 15th of December so we set about putting together his large artificial tree. It was my first fake tree but not my last. When Naomi came home from school that day she and I decorated the tree and the public areas of the house. The decorations were new to me but were half old style European sorts and half old American versions. Naomi and I liked them as we are both intrigued by such things as vintage homes, art, decorator items, and household implements. Christmas morning I was up at 5 a.m. The winds were really howling so I crossed my fingers that the electricity would not go out at least until the turkey was done. The stockings were stuffed and waiting for curious hands.

As the household woke up, the stockings were raided, the animals were all fed and taken care of and the horses given a special grain and molasses treat. Next we all ate a nice breakfast of Spanish omelets, toast and fresh fruit. Later at gift exchange time Stephen stunned me when I opened one of his gifts to me - a set of car keys and a pink slip! He gave me the 1988 Buick Regal. Keep in mind how expensive his gift to me was and that up to that time in our life together I had owned nothing. Although I have never been particularly materialistic there is a peculiar feeling of vulnerability when nothing belongs to you. It was a lovely gift. One of the gifts I gave him was a nice Panasonic cordless phone. He opened the gift, took one look at it and then tossed it onto my lap saying, "Take it back, I don't want it." That certainly was not what I expected. Stephen was a busy man and he became quite irritable whenever he had to stop what he was doing and cross through the house to answer a phone call. I was thinking that a cordless phone would be a real help to him since it could be carried to him wherever he was in the house. Seemed like a good idea but it turned out he did not agree. Stephen did not want cordless phones or computers in his home. He never allowed either until the day he died.

Other than that our Christmas was delightful. We packed the turkey, yams and dressing into the trunk of my car and the four of us went to visit my brother, David, and his wife, Joanne, in their new home in Vista, California (about a half hour drive away). My mother had come from England a month or so prior and had been staying in Oregon with my brother Pete and his wife Lin. All three of them had come down to David and Jo's for Christmas. My brothers both came out to greet us at the curb, my mother greeted us at the door. We all went inside and celebrated with a wonderful feast and lots of teasing and funny stories told. Other family members present at the celebration were David and Jo's children, Nate, Vania and Zack, my Aunt Hilda, my cousin, Jack Flanary, his wife, Suzie, and their daughter, Amanda. My extended family likes each other on top of loving each other so our gatherings are always warm and happy. Stephen was surprised at just how much he enjoyed himself, and my mother finally met the man in my heart.

The previous New Year's Eve I was supposed to go to a nightclub with Larry, but he began drinking early and I ended up going for a solitary night walk after the kids went to bed. My lone walk took me right past the Reeves ranch where (unbeknownst to me) Stephen sat alone with just his Christmas tree and a crackling fire to help him usher in the New Year. So we decided to relive and alter our history for that night. Just before midnight I changed into a tight, short leather skirt, a black knit lace top, a garter belt with black fishnet stockings and spike heels. Then I slipped out of the ranch house and started my lone walk. When I returned, I approached the front door with its arch of Christmas lights, knocked and waited. Stephen answered the door and I pretended to be a neighbor who had come to wish him a Happy New Year. He invited me in for a hot chocolate (I do not drink alcohol) and we allowed ourselves to get carried away in front of the fireplace on a tiger blanket surrounded by the mellow glow of the Christmas tree lights. We lay there afterwards for about two hours just talking and relishing the new memory. Then we went to bed and said our prayers. Stephen rolled over and I rubbed his back until he fell asleep. Good night God. And Happy New Year!

One of Deborah's all-time favorite pictures

Outside the Bodybuilding Museum
Oceanside, California 1993

CHAPTER 15
NEW YEAR - 1994

In early January, an agent from New York called and left a message about a movie offer he wanted to discuss with Stephen. The man said he would send more information via the mail. A few days later we received the information the agent said he would send. The agent proposed to cast Steve for the part of a modern day sheriff in a small Montana town. So it was something to think about - Stephen had indicated that if it was a western he might be interested. However, Stephen's idea of a western was not one set in modern times so he ultimately decided to decline the offer

One day, when my mother happened to be visiting us, a representative of his health insurance carrier, Family Health Plan, came by the house. She heard Stephen discussing with the agent the need to put his wife on the policy. Later she asked him, as only a mother can, what sort of future he had in mind for the two of us. He said he was trying not to rush me as I had a lot still to sort out.

On January 21, I made Stephen's sixty-eighth birthday as special as possible. We started the present opening before Naomi left for school. She gave him a Rand McNally 1994 map book of the United States and Canada as she knew how much he liked to travel. I still have it. Later that evening, I gave Stephen a very private, personal present that I had spent a considerable amount of time putting together. It was a beautiful, small photo album which had engraved on the cover, "STEVE REEVES PRIVATE COLLECTION 1994". Inside I placed a sensual set of our private photos - for his eyes only. He was really pleased. He said it was probably the best present he had ever received. We went on a really nice horse ride, with me on Monty and him on Torrey. Later, we picked up some take-out Mexican food and two videos for the kids to enjoy at home while we when out. Stephen and I had reservations for a table near the fireplace at the Fireside Inn in Escondido. I had filet mignon and he had prime rib - it was perhaps our best meal out, up to that point. We were both wishing the tablecloths were longer so we could have more fun but we managed to have little bits of private, spicy adventure without offending anyone. When we returned home we found the children watching their second movie complete with popcorn. We went directly to our room where we lit candles, set up a certain mirror and, with me in one of Stephen's favorite teddies, finished what we had started earlier. Happy Birthday Stephen! At sixty-eight years of age he ran circles around much younger men. I was glad to be his chosen sex slave.

Later in the month Stephen told me, "When you turn forty-five I'll buy you a new car, if you've been a good girl." Then he mused, "If only we had gotten together when we first met back in 1973 - we could've spent all those years together, loving each other. I don't ask for fifty years, just those twenty that we could've had." I loved it when he was in this mode. Stephen had purchased two almost identical rings some years back when he was in Sri Lanka. He decided to give me one of them. Mine had a yellow gold band with diamonds, rubies and sapphires. It was a beautiful ring in red, white and blue - Stephen's favorite color combination. He said he had the rings custom-made. I assumed that one was for Aline but always wondered who the other one was for - one slightly less quality gemstone wise. Some mysteries will never be solved.

A DAY IN THE LIFE

January 28, 1994
Friday
63 degrees
Clear

Was a gorgeous morning with frost, a moon going down in the West and Stephen's company for the walk and work out. Stephen had sanded the posts we hold while doing our thrusts-so the edges do not press into my hands where I grip the posts. Sure was nice of him. Joined Stephen in the bedroom. Enjoyed ourselves.

Left for Escondido at about 10:30 a.m. We went to buy a tuxedo shirt and tie, went to Boney's for bee pollen, then across to Marie Calendars for lunch with George Helmer, a fan of Stephen's. He has done a lot of research on Stephen and his background. Seems like a nice man. Finishing lunch we headed home via post office.

Stephen is still in a great mood. Oprah was boring, made dinner, picked oranges, ate with Stephen, juiced oranges, cleaned juicer then juiced limes, cleaned kitchen, cleaned laundry room, worked on photo album, experimented with my hair, and watched television. Gave Stephen a personal massage for a while - we both enjoyed that.

The End.

At the end of January Stephen replaced the 8x10 photo of Aline and him, which was sitting on the fireplace mantel in the living room, with an 8x10 photo of him and me. The photo of us which had been frameless before now had a rather nice looking golden frame. Such a simple change yet it made me feel more permanent. As I was cleaning the kitchen up after dinner on January 31, I mentioned to Naomi how the roses I trimmed a few weeks ago were producing little red leaves. Stephen walked by, leaned real close and whispered in my ear, "Since you trimmed your bush maybe you will produce too." I whispered back, "What, little red leaves?" He grinned that devilish smile of his and replied, "No, little white Steves!" This whole month had felt like a honeymoon.

CHAPTER 16
TENTH ANNUAL
AMERICAN CINEMA AWARDS

On February 6, Stephen and I went to Los Angeles to attend the Tenth Annual American Cinema Awards produced by David Gest and hosted by Robert Wagner. We arrived at the Beverly Hilton at around 3 p.m. and Stephen was instantly surrounded by fans seeking autographs and snapshots. We were handed the keys to room number 211, which Mr. Gest had arranged to be complimentary, and went upstairs to relax and then start getting ready. We arrived in the Grand Ballroom at about 6:30 p.m. where we were surrounded by familiar faces from the movies, television and the music world. For me it felt unreal. Martin Short accidentally stepped on my toe in the crush. We found our table, number 19, down near the front. One table away was Michael Bolton, Michael Keaton, Barry Bonds, Toni Braxton, Evander Holyfield, Babyface and others I cannot now recall. At our table was Leigh Taylor Young, Donna Mills, Dana Delaney and Alan Thick, with their spouses or dates. Robert Mitchum and Haley Mills later joined us. We were served very good food starting with salad, dinner rolls and wine (Diet Coke for me). There were so many people to look at, comment on and wonder about quietly with Stephen. There were beautiful women all decked out in incredible dresses, handsome men dressed to the tee in elegant tuxedos, and huge talent everywhere we looked. We were entertained by Joe Williams, Michael Bolton and the late Whitney Houston as we enjoyed Malibu chicken, pasta, vegetables and later a really yummy lime cheesecake with raspberry jam glaze. At one point Kenny G strolled in from the back while casually serenading us with his incredible talent on the saxophone. While everyone was focused on him, mesmerized by his music, I pretended to drop an earring and disappeared under the long tablecloth. Stephen's evening was instantly energized. Eventually I returned to my seat, earring in hand and none the wiser.

Up in our room later, Stephen squashed a lot of my pleasure in the evening by telling me that of the women at our table the one he would pursue, if he did not have me, was Donna Mills. He said, "She's really my type!" Donna is really sexy but there is no way I needed to have that image in my head. Stephen was voted the Most Handsome Man in the World one year — not by People magazine but by moviegoers worldwide. So he and I were not coming from the same world. Stephen often joked about how I suddenly became beautiful when I was viewed satisfying his sexual needs. He would say, "Now you're beautiful!" as he would come in my mouth.

Old fashioned "selfie" taken at Tenth Annual Cinema Awards

Portrait taken at 10th Annual Cinema Awards

CHAPTER 17
VALENTINE'S DAY,
FAN MAIL, MARRIAGE ISSUES

The "honeymoon bubble" which commenced on January 5th popped on February 14th. Valentine's Day dawned and things started out as usual - an intimate interlude. I tried what we called "ride the pony". In this position I kept my back to him because he found it more attractive. "Ride the pony" was the only position that enabled him to maintain an erection while inside me so I was damned determined to give it my all, especially on Valentine's Day. But a woman can only do what woman can do and my legs finally gave out so I had to finish him off with my mouth. I got out of bed that morning feeling like a failure. Stephen never said a harsh word but the words on the Valentine's card were not reflected in his eyes. Stephen decided to show me an IRS demand for money (which had arrived in the mail the day before). It was addressed to me and was for unpaid back income taxes my ex was supposed to pay pursuant to our divorce decree. After lunch he told me he had planned to ask me to marry him on this day but changed his mind when he saw the bill from the IRS for about $2,400. He showed me on his calendar where he had written "Wedding Day" on June 21 with hand drawn little mountains. He had intended for us to marry in the Tetons, at the Chapel of the Transfiguration in Moose, Wyoming. The next day I told Stephen that I would investigate the legal strength of my divorce judgment and, if need be, I would get a job to pay the back taxes. I also said once I was financially unencumbered, if he decided to ask me to marry him, I would wait the same length of time he had made me wait before giving him an answer - 385 days. I guess my feelings were hurt. When I checked into the liability aspects of my pre-marriage debts I was told that there was a high probability the IRS would seek to attach their tentacles onto the assets of my new spouse in order to collect any back due taxes. I started writing letters and buying newspapers to look for a job. Later, to make matters worse, I learned my ex still owed a significant amount to the state of California.

In the midst of all these financials concerns, fans of the female variety became an issue for me. One such fan, a bodybuilding model, sent sexy photos of her to Stephen with a proposition for sex. Next, a young woman who had her photo taken with Stephen during the Hollywood Collectors show sent a letter (which included a number of nude photos) propositioning him. She suggested that he let her know the next time he planned to be at the Beverly Garland so she could meet him there. Then she hinted that she would give her room key card to him when no one (me) was looking so that they could have a rendezvous. Which she spelled wrong, but then so did I until I looked it up.

That Stephen was receiving such mail was one thing but saving it, hiding it for later, was quite another thing. When I discovered the mail hidden among some of his files I was not exactly sympathetic. I went into the living room where he was watching a rerun of *JAG*, showed him what I had found, told him what I thought of him for saving such provocative enticements and then ripped up the offensive mail and threw it in the fire. Poor Stephen, I am sure I vexed him something awful sometimes.

On February 18, an insurance salesman named David Epstein came to the ranch to discuss annuities and end-of-life planning with Stephen. It was cold and raining outside. I heartily wished Stephen had not asked me to attend the meeting. They spoke of funeral and burial arrangements, which was one thing, but I became very uncomfortable when they began discussing the annuity I was to receive upon Stephen's death. I felt squeamish sitting there hearing about financial compensation I was to receive at the death of my man. Finance has never been one of my strengths but Stephen wanted me to take notes for him so that we could later discuss his wishes and plans. Despite all the uneasy topics covered earlier in the day we had a lovely episode at nap time and when we woke we made a pact to replay the episode at bed time. It gave us something to look forward to. Later we discussed our upcoming March trip to England.

Even though Stephen knew that I do not bolt and run when problems arise in a relationship, and even though he knew that I loved him with all my heart, Stephen started expressing concern about being alone again in the world. All I could do was reassure him that I was not going away and show him over time that I would not abandon him, no matter what. He actually said, "I take care of you now so you will take care of me later." I told him I would, God willing, be around like a long lived guard dog, ever present, ever alert and always protecting. Stephen sometimes teasingly referred to me as his favorite pit bull.

One day Stephen expressed considerable anger over the high electric bill. So I cut back to a shower every three days and started using baby powder on my oily hair to make it seem cleaner. I also did my best to be more judicious with the laundry - only using the washing machine when I had a full load and then hanging many items of the laundry either outside or on hangers in doorways throughout the house. I imagined and certainly hoped the electric bill would show some improvement.

A DAY IN THE LIFE

February 27, 1994
Sunday
65 degrees
Partly cloudy

Woke up and got up to make juice while Stephen did the horse routine, but just as he was going out he suggested we leave the ranch at 8:30 a.m. So instead of running back to bed after our early set of duties, I stayed up to get ready. Decided not to take a shower due to electric bill. So washed up in the sink and powdered oily hair, would fool anyone.

Got everything done and packed: towels and bathing suits for the mineral spa at Jacumba. As a treat Stephen took us out to share a breakfast burrito at Jilberto's. Got diesel, and headed out. We traveled via Rincon, Lake Henshaw, then we visited the property in Ranchita. We walked the property, examined the erosion and talked of building and fencing. After Ranchita we traveled desert ward through Ocotillo, passed Agua Caliente to Jacumba, to visit the Hot Springs. We soaked and swirled for about 40 minutes. There were a few people but we had a few moments alone to indulge in a sensual fantasy in the Jacuzzi, then in the dressing room we finished our session.

We left Jacumba, headed for Boulevard where we thoroughly enjoyed a roast beef sandwich, a diet soda for me and a Heath bar which we shared. Stephen had a turkey sandwich and his chocolate milk. Went over to Tierra Del Sol to check out the property there, sure has gorgeous oaks. From the Ranchita property I brought a cacti and a silver sage. From the Tierra Del Sol property I brought three tiny oaks. We will see.

You know something? Between Lake Henshaw and Jacumba Steve talked of Denise Fowler and some of Jim Ford's women. Denise Fowler was Jim Ford's ex-wife and was the only person Stephen had a date with from the time Aline died until he met me. Apparently it is more common than I would have ever thought, for men to offer their friends access to their ex-wives or their ex-girlfriends. Jim Ford had offered his ex-wife and a few girlfriends to Stephen, as dates. I had never heard of this particular practice but Stephen assured me it happens all the time.

We got home to the smell of a pot of beans and a ham hock in our crockpot. Stephen did some unloading of the truck, feed detail and brought up some loads of firewood for the fire. I built a fire, fed Daisy, gathered eggs and picked oranges. Then we ate. Was good.

I did the dishes, sorted through some laundry room cupboards and ironed some clothes. Began watching TV while I wrote a letter to Steve's friend, Stephen Vercoe, in Cornwall. Watched *Heaven and Hell* on TV. Just before it began, Stephen said he wanted to watch it, that it had the best looking English actress in it, Leslie Ann Downs.

The End.

I mentioned to Stephen one day that I wished he had been raised in a gentler time and place with brothers, sisters and both parents there to support and care for him. His childhood had been so tough on him. No siblings, no father and a mother whose hands were full just trying to keep food on the table and a roof over their heads. In those days there were not any government programs such as welfare or food stamps. No aid to single women with children. Eventually he told me that although he understood what I meant it was a "Catch 22". If he had been raised in such a gentler method and in such a protective environment, he would not have been driven to excel. He would have just bought himself a ranch after saving up his money at a "regular job", married and raised kids, cattle and horses. I could see his perspective and how who he was had a lot to do with when, where and how he had been raised.

Stephen made an appointment with an attorney by the name of Jack E Stephens in Del Mar. We were there to discuss my financial issues and how Stephen and I could not get married until my pre-divorce bills quit jumping out of the shadows at me. I presented the IRS notices along with a letter I had received regarding a defaulted loan from San Dieguito Bank (a business loan my ex and I took out and had made timely payments on until the divorce). I also showed him my divorce agreement. It was his opinion that the IRS would respect the court's judgment in this case. However, he advised me not to have anything in my name until the entire mess was cleared up.

Stephen received a lot of fan mail, and much of it was great. It was my job to organize the fan mail and write short notes to fans, most of who wrote in requesting photos and/or autographs. Mind you, by that time Steve Reeves had been retired for twenty-three years or so. Although I was impressed by the continued admiration I was disturbed by the obsession of some of the fans. My antenna went off once in a while when someone came across as too far off center to ignore. I maintained files on those few, just in case they became too pushy or an actual threat. We received mail from men who unilaterally decided Stephen was their best friend or even their brother. Some would even show up at the ranch claiming that Stephen had invited them over. I was the resident pit bull and would confront and send them packing. One even came back a little while later with a huge bouquet of flowers for me as a bribe. How bizarre. I set the real dog Zorro on him and he left post haste after calling me a cold bitch.

Around then, my dearest Lord Tyrant announced that if I suffered when he showed interest in other women then I was breaking my own heart. He said he took no responsibility for how it made me feel and that I should quit being a problem child. He said he might marry me if I did not have so many outstanding debts. He even went so far as to say that he loved me "in moderation" when I was warm and happy, but that I had to be happy first. He found any emotional turmoil repugnant and totally unlovable. He voiced a complete lack of empathy because he felt that I created my own problems. He said that he would never be the one to reassure me when I felt vulnerable.

CHAPTER 18
TRIP TO LONDON

On March 17, we said our farewells and left for the airport right on schedule. We boarded a shuttle plane from San Diego's Lindbergh Field to LAX where we caught a British Airways flight to England. Since we had a four seat row to ourselves Stephen was kind enough to allow me rest across three with my head in his lap. As a reward he enjoyed some midair "Tyrant's Delight". We arrived on time at Heathrow and took a taxi to our hotel where we were met by our hosts, Malcolm and Wendy Whyatt. We immediately liked them.

The next day, left to our own devices, we decided to go tour Windsor Castle. We both loved history and so we enjoyed all the antique furnishings, armor, weaponry, paintings and sculptures in the castle. We found the cathedral-like chapel, with its tombs of kings and queens, to be quite marvelous. After we left the castle we walked through the town and found a pub where the locals seemed to congregate. We ate a delicious and generous lunch while talking with two Welshmen who spoke both Welsh and English. They were an entertaining pair!

Of course eventually we had to return to the Marriott to take care of Stephen's commitments. Stephen was scheduled to do interviews with two different Irish companies. Then we left for the main event, the Oscar Hiedenstam Award Dinner. There was quite a crush of people in the room, all of whom seemed anxious to get photos of or with Stephen. Malcolm did really well at controlling and organizing the mass of fans milling around Stephen. It seemed like ten million photographs were taken that day. After Stephen finished signing autographs we were escorted to our table. Stephen was the center of attention since he was the guest of honor at this year's Oscar Hiedenstam; however, there were other people being honored as well. We visited with Russ Warner's wife, Jean, which was really nice. For me it is always nice to see familiar faces when so far from home. The menu included lamb, vegetables, potatoes au gratin, rolls, fruit in rum sauce as well as small cantaloupes full of fruit. It was all delicious. After dinner there were announcements, two other awards were given and then Stephen was introduced and presented with his certificate, two engraved crystal wine glasses, a pair of Dutch wooden shoes and a bottle of Irish whiskey. The head of the Italian Steve Reeves fan club, Giuseppe Alletto, who had visited the ranch the year before, also presented Stephen with a marble-like statue of Hercules fighting Diomedes.

Malcolm then took charge and organized the final proceedings so that all the guests paid their respects by approaching Stephen from the front of our table. No one was allowed to approach from the sides or from behind us. This process helped make everything run very smoothly. Stephen was gracious and friendly in spite of hating all the pushier fan behaviors. At 11 p.m. we headed up to our room but were waylaid by a few fans along the way. Giuseppe Alletto also caught up with us but we enjoyed his calm and friendly visit. He presented a personal gift to Stephen - an Italian taylored shirt and an Italian magazine with an article about Giuseppe's visit to the ranch last May.

Stephen was exhausted after the banquet and, as he had a flight to catch the next day and business to focus on, we did a rare thing for us and went to sleep. After all, we had already enjoyed three separate encounters: the prior evening we savored our first intimate interlude in England, then relished an affectionate wake-up call that morning followed by a delightful naptime episode. So after we said our prayers I kissed his big toe and rubbed his back until he relaxed into sleep. The next day I spent time with my Aunt Joan and Uncle Ken, who came down from Rochester, while Stephen traveled to Lausanne, Switzerland. It was wonderful to see my uncle and aunt again, absolutely wonderful. The following evening we met Stephen back at the Marriott Hotel. I felt so relieved and such a rush of love seeing him approach. Stephen was in his cool mode. While we sat and ate dinner with Ken and Joan he was courteous and polite. After dinner my aunt and uncle needed to start their long drive home.

On our last day in England, March 22, we went into the city to meet our friend, Jean Warner, at her hotel. We decided to tour London in her company. Stephen's mood cheered noticeably. At seventy-two years of age, Jean was such fun with a tart sense of humor we both enjoyed a lot. She is a dear lady. I remembered that today was the first anniversary of Naomi and I moving onto the ranch and I was so glad Stephen cheered up. Our flight home included several hassles including being seated nine rows apart. Still, when we finally got home it was wonderful to see Naomi and my mother (who took over while we were gone). The ranch was in good condition and Stephen was pleased.

In front of Buckingham Place
March 22, 1994

CHAPTER 19
BACK HOME:
SEX AND MARRIAGE, ALMOST

At that time, Stephen and I had the most active and experimental intimate relationship that I could have imagined. The only hitch in our sensual happiness was that I was not his ideal woman (figure-wise), and I knew it. One evening he asked me to share with him my most private fantasy. I only hesitated a moment before revealing my most secret thoughts as requested. My ideal fantasy begins with me off the ranch doing errands and Stephen out in the stables working. A young woman arrives riding a Morgan mare that she is interested in breeding to our stallion. The woman is firm and tanned with full breasts, a small waist and rounded derriere. Her brief knit-top hardly hides her nipples that grow erect under Stephen's intense scrutiny. He pretends to discuss her mare's finer points as she dismounts. She pretends to twist her ankle as she slides to the ground so Stephen gallantly comes to her aid. He puts his arm around her waist and helps her limp over to the groom's quarters where there is a bed she can sit down on. He decides to help her remove her boot so he can check out her hurt ankle. She coyly points out that her ankle is still covered by her tight-fitting Levis. Without hesitation he unbuttons, unzips and then slides her pants down and off her tense, quivering legs. His erection is obvious to her. Stephen gently massages her foot and ankle and then cannot resist continuing his ministrations up her legs to her parted thighs. He is pleased when he discovers that her panties are crotch-less. He expertly slides his powerful middle finger deep into her welcoming woman's entrance. Withdrawing his finger, at her gasp of pleasure, he pulls off her panties. He suckles one ripe breast briefly then turns her around, bends her over and plunges his hard, throbbing cock into her. Just as the two of them became one I appear from around the barn's corner and quietly witness Stephen fully aroused by a woman of his preferred taste. He is thrusting his manhood into her from behind as his hands grip her full breasts and pull her to him in that age-old rhythm. I can see the side of his mesmerized face as he grunts his passion and finally orgasms, every massive muscle heaving and straining. This is the fantasy I shared with him that evening - to witness him fully aroused and performing the sex act with someone he found a sensual equal.

I, of course, deeply wished I was that sort of woman but at forty-two years of age and getting older every second there was no work-out in the world that would ever make me the object of his full explosive desire. He was surprised at what my fantasy entailed. Silly man was thinking my fantasy would involve some smoking-hot sex between him and his so-called wife! Sharing my fantasy with Stephen that night succeeded in arousing both of us and we took advantage of the moment. Stephen frequently had me repeat the fantasy in order to get himself off (with some expert manipulations by that same so-called wife of course). He enjoyed having me create new sex scenarios that I would share with him as bedtime stories, as a sort of primer.

At the end of March, Stephen unexpectedly asked me who I would invite to our wedding if we got married locally instead of up in Moose, Wyoming. After thinking about it, I pointed out that we could have more friends and my relatives involved if we were married locally. It was cost prohibitive to invite my family up to a wedding held in Wyoming but at least his Uncle Claire and his wife, Dot, would be able to attend. I preferred a small, more intimate wedding in either case. When Stephen was twelve years old, Stephen's mother, Goldie, took Stephen on a road trip of the western state's national parks. On that trip they visited the Chapel of the Transfiguration in Wyoming. Stephen was so taken by the tiny church with its large window behind the altar which commanded a perfect view of the Grand Teton Mountains that he promised himself that he would bring the woman he loved there to make her his wife. His childhood dream never came to fruition, however. He married his first wife, Sandra Smith, in Sherman Oaks. He tied the knot with his second wife, Aline, in Switzerland because that is where he was living while he made movies in various areas of Europe and also in Baghdad. Of late, however, he had spoken with wistfulness several times of his boyhood intention regarding that special chapel. I suggested, therefore, continuing with the Wyoming plan and later having a reception at the ranch. I admit that his on again, off again talk of getting married really left me unsettled. A few days later Stephen asked me to write to the Episcopal Church in Jackson Hole, Wyoming that oversaw the small chapel to inquire about arrangements to marry there. I did so quite happily.

Around the end of March, I had begun the huge but entirely voluntary task of raiding the house's closets and cupboards for boxes and bags of Stephen's photos. The photos were not stored or organized in any order and there were hundreds of them. I was determined to organize, first by time period, then by event or subject, each bundle of photos. It was very much like a puzzle - except for a rare scrawl on the back of a photo regarding the place or name or date there was no labeling and few clues. I loved Stephen and in this wild assortment of photos was part of the history of his life. At first he pooh-poohed my plan as pointless and probably impossible to finish but as the project progressed he became animated by some of my discoveries.

The project took me years to complete because there were so many other projects and responsibilities that got in the way. Stephen's patience at times wore thin with all my inquiries and my need for guidance. Of course we had a ton of laughs and sometimes tears over some of the memories my discoveries brought back. There were long-lost photos (some from before he was even born) of his family, ranch scenes and others he could not remember ever seeing. It was a labor of love most often worked on while sitting side-by-side watching television in the evenings. As a routine, I would first record the events and feelings of our day in one of my journals and then work on the photos. There were movie set photos, photos of his bodybuilding years, photos of his early life, photos of his Switzerland years with Aline, and photos of his time in other parts of Europe, Oregon and Valley Center. There were quite a few vacation photos - some from very exotic places. There also were endless photos of his horses, prize cattle plus some of the dogs in his life. There were even a few of his various pickup trucks. Those last groups of pictures certainly illustrated his love of ranching.

Speaking of ranches, Stephen showed real-life Herculean stamina over and over in his five day a week exercise program: Power Walk followed by his work out in the gym, stretch, and then work out in the pool. He had intense interest in sexual pleasures off and on all day. His daily ranch routine involved various projects such as the care and training of the horses, maintenance of the barn, riding arenas, dirt roads, pastures, paddock grounds and fencing, and the fertilizing, irrigating and pruning of the orange and avocado groves. Naturally, it fell to him to maintain all vehicles, equipment and buildings. It often surprised me that he did not fall victim to a heat stroke or worse as he spent hour after hour hard at work outside.

That spring, we worked side-by-side for two days at another Hollywood Collectors show at the Beverly Garland. The show went quite well for the most part, fans of all shapes, sizes and sexual preferences came by. Some were very sweet in their admiration of Stephen, others were overly enthusiastic, and then there were those who were complete bores. Stephen's mood became upbeat when "those" women with bulging breasts oozing out of next to nothing tops and firm bottoms came and went. I did commendably well until one familiar, sleazy photographer came over with two well endowed (one real and the other a miracle of modern medicine), tiny waisted and plump derrièred females. He said one of his girls was an artist (I remembered her visually appraising Stephen earlier) and the other one he claimed was a model (I for one, wondered exactly what she modeled). The one fairly popped out of her low cut white knit top and was shameless in the tiniest excuse for a see-through skirt. After a few minutes of strutting their wares in front of our table, the photographer asked Stephen to pose with them. Stephen agreed. He did not gape or drool but he did discreetly check out what they were advertising. When they leaned up against him I felt sick inside. I did not blame Stephen. He would have to be dead not to appreciate these perfectly breed able wenches. I was having difficulty maintaining my composure as the two bimbos continued to snuggle up and press against him for multiple photo shots. My friend, Gordon Scott, attempted to come to my rescue. He leaned over and said quietly, "Think of it as a painful procedure in a doctor's office - sometimes it hurts less if you don't actually watch and if someone talks to you during it." I was so surprised at his perception and thoughtfulness! I added him to my prayers from that day until the day he died. Thanks Gordon. It reminded me of a quote I read from Jimmy Stewart. When asked why he did not associate with the Hollywood scene Mr. Stewart said, "I love my wife. If you are in a godless place you meet godless people who do god-awful things. I keep her away from those people." I have to agree. A bit later Stephen actually mentioned that he realized the cuddling photo shoot set up by the sleazy photographer was a really stressful scene for me to witness. That was not like him - he previously had said that I break my own heart when I let things like that bother me.

After the photo shoot I tried to turn my focus on Stephen making money at the show. We were both grateful to Ray Courts and his wife for providing great accommodations and such a pleasant working environment. Thank goodness that letter-writing vixen (the one who wanted to rendezvous with Stephen) never made an appearance. I appreciated the fact that Stephen never left my side except to relieve himself (and once to get me a muffin an elderly woman was selling). I had a lot to be grateful for.

Back at home, I took on more and more of the landscaping and gardening responsibilities on the ranch. I have always enjoyed both of those activities and although the ranch was set in beautiful surroundings it certainly had a deficit when it came to "outdoor decor". It was a shame to have such a beautiful home and not have gardens that accentuated certain focal points. I never had any money to spend so I utilized whatever free time I could manage out in the local hills gathering native plants and rocks for use on the ranch.

Stephen spent the majority of his time working with his horses. Since I was not a trainer I acted as his right hand man. Well, actually most of the time I was his "go-fer". On April 19, after he worked Sugarfoot in the small arena he went and mowed the entire large arena with our walk-behind mower. Covered with the dirt, dust and stickers, he paused and looked up when I drew attention to a Sheriff's truck that had just pulled into the ranch. He turned the mower off and went over to see if there was a problem. The Sheriff smiled and handed him an old black-and-white snapshot of Stephen with three or four other young men out in front of Ed Yarick's Gym. Turns out our Sheriff had purchased a used book on powerlifting while in San Francisco and found the snapshot being used as a bookmark. How cool was that!

Stephen received an invitation to attend the Saturn Awards Show in New Jersey which was being held during the last three days of October. He was also to receive a lifetime achievement award as a part of the Muscle Beach Celebration and Awards event in September. Invitations to various events were plentiful around then. Another item received in the mail was a group of photos sent by Malcolm Whyatt of the Oscar Hiedenstam Award event in England. I was always happy to receive photographs to add to our albums.

On April 23, a Saturday, we started the morning with our usual wake-up call followed by chores and a ride on Rocky and Monty. We came back and showered together for fun (the master bedroom's shower stall was large and done in Italian tile). We addressed some of the fan mail, paid a few bills and then we prepared for dinner with friends. We were invited over to Russ and Jean Warner's home in Escondido. Their home was large and beautifully decorated. We were, however, most excited about being with some very special friends along with Russ and Jean: Dr. Charles Moss with his wife Marge, George and Tuesday Coates, and George and Gerrie Eiferman. Jean and Tuesday kept busy putting the finishing touches on a sumptuous banquet while the rest of us visited and were treated to stories of some of their shared past - some of them went way, way back. Our meal was served and included thick steaks, salmon, meatballs, mashed potatoes with gravy, salad and dinner rolls, with two kinds of cheesecake and baklava for dessert. We were reluctant to leave but had to be mindful of our horses waiting at home for their hay and grain. Stephen felt it was very important for them to be fed every twelve hours so we rarely altered their feeding schedule.

On April 27, which was a Wednesday, it was chilly and rainy. Stephen had rented an X-rated movie which proved to be inspirational. I would not always feel comfortable with this sort of entertainment - it depended primarily on my current confidence level. We had done a lot of things, a lot of times, in a lot of places but this was new to me. This time it proved to be screamingly successful for me and initiated a double climax for him within twenty minutes. The sex was so hot I thought the curtains (oops, I mean drapes) would spontaneously burst into flames. I think I would have to consider X-rated movies as a guilty pleasure at best, and appalling at worst.

On Saturday, April 30, George Helmer arrived on the ranch. He brought with him photos of the Oakland, California house on 76th Avenue where Stephen lived after his mother, Goldie, married Earl Maylone and up to the time he was approximately twenty-one years of age. George had traveled to Oakland and not only took pictures of the outside of the house but also, with the current owner's permission, took pictures of Stephen's original workout schedule which had been written on one of the inside garage walls when Stephen was sixteen years old. Enterprising man that he was, George not only took photos but he purchased the entire section of the garage wall which contained Stephen's handwritten workout schedule. Now that is a fan!

George informed Stephen that he wanted to start a new fan club but Stephen was reluctant. I was curious so Stephen explained to me the requirements for starting fan clubs - including the fact that anyone could establish a fan club, with or without the permission of the person being honored. Even though George did not need Stephen's permission he took the time and trouble to approach Stephen about the project and obtain his blessing. I encouraged Stephen's participation in the new fan club just as I had encouraged him to cooperate with Chris LeClaire's proposal to write a book about his life and contributions to health and fitness. I felt that it would be better to have a known person rather than a stranger to start a fan club here in the United States. George left that day without obtaining Stephen's favor so I made a point of bringing up the subject now and then. I did not realize that Stephen had changed his mind about the fan club until I heard him agree to it while talking to George on the telephone some time later.

After dinner on May 1, Stephen gave me "The Poem". It is an original poem by my Stephen to and for only me. I did not have amnesia about all the poems he had written and given to other women but this one was for me and it was his proposal of marriage. Only God knew that exactly six years later, on May 1, 2000, my dearest Lord Tyrant would slip from this life and go to his rest. The poem is as follows:

> Deborah:
>
> Marry me, marry me soon,
> On the twenty-first of June.
>
> The "summer sails" will light up the clear blue sky,
> The majestic snowcapped Tetons will stand like sentinels proud and high.
>
> The near full moon will shine brightly, lighting up the darkness of the night,
> As we walk hand-in-hand together we hear night birds taking flight.
>
> The wind blowing softly through the trees and making ripples on the lake,
> These are the sights and sounds that only God can make.
>
> If you want to make me happy and enjoy my way of life,
> And if you truly love me I want you to be my wife
>
> SR

A month earlier, when we were once again planning to get married, he asked me to write to the church in charge of the small chapel in Wyoming. We needed all the information required to pursue that wedding locale. The Episcopal Church in Jackson Hole had authority over the wonderful chapel. The information they sent in response to our inquiry stunned and dismayed us. If either petitioner for marriage had been divorced then the couple in question would have to undergo the church's counseling program for three months prior to the arrangement of any wedding. When we inquired if we could undergo counseling at a local Episcopal Church as we lived so far away, they replied, with apologies, in the negative. Well, that dashed Stephen's dream of a wedding in the Chapel of the Transfiguration located in Moose, Wyoming. He was really not good at accepting other people's dictates. So he hatched his own private plan which I did not know about for a few weeks or so. Knowing Stephen, he would probably change his mind a few times in the interim anyway.

CHAPTER 20
BREAK UP AND MAKE UP

Not long thereafter, I hesitantly inquired if he was asking me to marry him out of some feeling of obligation. He had told me that after all Aline had done for his career, and after she told him she had gotten pregnant but had lost their baby due to a fall, he felt he had to propose marriage. He denied feeling obligated this time but his denial was without any reassuring smile or warmth. The next day, on our Power Walk, I asked Stephen if I could buy a new dress to get married in. He said, "Yes." I asked what he thought he might wear. He answered, "My best blue suit." Then we spoke of other things and began our workout in the gym.

After a while he started to complain about the cost of our wedding. He said that I was not like his previous wives who were so much younger and had relatives who paid for the wedding and the reception. I know I should not have been surprised but I could hardly believe he would complain about the expense of our special day. He had told me all about his other weddings, receptions, dresses, rings and even a honeymoon in Europe. I had not asked for nor expected any of that (well, I would have liked a ring). It hurt me down deep to think that for him marriage to me was regretful because I cost too much. I said, "Forget about the dress!" As soon as we were done in the gym I asked if we could go up to the house to talk it out. My honest impression was that Stephen was lukewarm about getting married on a good day and the whole idea left him cold on a bad day. So I gave my pre-engagement ring back to him and called off our wedding saying, "I can't get married to a man who thinks so little of me." There were tears running down my cheeks as I turned to go. As I left the room he retorted, "I will just replace you with one of the women who will love me with the total abandon you used to love me with!" I was shattered.

I went from being excited about getting married in June with this sometimes wonderful man that I loved, to realizing Naomi and I had to get off the ranch and out of his home. Stephen asked me to stay long enough to help him prepare for the Western Film Caravan in Tennessee. By May 6th I had found a little house on Lilac Road to rent and filled out a pile of employment applications. Stephen made us dinner that night, his excellent chicken-in-rice that we had long since come to love. While I was busy filling out applications he unexpectedly brought me a bowl of ice cream.

A strange thing occurred the next morning. Naomi found a medium sized brown tarantula in the hallway by Lynx's door (the room he used on his visits). We picked it up and took it to a sunny location down by the garage. Tarantulas are not normally out and about in May. They are relatively rare in the area but can be found walking across hot, dry acreage or roads in August or September. That evening Stephen nearly stepped on it, or its twin, in the kitchen! In twenty-two years he said he had never seen one on his property. We could not figure out how it got indoors - not once but twice. Naomi transported the poor lost arachnid to a location down beyond Daisy's pen.

The following morning Stephen was quite chipper and upbeat. If my impending departure was bothering him, he sure was doing a great job of covering that up. I had noticed the last evening he had spent quite a bit of time on the phone talking to someone who made him laugh. Stephen was not one who usually enjoyed talking on the phone. It occurred to me that I had perhaps already been replaced. Oh well, onward and upward. I had agreed to stay on the ranch and do my share of the chores until after the Tennessee show. I was hoping an opening at the Wild Animal Park would be given to me.

The weather that morning was ripe for rain with low, dark menacing clouds marshaled all around us. Stephen wanted to ride Rocky, his green-broke gelding, once the rain came and went. It was not safe to be riding such an untrained horse when the ground was wet and slippery so I offered to accompany him on the trail ride down toward Pauma Valley. During the ride I kept thinking that this was very likely my last ride with Stephen. The thought also occurred to me that on his next ride he would likely be accompanied by "one of those much better horse women than me" that he was always referring to. I was glad that I was riding behind Stephen that day. After our ride we groomed the horses and I went indoors and made lunch. Stephen came in and offered, while I was preparing our lunch, to pay for my first and last month's rent on the little house on Lilac Road. I accepted his offer because I realized it would take me some time to come up with enough money via a job (that I did not have yet).

That evening Stephen asked me to join him for a talk in the living room. When I entered the room I decided to sit over on the hearth rather than next to him in my chair. I forestalled whatever he was about to say by asking, "How would you have liked things to have gone between us?" He answered that but for the financial issues involving my ex (including his failure to pay child support and provide health insurance for Naomi), he would marry me without hesitation. Well, that is not what he said some days ago! He then confessed that he wanted us to maintain our previous status quo but be engaged to someday, sometime get married. He wanted me to tear up the applications for work and call the landlord of the little house on Lilac Road to let him know I had changed my mind. After some discussion, I agreed.

CHAPTER 21
WESTERN FILM CARAVAN
IN KNOXVILLE, TENNESSEE

About that time, we were getting ready for the Western Film Caravan in Knoxville, Tennessee. My mother, Audrey, committed to stay at the ranch with Naomi while we were off selling Stephen's autographs and photos while giving his fans pleasure at meeting one of their heroes in person. On Wednesday, May 11th, we flew first to Atlanta where by sheer coincidence we bumped into Gordon Scott. We ended up on the same flight with him to Knoxville. It was always good to see his smiling face. The next morning at 10 a.m. the photo signing began. We quickly discovered a huge difference between Knoxville and Southern California. A majority of the attendees at the show in Knoxville felt, after paying a nominal fee to get into the show, that the autographs should be free! They had difficulty understanding that Stephen was not there to stand around, be admired and hand out free pictures and autographs. It fell on my shoulders to carefully outline the costs and our expectations to the fans that paraded passed. Some fans even got angry and rude at the audacity of the celebrity who thought he should get paid for autographs! There were even some who thought the 8x10 photos should be free as well. A choice few were not surprised. They were happy to pay and were delighted for the opportunity to shake hands with, or pose for a snapshot with, Steve "Hercules" Reeves.

Stephen and I agreed to never, ever do a Knoxville show again. We sorely missed the way Ray Courts did his show in Southern California. He and his wife always provided fresh donuts, coffee, tea and sodas for the celebrity sellers. They would also come by periodically to ask if they could get you anything else. At the Knoxville show, I had to go in search of something to whet our whistles and when I finally hunted down a promoter/manager person, he at first looked puzzled then suggested I go outside by the far door where he heard some lady had sodas for sale. Real red carpet treatment there at that Western Films Caravan. Now to be fair, that was in 1994, their show may have gotten more sophisticated in the years since.

Our last day in Tennessee we woke up at 5 a.m., readied to vacate the hotel then left in a rental car for Asheville, North Carolina. If you have never experienced Tennessee's north-eastern area or the countryside around Asheville, you really should fix that deficit in your life. The mountains, valleys, forests, and rivers are breathtaking. We were planning to visit the Biltmore estate but when we got there Stephen said it cost too much so we did not get to go in. We had lunch at the beautiful Grove Park. On our way back to Knoxville we stopped at a McDonald's for a chocolate shake. Then it was back to the airport and fly home. We arrived at the ranch at 9:55 p.m. Naomi was in bed but we talked and hugged and then talked and hugged some more. My mother was fine as was the ranch - she had held down this rancher's domain with true British competency. In our afterhours I asked Stephen to "help me out" and he very generously left me gasping. It had been too long since I had been happy enough to be comfortable with him in bed.

Taken while at the Knoxville, Tenn Show on May 12, 1994

CHAPTER 22
LIFE GETS BACK TO "NORMAL"

I attempted to attract Stephen's interest one morning by wearing some Lycra workout pants during our daily exercise routine but he was out of sorts and told me I looked really awful in them. A few minutes later, Dave Morris was a welcome sight pulling into the ranch driveway. If anyone could turn sour Stephen into nicer Stephen it was his great friend Dave. And, with Stephen's attention on Dave, I could escape the gym and Stephen's ongoing insults. Stephen headed up to the barn to greet Dave then began rounding up the horses one by one for Dave to inspect and work on. While Dave worked his magic on the horses' hooves, he would share "horse talk" and tell jokes with Stephen. I was not worried that Stephen would tell Dave about my morning's audacity. Although Dave, like Stephen, was a reality-based horse and ranching man, he did not share Stephen's obsession of physical perfection in women. If Stephen related my personal fiasco, I honestly feel Dave would think that Stephen was being too harsh in his criticism. As for me, I just wanted the day to be over.

The next day Stephen purchased a 1994 Jeep Grand Cherokee Laredo package in hunter green. Then, when I went and retrieved our mail there was a check he had been expecting since the first of May. All good events. A bit later Stephen received calls from Harold Smith from Knoxville and George Helmer. He was not entirely pleased with the calls but he never really liked talking on the telephone so one could not expect him to be pleased. I tried making him one of his favorites for dinner: Tuna Casserole, green salad and steamed broccoli. After dinner dishes and Bible reading I wrote in my journal then we watched some television as he checked on the lineage of a stallion he had heard was for sale. I was hoping that buying the new Jeep would improve his mood but not so you would notice. We later had our evening after-hours episode, a bit less inspired than some. We then said our prayers. I realized I had forgot to reset the thermostat so I jumped up, went to set it to 55 degrees and returned to kiss his big toe and rub his back. Good night Stephen, good night God, I love you both.

The following Sunday, after chores were completed, we left to put the initial mileage on the new Jeep. We drove up to Temecula and on to Indio where we stopped to share a burger and a date shake. Then we drove through Palm Springs and over to the Salton Sea. As usual we talked during some of the drive. At one point he asked me about that sexual fantasy of mine - the one where I imagined him fully aroused and fully involved in sex with a young, firm, pretty woman. He wanted to know why I did not fantasize about him having sex with me (as I admitted to doing in the earliest months of our relationship). I answered his question, not entirely sure he would want to know the truth. I told him, "Stephen, I imagine you holding, stroking and pulling the clothes off warm, firm arms and legs, I visualize you tasting full youthful breasts then sinking yourself up to the hilt in this warm welcoming woman because I cannot imagine you wanting me." Then as we drove I started to cry quietly and he said, "Oh sweetie, don't cry!" I was really moved that he sounded just like a man who cared his mate was sad. I quickly changed the subject but I would never forget how he sounded for those few seconds. We continued our journey on through the desert then up to Julian the back way. From there we drove the new Jeep down, down, down to San Diego's Mission Valley Center Mall to pick up Naomi who was coming back from visiting with her dad.

We were able to accomplish a lot on the ranch that late May. The training of Stephen's green horse, Rocky, was going pretty nicely. I had learned so much about living on a ranch: fence mending, concrete mixing, horse care and training. It seemed I was always part of some project and I liked that. Stephen could be really gruff as he gave orders and sometimes fairly hissed directions but at the end of the project he now and again said, "You did well." I would float on air for a few hours.

Stephen decided to rent a couple of porno videos to spice up our after-hours. I was not entirely happy with his decision and, when I saw a bunch of pretty young things sans clothing, I had a sinking feeling of dread. Stephen used his best imagination and pretended I was one of them (I understood the value of the videos for him). I tried to get into the spirit of the event and Stephen seemed pleased, which is mostly what mattered to me.

Around that time he explained something that sort of amazed me. He believed that when I felt down, insecure or sad that he should withdraw all affection because giving me a hug or a kind word would only encourage my bad behavior. He assumed my despondency was just some sort of female manipulation ploy. He tended to view himself as the right person to teach me a lesson in tough love. In the next breath he also compared me to his Jaguar, saying that everyone is as replaceable as his expensive car. Stephen said when and if I became someone that did not suit him, he would replace me. I insisted that people are not like Jaguars and he simply said, "I disagree."

That evening the kids did the dishes which left me free to join Stephen in the living room where I attacked a bag of his old photos - sorting and labeling them for later. During part of the television program *Inside Edition* actress Kim Basinger was shown baking various foods in the kitchen. Stephen asked me what program I preferred to watch. I made a Freudian slip by saying, "I want to see Kim Basinger bake in the oven." Boy, was that a blooper! But it gave us a good laugh.

A DAY IN THE LIFE

June 13, 1994
Monday
76 degrees

Well, we had a really nice morning. Started with one of Stephen's spontaneous monuments to pleasure. Had ourselves a good time—all before 5 a.m. I got up, got the Sky up for her shower and returned to our bathroom to get face clean and done up. At 5:54 a.m., I went back to my dearest Lord Tyrant's den for round number two. Then we both got up.

Good walk, good workout. Rinsed the car down, squeegeed to the windows. Changed my clothes and put Naomi's lunch together, then kissed that warm, loving and lovable man of mine a reluctant goodbye. Took off to take Naomi to school then went on to my appointment with my mom. I dropped my mom off at her art meeting and sped off for home. I did stop by the post office - then hurried on, to get home. I found Steve in bed - where I helped myself snuggle into his arms and the inner curve of his body - spoon style. Off to sweet sleep we went.

Went to go get Sky. Fed critters, helped Stephen with Rocky and Sugarfoot, made dinner, assigned Naomi the dishes, moved the microwave to the groom's quarters, hoed a few weeds in the small arena, then helped to measure the area behind the hot walker for a new training ring Stephen is thinking about building, to work Rocky and later Traveler. Spent some of the evening altering the hem of that beautiful dress Stephen bought me, so I can wear it tomorrow. Been a great day living beside Stephen!

The End.

The next day I was watching Stephen working Rocky in the small arena when he rode up and paused to say that he had been thinking about me lately. He then said, "You have a lot of need to love - it might as well be me!" I smiled up at him and said I could not agree more.

In the early afternoon of June 15, we were at San Diego's international airport, Lindbergh Field, to pick up Chris LeClaire (the friend who was writing a book about Steve). Everything went well and Stephen seemed relaxed. It was always good to see Chris. After we returned to the ranch I made baked chicken, potatoes, steamed cauliflower, green salad and our usual cottage cheese with fruit for dinner. Stephen and Chris talked about everything from the book Chris was writing (to be entitled *Steve Reeves, Worlds to Conquer*), to general subjects such as ranch work, local weather and Chris' life back east. Chris' visits always accomplished two purposes. First, it gave Chris ample opportunity to interview Stephen as a part of writing the book. Second, Chris served as a hired hand to help Stephen with ranch projects and as a steward over the ranch when we were out of town. Chris was a really good worker. His parents did not raise a lazy son and Stephen made sure Chris worked for every moment of interview time.

We spent most of June 21 (our previously planned and now canceled wedding day) purchasing the supplies Chris would need on the ranch while we were gone on our trip to Montana. That night in bed, talking in the dark, I said something about liking it kept dark on these really hot nights so I could lay naked without covers under the ceiling fan. Stephen asked why I liked it dark and I confided that age had caused my breasts to flatten and it was depressing for me to look at them. I was expecting Stephen to say something critical or condescending. Instead, he surprised me when he said, a "Well they suit me just fine." And the seed of hope germinated again inside of me.

CHAPTER 23
DRIVING TRIP TO MONTANA AND BACK AGAIN

We had planned for Naomi and Lynx to stay with their father while we were on our road trip. Larry had agreed to care for the children but he unfortunately changed his mind at the last possible moment. So Naomi and Lynx joined Chris LeClaire at the ranch. I am sure that was not what Chris bargained for. Although I did not think the kids would be much problem, I understood that having one's itinerary changed unexpectedly can leave a bad taste in anyone's mouth. No one was happy with the sudden change in plans.

At 6:07 a.m. on Thursday, June 23, we left for Montana. We stopped to get gas in Las Vegas, 306 miles later, and then arrived at Ely, Nevada at 3:30 p.m. where we checked into a Motel 6. I was up to shower and pack by 4:15 a.m. the next morning because Stephen wanted us to be on our way by 5:45 a.m. Our morning wake-up call was never forgotten just because we were out of town so we worked it in right after my shower. And we still made it on time! We headed due north, through the back country. The next stop on our itinerary was Jarbidge, Nevada. It took us three hours and forty minutes to travel there via an eighty-eight mile dirt road. We were pleased to see a half-dozen antelope, lots of cattle, some beautiful mountains, rock formations and trees, trees, trees. We loved the scenery.

Continuing north, we stopped and washed the Jeep off in Twin Falls, Idaho, then headed through Ketchum to Stanley, Idaho, where we had hoped to spend the night. Stephen decided, however, that we could not afford the lodgings so we continued our journey and found a quiet motel in Challis called the North Gate Inn for $34 per night. I had packed some Victoria's Secret lingerie to wear at the appropriate time. Even though Stephen was exhausted from all the driving that day, Victoria's Secret did the trick. We had to get at least one in while traveling through Idaho.

Saturday morning I was up again by 4:30 a.m. so we could get an early start for Montana. We paused at Stevensville, Montana and visited their Riverview Cemetery which Stephen selected for our final resting place. We both loved its atmosphere with the river running through it and all the beautiful trees. Stephen said he wanted a pyramid shaped headstone. I just wanted to be next to him forever. We arrived in Missoula, Montana just after noon.

Stephen was excited and pleased to be the first to show me "his Montana". Driving north we arrived at Flathead Lake which was really impressive. He decided to drive along the eastern shore - the lake seemed endless. A touring group of motorcycles rumbled past us when we pulled over briefly in order to take a couple of photos. A few minutes later, as we continued along the curving shoreline, we came upon an accident involving one of the motorcycles. We could see a young woman lying on the road with a river of blood running from her helmet into the drainage ditch. Even though we knew she was probably dead, we said a prayer that she did not suffer and that everyone who loved her would find a way back to happiness. Sure did feel sad for quite a while after that.

We continued through incredibly beautiful land to secluded Swan Lake. Stephen already knew these places and had selected Holland Lake lodge as our destination. Everything about the area was breathtaking - so much green and the bodies of water were awe inspiring. Neither Stephen nor I were snow people anymore - been there and done that - but we loved the forests, rivers and lakes which a snow climate creates. We observed diverse varieties of wildlife including so many deer we lost count.

The next day we began as usual with our special wake-up call then, while I showered, Stephen prepared a pre-breakfast snack of Triscuits, cheese, half a banana and juice. We then drove toward Lincoln, Montana which was one of the best childhood memory places for Stephen. He spent two of his favorite childhood summers there. It was and is a small town with a popular restaurant called Lambkins that happened to play a significant part in his fondest childhood memories. We spent the day checking out all his remembered places and also the somewhat distant old cemetery where the earliest local pioneers and settlers were buried. We found reading the headstones a true historical journey.

Back in his childhood years, his mother, Goldie, was able to get work in Lincoln's General Store during the summer months. Little Stephen spent those months of delightful freedom in the Lincoln area surrounded by mountains, rolling hills, meadows and forests. Stephen became fast friends with the Lambkin children, Leonard and Betty. He remembered many hours spent riding horses with them through the woods, grasslands and all around the town. They sometimes tied the horses behind the Lambkin's Restaurant and went into their kitchen to eat. They took turns riding five mounts: a roan they called Tiddlywinks, a black called Smokey (that once reared up and landed on Stephen cracking his rib), his favorite horse called Popcorn, and two others called Jack and Jill. He remembered giving out some of the General Store's sodas to his friends. His mother did not appreciate his generosity since it fell on her to reimburse the store owner for the pilfered soda pop. There were other kids that he and the Lambkin children played with, but their names had grown foggy over time. The kids sometimes visited the old cemetery that he showed me. Another time Stephen, Betty and Leonard decided to mess with some of the customers of the bar portion of Lambkins Restaurant. Locals would sometimes place their beer mugs on the nearby windowsills while they drank and visited inside. The three kids decided that it would be funny to sneak a mug or two outside, partially refill them with their pee and then replace the mugs back on the windowsill. The mischief makers were tickled that the drunk customers did not seem to notice any change in their drinks.

During those hot summer days the children would play in the local creeks catching pollywogs and building small dams. They would catch crawdads and place them in buckets they had found in the trash behind the general store. The crawdads were sometimes used to scare or startle people in town, mostly girls or women of course. The kids could and did also play in and around Blackfoot River. They fashioned fishing poles and tried various sorts of bait and lures to use while fishing. The creeks did not run deep enough to have fish for catching but the Blackfoot did.

The children enjoyed near total freedom those summer days in the early 1930s. From breakfast to dinner time they were free of supervision by their respective parents because the adults worked for a living. Hide and go seek was played in and around town or out in the rabbit warren brush areas. They would also take turns out at the river enjoying a rope swing someone had put up as part of their summer experience.

We asked locals about the Lambkins and the Dietrichsons who had owned the store where Stephen's mother worked and where the two of them stayed in rooms. A waitress we spoke with knew the local history of the families. We ate lunch while we were filled in about the current state of the town of Lincoln which just happened to be celebrating its centennial. The whole day was a wonderful trip back in time for Stephen. We did a cursory scan of bulletin boards to check out the possibility of buying a summer place in the area. We even checked out a few of the currently offered smaller homes that had some acreage but we were not really in the market yet. We had thoroughly enjoyed our day in Lincoln including a late afternoon sensual episode at a place called Snowbank Lake before we headed for the Holland Lake Lodge. That night at the Lodge we feasted on roast pork, baked potatoes, squash and a small loaf of warm bread, Yum.

At 4 a.m. the next morning we tried to be quiet as we dressed and packed, despite very squeaky floors, hoping not to wake fellow guests. By 4:45 a.m. we were on our way to Red Lodge, Montana. We saw four deer in the front yard of the lodge and others scattered along our way for the next thirty minutes and then none. By then they were settled down for their day of hiding. On our trip to Red Lodge we stopped in Deer Lodge to eat at 4B's restaurant. The food was generous and quite delicious but the most memorable thing was the paintings on their walls that were for sale. Stephen bought one called Wild Horses for us. He was rarely impulsive about spending money so buying the painting was really special.

We went through Yellowstone on Tuesday, June 28. In addition to enjoying many of that park's unique and wonderful sites we were fortunate to see antelope, lots of elk and buffalo on this day. We stopped at the painted mud pots and we observed the enormous devastation caused by recent wildfires. We arrived at Old Faithful about a minute before it went off. Stephen had his arm around my shoulders which was extremely rare. Afterwards we drove on to Moose, Wyoming which is sort of near Jackson Hole. Stephen wanted to take me to his specially chosen chapel, the Chapel of the Transfiguration. I was totally enchanted with the small wooden structure with its serene atmosphere and unforgettable view of the Grand Tetons over the altar. We waited for the other visitors to vacate the chapel so we could be alone. Then we knelt by the altar rail and said our vows to each other. I said, "I, Deborah, take you Stephen to be my spiritually wedded husband." Whereupon Stephen responded, "I, Stephen, take you Deborah to be my spiritually married wife." Then we said in unison, "Amen." That day would stand out forever between the two of us as our special day. When we returned home we created a photomontage of various pictures from our wedding and hung it in the living room. The powers that be over that chapel may have squashed our official wedding, but you just did not get away with saying no to Steve Reeves.

The next day we had breakfast in Paris - Paris, Idaho that is. The restaurant was partially decorated with rows of cowboy hats in various stages of wear and tear. The food was good and we were glad they were open because we were ravenous. After a very long day caused by detours due to highway closures, we arrived at the Days Inn in Cedar City, Utah. We checked in then washed the Jeep and shared a Subway sandwich for our dinner. We started watching television in our motel room but ended up having really great sex instead. Afterwards he rested his head on my chest for several moments in one of those precious, fleeting spells of closeness and harmony. I wrote in my journal, "Something special was going on that day."

We began yet another day of appreciating our relationship. Our Jeep carried us effortlessly over the highways from Cedar City, Utah to the Luxor in Las Vegas. Staying in that modern day pyramid was very special for Stephen as he had ventured into one of the ancient Egyptian pyramids decades before. I do not remember how much it cost to spend the night there but it was well worth it. The room was a beautifully decorated trip to Egypt. We were pleased with the atmosphere of the whole of Luxor. We checked into room 148 on the twelfth floor, which provided us a marvelous view of the back of the Sphinx, the outside obelisk and the fountain. Stephen and I meandered around the hotel taking in its decor and special features. We were amazed at the number of restaurants and places to eat. Stephen purchased tickets to one of the shows at the Luxor which featured chariots and both men and women, not just naked women. It was great. I was feeling exuberant pleasure at the lovely treat at this end piece of our vacation. Staying in a luxurious room at a beautiful hotel, dinner of prime rib followed by a great show was so extravagant. I made absolutely certain Stephen knew of my appreciation. I let my love bubble up from my inner well - the intimate finale of our evening was just the cherry on top. Thank you God!

The last day of our vacation was not going to be a pleasant one as the drive from Las Vegas to San Bernardino is an uncommonly boring trek. Knowing ahead of time that the final road trip would be lackluster, I made sure Stephen had an especially exciting session on the carpet of our Luxor room. It was a delightful treat at the end of our remarkable first trip to Montana. Stephen took first shift, driving as far as Victorville where I took over. All in all it took us a bit under five hours to cover three hundred miles.

The Chapel of the Transfiguration in Moose, Wyoming
where we exchanged our private wedding vows on June 28, 1994

View from inside the chapel

CHAPTER 24
BACK HOME

It was marvelous to return home but we also had to get back to reality. As I was to learn over time, coming home for Stephen would nearly always be accompanied by a dramatic drop in his mood. Most of us feel let down to one degree or another after all the pleasure of a vacation, but for Stephen the return to backlogged ranch work and responsibilities probably accounted for most of the crash his humor took. He was nearly always depressed upon returning home. In this particular case he was dismayed at the condition of the ranch when we returned. There were not any emergencies while we were gone, which to me was huge. There was a broken faucet handle, a water line on the front lawn that was not working right and all the lawns were a bit browner than we would have preferred. However, Stephen was on Chris' case about everything.

I knew from experience that even when we were home faucet handles broke occasionally and Stephen often had to work on those irrigation lines. So I felt it was not a sign of Chris' neglect to find these minor problems upon our return. The condition of the lawns though was a disappointment, particularly since we were hosting a Fourth of July gathering in a couple of days. So my dearest Lord Tyrant was not a happy camper. Chris, Stephen and I worked our tails off in order to bring the house and grounds shipshape in honor of the friends we were expecting on the Fourth of July. Stephen was angry with me for taking Chris' side. Fortunately, most of my chores involved work inside the ranch house while Stephen and Chris concentrated on the grounds. Stephen's anger towards me consisted of coolness at meals and in bed. Still, when our first guests arrived for our fourth of July celebrations, Stephen was his warm, welcoming, gracious self. A bit later Russ and Jean Warner arrived bringing a lovely basket of mixed plants for me. George and Tuesday provided various light and dark beers. It felt so good to hear everyone's cheery voices as George and Gerrie Eiferman came in and met my mother, Audrey and Chris LeClaire.

We visited in our living room for quite a while with Stephen, full of wit and friendliness, acting as the perfect host. Later we ate outdoors on tables the children had set up. Stephen made his own recipe of Three Bean Salad, we cooked a large boneless ham, I prepared a potato salad and a tossed green salad, and we had chips and dips. Lynx made cornbread muffins before he had to leave for San Diego. After dinner, it was time for photo taking which is the part Stephen hated the most. He was wearing blue slacks with a white Egyptian cotton shirt (which was almost sheer). He had purchased the shirts, about six of them, some thirty years before. They were custom-made but he no longer liked their long sleeves so he had me alter them. He looked good. George and Tuesday had to leave around 4 p.m. and everyone else left after going on a quick tour of the barn and stable areas. We sent my mother home with a care packet that included the remaining sliced ham, Three Bean salad and some of the apple pie we had served for dessert.

We did our evening chores and felt really good about how everyone seemed to enjoy the celebration. Chris was able to get to know some of Stephen's friends he had not yet met. We had managed to bring some old friends together where they could reminisce and catch up on each other's current events. Two days later, on July 6, Chris went back home. I sincerely hoped that he had been able to gather the information he needed to finish his book on Stephen's life. He sure worked hard around the ranch as trade for all those interviews with Stephen. I felt for him.

CHAPTER 25
GOLD'S GYM EVENT IN OAKLAND

We barely had time to catch our breath before we were again preparing for a very brief trip out of town. This time we were heading to Stephen's hometown, Oakland, California, in order to attend another Gold's Gym event. Once again, our plans for the kids to stay with their father in our absence were laid waste by Larry changing his mind. Stephen almost went ballistic. When my secondary plans for the children also fell through I volunteered to stay home. Stephen was torn between his desire for me to go with him and his oft expressed fears of the ranch burning down if left in the hands of the children. In the end, Stephen reluctantly agreed to leave his ranch, the animals and all his worldly possessions in the hands of Lynx and Naomi - it was a first.

On July 16, we flew to Oakland, arriving there at 10:50 a.m. We were greeted by a very nice escort by the name of Bob Thomas who whisked us off to visit Stephen's boyhood home and neighborhood in Oakland. I approached the home and spoke with Mrs. Hartman, the current owner. When I offered to introduce her to Steve Reeves she exclaimed, "Oh my God, Oh my God!," as she came forward to meet one of her heroes. I give full credit here to George Helmer who had obviously briefed her on Stephen's childhood history with her home. Mrs. Hartman graciously gave us a short tour of Stephen's old home. It was quite an experience. I was very intrigued by the large brick barbecue outback. Stephen said it had been hand built by his stepfather, Earl, back in the day.

Our escort, Bob Thomas, then took us to the new Gold's Gym by Lake Merritt. It was really modern and had everything any customer could need. Our hotel was nearby and our benefactor provided us with a lovely room on the twentieth floor with views of Lake Merritt out one side and the bay out another. We met that benefactor, Mr. Odd Haegan, with George and Gerrie Eiferman in the hotel cafe. We were really happy to see George and Gerrie. George was so easy to keep company with and no one was sweeter natured than Gerrie.

We returned to our room for a nap and initiation interlude then put on our Sunday best and went downstairs to be taken to the evening's event. There were tons of platters of fruits, veggies, cold cuts, cheeses and mile-long Subway sandwiches. When awards were being given and speeches spoken I watched Stephen with pride and pleasure. During most of the event we sat side-by-side while we visited with some of his old associates including Pepper Gomez, Jimmy Payne, Russ Warner and the Eifermans. Photos were taken and hands were shaken for a couple of hours. Eventually we ended our participation and headed for our room. That hotel room was the scene of our hottest, steamiest, wildest, torrid, full blown sensual session ever which lasted for more than two hours. Adult videos were always the best primer for Stephen - even the milder sort you get in a hotel. The man was awesome and then some!

CHAPTER 26
BIRTHDAY PARTIES, THE BEST SEX AND A HIGH SCHOOL REUNION

We returned home the next afternoon about 1:45 p.m. and found the house clean and the ranch in exactly the same shape as when we left. I guess we were not gone long enough for our two favorite fire-starters to burn the place to the ground! Not long after our return, Stephen changed my workout routine and added more weight on my leg press sets. He said the change was designed to add to my fanny. My workouts included more exercises for my fanny than any other body part. I did six sets of exercises, five days a week, which were specifically focused on my backside. That might sound like next to nothing for bodybuilding persons, but it seemed like a lot to me. I knew it was practically sacrilegious not to eat-up every instruction out of this man's mouth about my workout. Sometimes, I will admit, since it was not part of my nature to cherish bodybuilding, I just wanted Stephen to find me lovable. I was always trying to become what he wanted. The next day he said my back needed more work, which he said he had realized when I tried to "ride the pony" a few days before, so he added more weights to my back exercises. Sigh.

John Kendrick, our rental house tenant, started helping Stephen more regularly with horse training that month. I worked with Stephen in the mornings, first with Sugarloot and then Rocky, and John helped out in the late afternoons or evenings. Stephen's place was essentially a horse ranch and was run as such. Naomi and I always made sure that a resident lizard or two roamed the house. The purpose of resident lizards is to rid the house of flies, moths, mosquitoes and other pesky insects. One afternoon while I was washing the windows in Lynx's room I found one of our little reptile helpers. I returned him to the large windowsill in the living room where he promptly caught a huge fly. Stephen was properly impressed.

On the afternoon of the full moon on July 22, Stephen rented two adult movies for viewing together during our after hours. The rest of the day was full of ranch chores, citrus picking, juice making, doing laundry, irrigation of some of the pastures, horse training, critter feeding, bathroom scouring and the like. Then, finding ourselves alone after dinner, we decided to play some adult games. Sometimes I found it difficult to let Stephen's admiring comments about the female actresses in the adult videos slide over me. Watching sensual scenes between men and women does tend to light a fire even in me and, in spite of the dampening effect of Stephen's words of praise for the women's looks and abilities, he was able to cause me twice to climax while he enjoyed three orgasms. It was not the same insane tempest as our recent Oakland episode, but to me it still seemed like a miracle. When people said Stephen was one of a kind they had no idea.

Stephen decided to build a tall, walled smaller arena within the adobe walled arena for horse training. The goal was to cause the horse they were training to concentrate better. Stephen and John devoted a lot of hours and labor to that project. The temperature was in the nineties. John had wisely brought a supply of Dr. Pepper to keep himself hydrated so several times a day I would take drinks out to Stephen as he always refused to taking a break. The drinks I made consisted of orange juice, cranberry juice, lemon juice and some water. All his long hours in the sun doing various hard, dusty chores required frequent hydration.

Our workouts in the gym were always right after our early morning Power Walks while it was reasonably cool. We did one exercise called a thrust. A wide leather belt was strapped around the hips (not the waist) and then the back of the belt was attached to pulleys and weights. Facing the wall you would hold onto two wooden supports and then thrust your hips forward against the weight. I did 125 pounds at 40 reps and he did 150 pounds and 100 reps. One day in late July I knelt in front of him, pulled his sweat pants down and offered my mouth as his workout partner.

The end of that July was Russ Warner's seventy-seventh birthday party at George and Tuesday's home. I cannot expound enough on what good hosts George and Tuesday always were! I noted in my journal the names of the people who attended (as best as I could remember their names the next day): George and Tuesday Coates, Glen Sunbe and partner, George and Gerrie Eiferman, Jack and Elaine LaLanne, Dr. Charles Moss and wife Marge, Ken Dawson and wife Millie, Armand Tanny, Mike Glass, Malcolm and Wendy Whyatt, Henry and Betty Atkins, Ray Wilson, Eddie Sylvestre, Ray Reardon, Harold Zinken, Artie Zeller and Terry Robinson. We feasted together, had photos taken, talked to friends, had photos taken, laughed, had photos taken, watched Russ open presents, had more photos taken, then we ate great Greek food and thoroughly enjoyed everyone's company except Eddie Sylvestre, who made it his goal, whenever in Stephen's presence, to be an ass. Sometime after this event, Stephen told his friends that if they invited Eddie Sylvestre to their events we would not attend. While I find something to like about almost anyone, Stephen did not. As far as male friends are concerned, at this time I would have to say Stephen was attached to Dave Morris of Valley Center, George Coates, Jim Ford, and Jack LaLanne.

Sometime later we sat down to watch *Hercules Unchained*. During the video he shared with me that during the making of the movie he and his co-star, Sylvia Lopez, had an affair. This romance was apparently pre-Aline. Unwise man that he could sometimes be, he kept talking about how much he enjoyed her. He rewound the video to the scenes where they kissed again and again (well three times) which was not pleasant for me. He seemed to find my displeasure quite amusing. Anyway, after we watched and re-watched the video, Stephen was ready for some sensual release. Even though I was still feeling a bit edgy I did comply and, after I brought him to his climax and he fell asleep, I whispered, "Off to your sweet, sexy dreams and memories my love, I release you." I kissed his big toe then I said my prayers.

The next morning, after our regular interlude, Stephen made a reference to other women's desires for his body and I said, "Well, I hope you never receive an offer you can't refuse." His response was "Me too." Later in the day I told him to do me a favor next time something like that came up. I said, "Lie to me, tell me no one could ever tempt you to do that to me." Somehow the rest of the day was a lot better as I resolutely focused on anything and everything else.

One day in early August, after again insulting my sexual abilities and talking way too much about all the women he had enjoyed in his earlier years I stood up and walked out. Lord Tyrant must have realized that he had crossed the line because he came after me and apologized. Then he topped it off by looking me square in the eyes and saying, "The best sex I've ever had, has been with you." If it was not the truth, it was a really, really kind lie. Either way I loved it.

August and September are generally the hottest months of the year in Valley Center. I continued to be concerned about how many long, hard hours Stephen worked outside on the ranch. On August 9, the temperature was in the high nineties. In addition to his regular Power Walk, workout and care of the horses and upkeep at the barn, he unloaded and spread a load of coarse sand, mowed the lawns around the ranch house, worked Sugarfoot, worked on the large arena, then gave Traveler his groundwork. I spent a good part of my day trying to gauge when Stephen could pause for a hydration break of the fresh fruit and water combination drink. He was totally deaf to my efforts to get him to slow down or consider doing some of the work the next day. To top off the day's activities, that evening he fit in another full training period (with John helping him) with Rocky.

Two days later, having somehow avoided having a heatstroke, he brought up another scenario he wished had been our life. This time he said we should have started our relationship in the summer of 1976. He talked of how our lives would have been so different, the children we might have had and the wasted years we could have filled with our passions. He had not shared one of his wistful regrets of that sort in quite a while.

Naomi and Stephen had been getting along really well, teasing and joking around. They each had a quick wit and loved plays-on-words. I could not help but wish Stephen would get past his sour view of Lynx. A large part was the obvious fact that Lynx was the son of a man who regularly interfered with our life and plans. There was a lot of built-up resentment. Unfortunately, Stephen visited an unfair amount of that resentment on Larry's son.

In the middle of August we attended my twenty-fifth high school reunion, the San Dieguito High Reunion of the Class of 1969, held at de Auberge Hotel and Resort in Del Mar, California. I felt confident that the people I went to school with would either not recognize Steve "Hercules" Reeves or, if they did, they would be totally cool about it. There was one friend, Steven Taylor, I was hoping would be at the reunion as he had been quite a fan of Stephen's when we were in high school. I was hoping he would have the opportunity to meet and talk with Stephen for a while as I knew it would be special to him. Unfortunately, he did not attend. I was really happy to spend time with a friend I had known since third or fourth grade, Laura Fowler Stout, and another high school classmate, Paul Madden, who was dying of AIDS. I was impressed that Stephen was not fazed with the idea of spending part of our evening sitting with an AIDS patient. Back then AIDS was a relatively misunderstood disease and many believed that any proximity to someone with the virus was dangerous. It was the last time most of us would see Paul as he lost his battle with AIDS shortly thereafter. After the reunion, we naturally had a rendezvous planned. Stephen always liked role-playing so he came up with a teacher - student illicit affair fantasy which we acted out on a beach in Del Mar.

A DAY IN THE LIFE

August 16, 1994
Tuesday,
96 degrees
Thunderclouds

Not a wonderful day, but it was live-throughable. Eventually I confronted Stephen with the fact that I am the mother of two children, not one, and that we had spoken earlier in the relationship about the possibility of Lynx coming to live with us sometime. I cannot be expected to rule out Lynx - he is my son. No impact of any noticeable level.

But by the evening we were on an even keel - it seemed to me. So we watched TV, Steve had watermelon and I had ice cream.

A late phone call came from Claire Timmons who apparently grew up, at least part of the time, with Stephen in Oakland. She is quite a character - very entertaining, has not seen Steve in donkeys years she said. Anyway she told me a lot of funny to interesting things, among which was the following story. Steve used to wear big oversize shirts and pants in high school. Then one day at the end of school, he shows up for the big school picnic wearing a tightly fitting T-shirt and well fitted pants. I will tell you, if I had false teeth they would have been on the floor! They would have just fallen out with my mouth hanging wide open. He looked so good. I asked him how he did it and he said he just worked out with weights. I thought I knew him. Boy was I surprised. Then later the girls were talking about how olives are supposed to be an aphrodisiac and I said, "Well get me a whole can of them and I will take him in the bushes!

This Claire Timmons is quite a talker. She was very nice to me though she obviously had quite a lifelong crush on Steve. She said some snotty woman (who claimed she was a Baroness or something) was very rude to her every time she tried to get hold of Steve to let him know about the different high school reunions. She said, "The Baroness hung up on me whenever I called." Anyway, she was fun to talk to.

Stephen paid to have Naomi's front tooth repaired and even went with us to Dr. Adair's to get it fixed!

The End.

On August 23, my mother and her sister, my Aunt Hilda, joined us for lunch to celebrate Hilda's birthday. Stephen had been pretty good natured about most of the family he inherited when I came into his life. In this case he had inherited two middle-aged, eccentric English ladies who had unique, strong opinions about anything and everything that they were only too willing to share. Both of them, like me, were Democrats to his very Republican convictions. When Stephen returned from a quick trip to Escondido, he came into the house carrying a fresh baked apple pie, some Brie and a big welcoming smile. I prepared chicken in rice, mozzarella and tomatoes with a fresh fruit salad. Now that I look back, I think the only thing Stephen did not like about family get-togethers was the photos people wanted to take. Around the time of Hilda's birthday we were doing better in our relationship. Stephen told me that he loved me and danged if his eyes did not seem to say the same thing. It was a good spell for us.

Two days later, as we were lying in bed just prior to starting our prayers and his back rub, he turned to me and said that he had been thinking about our spiritual marriage ceremony in the Chapel of the Transfiguration in Wyoming. He pointed out that we had spoken our vows before each other and God, and that to him meant we were married, just not officially married. I agreed.

Lynx turned sixteen on August 29. His friends, Cale Beck and Travis Devlin, came to help him celebrate. Eric Woods came a bit later but could only stay a few hours as he had an early football practice the following morning. Cale and Travis were spending the night while Naomi had her friend, Nicole Robey, also staying for the night. It was a recipe for disaster so far as Stephen's peace and quiet were concerned. However, not only was he good-natured about all the kids in the house, he gave Lynx $100 for his birthday plus he contributed $14 for a Baskin & Robbins Mud Pie to compliment the birthday cake! At one point Stephen invited the boys down to his gym to show them guy stuff, I guess. We were all impressed with his generosity and good spirits.

I waited until the day after that to tempt Stephen with some new sex wear I had recently purchased. I played coy by initially sticking to our usual routine: the wake-up, the after workout rest and then the afternoon naptime warm-up. Stephen was a bit unusual in one aspect of his sexual preferences. He enjoyed having sex multiple times during the day without climaxing. His favorite pattern was to hold off his orgasm during our three regular, daily sessions and then attempt to explode during the evening session. So in the after-hours of the thirty-first day of August I put on my new black lace garter belt with black stockings and long black lace gloves. I lit two candles and set up the mirror his favorite way. And then I proceeded to tempt him, to seduce him which ultimately resulted in our having the very best session ever (at least to that point in time). Stephen told me he had never before come like that! It was a pretty incredible feat for a sixty-eight year old man. After his back rub and our prayers were finished we both slept like babies. Good night Stephen, good night God.

In early September, on a Saturday, after he had finished working Traveler with John, Stephen came over to the half circle garden where I had been working for a couple of hours. He said, "Put those pruners and the shovel away and come join me in the pool." I put the tools up by the house as I went in to change into a black and white one piece swimsuit that hid the little wrinkles just above my belly button. I found my dearest Lord Tyrant already relaxing in the pool. He saw hesitation on my face when my toes tested the chilly water and so he said, "If you love me, you'll come out here and touch me." In next to no time I was with him and we enjoyed a wet romp.

CHAPTER 27
MUSCLE BEACH CELEBRATION ACCEPTED AND LONDON DECLINED

A man named Steve Ford arranged for Stephen to appear at the Muscle Beach Celebration event held on Labor Day in Venice, California. Mr. Ford and his wife were very attentive to Stephen, Naomi and me when we arrived at the event. It was the only public event Naomi ever attended with us. Stephen took the photo-taking sessions reasonably well. When it was time to leave, Steve Ford provided bodyguards to escort the three of us back to our Jeep. I was the chauffeur all day that time. The Muscle Beach Celebration left Stephen in a great mood and he treated us on the way home with a yummy KFC special chicken dinner, which included a small apple pie, for only $14.99 plus tax.

David Gest called and invited Stephen to an awards evening in London which was to be held on the eighteenth of December. The offer seemed wonderful to me - business class airfare for two, first class hotel accommodations with all meals included for five nights! There was to be an elegant evening of awards and top-notch entertainment. Anthony Hopkins, Ginger Rogers, Princess Diana and many others were scheduled to be there. Robert Wagner was slated to act as Master of Ceremonies. It sure seemed a lovely invitation to me but Stephen declined. He had visited London on multiple occasions in his past and he could not think of any reason he would want to make a return trip. I was understandably disappointed. But no one would enjoy a long, overseas flight and five days in a London hotel with a grumpy Steve Reeves.

CHAPTER 28
NEW SCHOOL YEAR; A BLACK HOLE AND NAOMI'S BIRTHDAY

The school year began for the children and Stephen contributed sixty dollars (in addition to the $100 he gave Lynx for his birthday) to help Lynx purchase the necessary back to school supplies. We were really grateful.

The middle of September Stephen and I fought over expenses. The fight was triggered by a simple mistake I made in not making sure the toilet out in the groom's quarters turned off when I finished cleaning and returned to the ranch house. Hours later Stephen discovered that the toilet was still running. He stormed into the kitchen and vented his anger which then turned into a verbal battle over all the extra expenses I caused him each month. I was about to get into my car and resume my employment search when the weight of the upheaval made me pause. I went and asked Stephen if we could talk. He agreed. We sat down at the dining table and talked at length about the various financial and personal issues involved in our dispute. After due consideration, he offered to forgive all of the debt I owed him, including the $150 balance on Sky's dental bill. He considered his offer a bargaining chip to keep me on the ranch full-time. I understood, appreciated his offer and agreed to forego seeking outside employment.

During our discussion, I asked Stephen what he needed to become happy. His answer surprised me. He had only three requests. First, he wanted me to load the grass clippings from his lawn mowing into the wheelbarrow and haul the clippings to the horse arenas. I happily agreed. Second, he wanted Lynx to do more chores and use less electricity. No problem. Finally, he wanted me seated in my recliner next to his by 8 p.m. every evening. I managed to fulfill this request most but not all evenings. Since he did not ask, I wrote my needs in my current journal along with his requests - knowing that he would read what I wrote sometime later. The needs I included in my journal that night were as follows:

<u>Number one</u>: No more nasty accusations, not ever.

<u>Number two</u>: Only get angry with me when I willfully do something hurtful or damaging not when I accidentally break something or make a mistake.

<u>Number three</u>: Do not throw expenses in my face and I will promise to continue being economical.

<u>Number four</u>: If you actually intend to keep me in your life as partner or wife, supply me with security. If there is anyone you would rather leave your home and or assets to, if you should die, please let me know. If not, provide me with security.

Stephen admitted having regrets about two of his behaviors - being angry with me about Larry's irresponsibility, which I had no control over, and for going in a fit of anger down by the pond and using a machete to destroy our initials that I had carved on our special tree. When I came across the results of his bout of anger it really wounded me. We did not have sex for thirty-two hours which was a record of abstinence for us.

Sometime later, Stephen discovered my old journals and read way too much information about my life with Larry. As a consequence, he was full of resentment at what he referred to as me wasting years of my life. I tried to compare my commitment to Larry to his self-admitted obligation to offer marriage to Aline for all she had done for him. He had stayed with Aline for thirty plus years, until she died, although he freely admitted to me that he was very unhappy most of the time. His relationship with Aline and my relationship with Larry left a lot to be desired. We each, in our time, had good days and bad. Unfortunately, in the final analysis, the bad outweighed the good, at least in my case.

The ranch business was going well. Rocky's training at that time entailed going over obstacles while on the long-lines (reins rigged to go from the horse's head to the guiding hands of the trainer standing in the middle of the arena). The trainer gives instructions to the horse by using his voice, physical contact via the reins and a long training whip. With continued training, Sugarfoot spooked less and less and was steadier under saddle. The Araucana chicks (a South American breed of chickens) were feathering out nicely and would be laying pastel colored eggs for our breakfast by the New Year.

Naomi's fourteenth birthday arrived on September 23. Lynx was the only boy among a half-dozen cute girls but he was not complaining - he even set the party table and put the candles on her cake. Stephen arrived in time to watch Naomi blowout the candles. He gave her the same generous $100 to spend on school clothes.

CHAPTER 29
JACK LALANNE'S
BIRTHDAY PARTY

Lynx agreed to stay and hold down the fort while Stephen and I headed north to Morro Bay and Jack LaLanne's birthday celebration. Stephen was really fond of Jack. Their friendship spanned back to the early days of Stephen's bodybuilding as a young man. These two men thoroughly respected each other.

We drove the 330 miles and arrived in time to check into our motel, change clothes and get to Jack and Elaine's by 5:30 p.m. A considerable crowd had already gathered, but not a lot of familiar faces. We were really pleased to see Russ and Jean Warner, Lou Ferrigno's wife, Carla, and, of course, Jack and Elaine. We were assigned table number seven in a huge white party tent and given a name card each to place where we wanted to sit. No one else had arrived at our table so we had first choice in seat selection. We put our name cards down and propped up our chairs against the table to indicate the two seats were taken. We later put our drinks and my purse at our selected place at the table and then stepped away to socialize. Upon our return to the table we discovered that my name card, purse and drink had been replaced with Betty Weider's card, purse and drink. Betty was the wife of Joe Weider who produced a large line of workout equipment. I located my things and put them back where they belonged next to Stephen. Ms. Weider's card, purse and drink were unceremoniously deposited where she had dumped mine. There was a verbal protest about my removing her things, but not from Stephen.

Carla Ferrigno took the seat on the other side of Stephen. Both Carla and Betty were gorgeous women decked out in beautiful outfits, with manicured nails, perfect teeth and killer figures. I quietly mentioned to Stephen that I felt like a toad with my ranch rough hands, crooked teeth and modest skirt and blouse. That is when another of his miracles happened. Stephen beamed that heart stopping smile of world renown and whispered, "But you forget, I love only my wife, Deborah." He continued to chat with Carla and Betty in their turn but he touched me often and was openly affectionate. Now that is a loving response to calm a jealous spouse. I was on cloud nine.

A little later I went to the rest room and removed my panties. We enjoyed playing games with each other - some of them sensual. It took my dearest Lord Tyrant all of about ten seconds to discover their absence. As soon as I sat back down at the dinner table he put his hand on my leg and then slowly moved it along the inside of my thigh until he discovered my lack of panties. With the tablecloth hiding his actions but not the bemused smile on his face, he took full advantage of the situation. We were amazed at how much we got away with despite the presence of nine other guests sitting at the table. He spawned even more miracles by kissing my ear three different times. I tattooed each little rarity on my heart.

At 10 p.m. we left the party after spending a little time with Jack in his home. Once back at the motel, our games continued all the way from the Jeep, up the stairs and into our room. Of course, once in our room the serious stuff began. I put on black fishnet stockings, a black lace garter, a black lace Teddy and black patent leather heels. We drove each other crazy then granted each other release. We said our prayers, I rubbed his back and then we slept deeply.

We had a nice, uneventful drive home the next day. When we arrived home we found all the animals alive, well and the ranch still standing. We were tuckered out but happy.

CHAPTER 30
GEORGE HELMER; CARROW'S PRIME RIB DINNER

October 6, was a Thursday with fair weather and a 10 a.m. appointment scheduled with George Helmer at the ranch, so I did a little extra spiffing up. I was just finishing wiping down the dining room table when I saw George arrive at the ranch, so I scurried to rush a quick brush through my hair and retrieve my pen and clipboard. During their meeting Stephen and George discussed several subjects but focused mainly on new products George hoped to develop and sell through the Steve Reeves International Society. It all sounded good to Stephen with one exception. The fact that George wanted to include black as one of the color options for the new t-shirts. Stephen believed that black clothing, at least on men, represented either death or some criminal activity. Stephen did not have the same objection with respect to women wearing black - he loved an elegant black evening dress or sexy black lingerie on a woman. I needed to postpone any attempt to change his perspective until he was no longer ticked off at me, which he was that day. I also decided to enlist Sky's help, as I knew Stephen trusted her opinions on several things including what the younger generation might be interested in purchasing. Regardless, once George completed production of those t-shirts, I obtained a couple for myself (which I still have).

The following Saturday morning we had intended to have an interlude after Stephen returned from watering and feeding the horses. However, we promptly fell into a deep sleep when he snuggled back into bed. Stephen bolted out of bed a short time later when he woke and remembered he had to meet John out at the barn for their scheduled 8 a.m. training of Rocky. After scrubbing the pool walls with a long handled brush, I went out to the barn and inventoried the large bin of chrome handiweights leftover from Stephen's Power Walk project - George Helmer was proposing to use or sell the weights. Stephen finished training Rocky with John and then went over to the tack room and installed a large set of red brackets for hanging bridles on. After lunch we had a nice little episode, took a nap then we went to see the movie *The Specialist*. If the movie theater was relatively populated we always sat in the middle of one of the back rows so we could, like a couple of in-heat teenagers, put the dark to good use. In this case, the movie theater was nearly empty which was even better. Some wild moments of buildup which culminated in ecstasy (or so he always said).

When our movie was finished we went to a new Carrow's Restaurant in Escondido that was promoting a special on prime rib dinners. Wow was that great! The Carrow's prime rib dinner specials would become one of our traditions. Years later, when Stephen was in the hospital, he said to me, "When I get out of here you're going to take me to Carrow's for prime rib." I replied, "Absolutely guaranteed!" A little bit later Stephen said, "And tomorrow don't be late, you were five minutes late today." That is the last thing he ever said to me. But that is jumping ahead in our story to May 1, 2000, the day he died.

After the movie we returned home and worked the horses together, in this case Traveler and Sugarfoot. When Stephen turned his attention to unloading the hay he had picked up at Terry's Hay and Grain I went inside and vacuumed the house. Afterwards we worked on correspondence together. I prepared answers to fan inquiries while Stephen signed photos and sent in posters. It was there, while working at the table, that he handed me a small jewelry store brochure with really pretty rings in it. He pointed to one ring in particular and asked me if I liked it. I did! He then said he would buy me any of the rings in the brochure for my wedding ring. It was a stunning offer and I was so excited. I really loved the one Stephen favored. When I mentioned that it was not the least expensive Stephen noted that it was not the most expensive either. I had butterflies in my stomach instead of knots. Pretty cool, huh!

My mother had been under the weather for several days. While discussing her condition, Stephen said that if she should become seriously ill or incapacitated in the future he would be willing to let her stay in the rental house on the corner of the ranch. It was a very gracious offer since it would enable me to care for her, as he had cared for his own mother, Goldie, before she decided she wanted to live in Oregon again.

Stephen, as I have previously mentioned, enjoyed reading my journals - usually at the end of each week. He started this habit early in our relationship. Most of the time, he was really pleased with my rendition of our weekly history. He was less than thrilled with those journal entries which revealed some less admirable parts of his behavior. Be that as it may, he often told me that he considered my journals part of his legacy.

CHAPTER 31
TRIP TO THE EAST COAST

On October 19, we commenced a six day trip to New York and New Jersey. On our flight from San Diego to New York we, by strange coincidence, found ourselves sitting across the aisle from a Valley Center couple named Haas who said they knew our good friend Dave Morris! Once we landed, we were escorted to the Meadowlands Hilton in Secaucus, New Jersey. The next morning, Stephen somehow twisted his knee which plagued him often on that somewhat rainy day. We went by city bus over to New York City. One of our first goals was to find a Hard Rock Cafe in order to purchase a t-shirt for each of the children, as I had promised. Stephen unexpectedly opted to pay for them. Another goal of that trip was to go to the Carnegie Deli which figured prominently in Stephen's past. He used to eat there back in the 1950s when he was a young, starving actor. He was just beginning his career when he landed a role in the off-Broadway play *Kismet*. He and his friends, and later he and his first wife, Sandra, enjoyed eating at the Carnegie Deli. When we arrived there, Stephen ordered his favorite corned beef sandwich for us to share. My makeup had washed into my eyes from all the rain so I went to the restroom to tidy up. The deli was packed with patrons having their own favorite meals. A customer came over and focusing only on Stephen said, "I remember you, you're Steve Reeves!" Stephen gave him a blank look and said, "Sorry, you're mistaken." As we left, a man near the door opened it for us and, reaching for Stephen's hand to shake it, said, "Mr. Reeves, welcome back!" Once again Stephen blew me away by saying, "Sorry, I've never been here before." I could not see the harm in giving these two seemingly warm strangers a moment of his time and a little something to tell their wives when they got home that evening. Several times through the years I witnessed Stephen denying who he was when someone approached him.

That evening we had tickets to attend my first Broadway show. Getting to the show, however, became a bit complicated as you will come to understand as you read the rest of this description of the night's events. Stephen looked sharp in a spiffy dark suit and tie. I wore my black sparkly dress, black stockings and high heels. Before we left the hotel room it occurred to me that the cost of the taxi ride would most probably be prohibitive so I asked Stephen how we were going to get to the theater. As I suspected, Stephen was planning for us to take a bus for our outing to New York. I realized that a change of clothes was in order - there was no way I could risk looking "all that" in a rather short dress as we waited for and then rode a city bus to and from the show. It just felt like we would be asking for trouble and my gallant escort was no longer in his prime. So I put on some jeans, stuffed my dress into the jeans and wore tennis shoes instead of my heels. My stockings were no problem since they were hidden under my pants. I wore my jacket to cover the top portion of that pretty dress and stuck my fancy earrings in the jacket pocket. I traded my evening bag for a large black everyday purse - perfect to carry my high heels in for later. Stephen stood with his mouth gaping wide with surprise when I came out of the bathroom a few moments later. As I showed Stephen the elements of my transformation and explained to him my plan he nodded his head in approval.

We caught a ride on the right bus from our hotel over to the city and then Stephen opted to take a taxi for the short ride from the bus stop to the theater. While in the taxi I slipped off my tennis shoes and pants, and then slipped on my high heels and ear rings while Stephen rolled my pants and stuffed them and my tennis shoes into my large purse. Presto, my handsome one-of-a-kind escort and his somewhat sexy wife, in her awfully pretty short cocktail dress, arrived ship-shape to see the Broadway hit show *Passion*. We were safe and chuckling at my transformation. The play was wonderful and we both had a really good time. Stephen sprang for a taxi ride all the way back to the hotel. Once in our room I made sure he understood how grateful I was. I rubbed liniment on his injured left knee and then his back. We said our prayers and snuggled into bed. Good night Stephen, Good night God, sure do love you!

The next day we had an appointment at the Downtown Athletic Club (DAC). One of Stephen's depressions descended on him that day but we were determined to try to make the best of our day. After a harrowing ride in a taxi with an insane driver, we went into the DAC and I met Johnny Mandel as well as Rudy Riska. We had lunch in the Heisman Room. Mr. Mandel had the look of a Capone-era gangster and yet he was really interesting and often times amusing. Later Stephen and I went over to the Empire State Building where the black cloud within Stephen erupted into a full-blown verbal assault about my character - humiliating me in front of total strangers. I was left terribly hurt and really angry.

The underlying purpose for our trip back east was to participate in a Ray Courts' Hollywood Collectors Show - which was all about Stephen making money. Ray's shows were the best run and most profitable for the celebrities involved. On Saturday morning we came downstairs to the appointed showroom and set up Stephen's display and materials on a generous sized table. We were disappointed that Gordon Scott did not attend the show as he made the atmosphere lighter and somehow always managed to make us laugh. Stephen's depression had lessened but was not entirely dissipated. It sometimes took as much as a week for Stephen to get out from under his funk. I sat on one side of Stephen and an actress named Terry Moore sat on the other side (where Gordon usually sat). She was very attractive but as she was much older than me I knew Stephen would not have the urge to breed her.

During a lull moment, Ms. Moore started massaging Stephen's shoulders and said, "My male companion insists that Steve's shoulders couldn't really still look like that - they must be padded." Which I guess was her excuse for having decided to reach out and feel for herself. I stood up, looked her square in the eye and said, "Keep your hands off, lady!" She quit, saying almost defensively, "Well, you can massage my companion's shoulders if you want." I politely ignored her suggestion. Stephen stood up at one point and went and bought a Mounds bar which he split with me. I understood this gesture to be his peace offering. Although he was fairly buried in his misery I guess it had not been lost on him that it was hard on me too. The tension of the last two days finally started to dissipate. We still had a few rough patches during that day and evening, but I ignored them. Eventually my smiles and responses to both the public and Stephen became more natural. His did as well.

By the time we left New Jersey the next day, Stephen was in one of his joking, adventurous moods. As we were moving through the Newark airport we each helped maneuver our large, heavy bag full of photos and other show-related paraphernalia. Stephen suddenly said, while looking down at our bag, in a loud voice so others could hear, "Gee, I hope the baby can breathe okay in there!" I had to laugh as did a couple of other travelers standing near us. Since we were seated in the very last row on the plane (you know the seats where there is no window and the seats cannot recline) we took advantage of the privacy and entertained ourselves like a couple of college kids. While we waited at the Denver Airport for our connecting flight we headed to the restroom for a small episode of the kind we could not manage in our seats. For Stephen it was always a game. He somehow found a way to make every new experience or new place a first. And he was checking them off his mental fantasy list.

On our drive home from the San Diego airport we stopped at the Apothecary Shop in Escondido for some quinine as Stephen had developed a cold from getting rained on in New York. As we pulled onto the ranch, John Kendrick was there starting a training session with Rocky. Stephen stepped out of the Jeep and paused near the lime tree in order to relieve himself -which elicited an appreciative wolf whistle from Mr. Shivers. Then he headed up to supervise Rocky's groundwork. It was so good to be home. The animals were fed and watered, the house pretty much the way it was when we left and all the buildings were still standing. The kids were pleased with the Hard Rock Cafe - New York t-shirts. Then to top it off, the next day he gave each of them twenty dollars and said he wanted to share some of the money he made while we were gone. I was not the only one who felt he was being generous. That was a special day.

CHAPTER 32
OUR SECOND NOVEMBER TOGETHER

Within a few days of our return Jose, a day laborer, showed up looking for work. I was really glad to see him as he helped Stephen so much on so many projects. The ranch always looked better, tidier, after Jose spent a day helping out. The next day Stephen and John took Torrey and Rocky on a trail ride. Stephen said Rocky did really well. They had worked and worked with Rocky so it was gratifying that he did so well. After John went home Stephen and I mucked out the front paddocks and then cleaned up so we could take the kids to a movie. Lynx and Naomi watched *Stargate* while we saw *River Wild*. As Stephen was ever mindful of cost we almost always went to matinees. The kids were just pleased to be taken to the movies. Afterwards came the cherry on top - Stephen bought us each a burger at Burger King.

When we returned to the ranch it was time for a nap. Stephen woke up in a good mood and when he turned to speak to me, he smiled. He transformed from his stern and pensive self to the handsome and happy man I fell in love with. When I expressed my delighted surprise at his transformation he found it amusing. Those who have been close to someone who suffers from depression understand how sad it makes you to know that your loved one is unhappy so much of the time. I wished I could have made a bigger difference. Later that afternoon we sat together to watch a copy of his *Romulus and Remus* movie (also known as *Duel of the Titans*). Even with its really faulty dubbing we took pleasure in watching the movie.

George Helmer brought his wife, C.J., and two daughters with him for his meeting with Stephen on November 5. I was pleased to welcome them to the ranch and found C.J. to be a pretty, obviously intelligent woman, and their daughters - two blonde athletic youngsters - had great manners. The girls really enjoyed the horses. During the business meeting with George, Stephen signed forty movie photos and thirty body-building photos for George to sell. After the Helmers left, Stephen, Naomi and I went to Escondido where he bought me a pair of Reebok athletic shoes (my old tennis shoes let the rain in when we were in New York City). He told me the Reeboks were my Christmas present. Then he took us to Pizza Hut for an early dinner. Nothing really decent was on the television that evening, we only received channels 6, 8 and 10, so after Sky went to bed Stephen and I watched two of his movies - *The White Warrior* and *Goliath and the Barbarians* on VHS videos that were given to us by George. I was amazed when Stephen told me a few days earlier that he had never watched them. I will be forever grateful to George Helmer for bringing us a copy of those two movies so Stephen and I could watch them together. We particularly enjoyed *The White Warrior* and celebrated by having our third interlude for the day there in the recliner.

In an effort to stretch my meager household allowance to cover both the usual monthly expenses in addition to some Christmas related expenditures, Stephen requested that I cut in half whatever monies I had planned to spend on him. He also offered to pay for Naomi's much needed new shoes, which I planned to get her for Christmas. Then he added with uncharacteristic but much appreciated generosity to also purchase the leather vest which was on Lynx's Christmas list. Then on top of all of that he gave me twenty dollars to replace the money I spent in New York. Sometimes he was particularly thoughtful and I was touched.

Shortly thereafter we had a working Sunday where we stayed on the ranch, all four of us. While the kids ate their breakfast Stephen and John took Sugarfoot and Rocky for another trail ride up over the hill and down toward Palma Valley. When they returned Stephen was obviously pleased with the progress the horses were making. Lynx, Naomi and I raked leaves into piles and then began the long, slow, repetitive process of loading piles into Stephen's Dodge pickup. There was a section of land beyond all the pasture fences where ranch debris was piled and allowed to decompose. Lynx drove the loaded truck in reverse all the way down the long hill to this section of land so we could add the leaves to the debris. Once we unloaded the truck we all jumped in and he drove us back up to the next set of piles.

Stephen came to help us once he was done with the horses. After unloading the leaves, Lynx sat on the side of the truck bed while Stephen drove the truck back up the hill. Stephen's old dog, Zorro, began to run alongside the truck - on the same side that Lynx was riding. Without warning, Zorro jumped up and bit Lynx knocking him headfirst into the wheel-well inside the bed of the truck. Stephen rushed him back to the house. Turned out his injuries were not serious. The bite would heal after a thorough cleaning, some Neosporin and bandaging. His poor head had a painful lump but an ice pack and Excedrin seemed to help. I wanted to, but did not, throttle Zorro.

November 8, election day, began as any other weekday with our standard wake-up call session, horse feeding and walk but we threw in an erotic escapade down by the pond (on the other side of the orange grove), just for good measure. Then we did our gym workout with my routine customized by Stephen that morning as he was still trying to help me develop a decent fanny. While he finished his work out, stretch and pool exercises, I climbed two Valencia trees to pick enough oranges for his morning juice and some to store in the freezer. We left the ranch after breakfast to go vote at our assigned location, St. Stephen's Catholic Church over on Cole Grade Road. Since Stephen was a strict Republican and I tended to vote Democrat we canceled each other's votes on most of the positions and issues on the ballet.

That evening I sensed a little ghostie of anger trying to ruin Stephen's good mood but he fought it down and treated me just fine. We spoke of the delightful moment we enjoyed during that morning's walk (in the pre-dawn darkness) when we surprised three coyotes. Actually I am not certain whether the coyotes or Stephen and I were more surprised. Wildlife was being forced out of our area due to continued development so it was a rare treat for us. Personally I miss the raccoons, coyotes and quails the most. As the television options that evening consisted of coverage of the election, we decided to watch a video of *Sandokan the Great* in our bedroom. Turned out to be a pretty good reproduction with decent color and dubbing. In any case, I really had a good time watching the story. After the movie I read Stephen one of those sensually stimulating scenarios. We opted to forgo the candles, incense and sex wear but I treated him to a loving climax. Then we said our prayers. When I finished my prayers I said, "Sweet dreams and may you wake up in a great mood." To which he replied, "May you wake up in a good mood - but you always do - unless you're given a reason not to." That small acknowledgment certainly surprised me.

Jose showed up unexpectedly the next morning, so he and Stephen were able to get key things done around the ranch prior to our promised rain. The fact that Jose was there naturally meant that Stephen would not be asking me to help as much outside. So I tackled the bills and correspondence with fans. Jose was a good worker and got more done in a shorter time than I did doing the same chores. By the time I prepared lunch they had cleaned all the paddocks and stalls, Stephen had replaced a hinge on one of the stall doors and Jose had cleaned out Daisy's pen. The work continued after our shortened nap and session in order to make best use of Jose s presence.

Later in the afternoon, just prior to John Kendrick coming to help with the scheduled horse training, I was sitting on the floor in Naomi's room sorting through a pile of magazines when Stephen entered her room and sat on the bed. I asked him, "Do you need me for something?" And he tenderly replied, "I need you, I always need you." There is an old cowboy saying, "Making it in life is kind of like bustin' broncs - you are gonna get thrown a lot. The secret is to keep getting back on." Loving moments like these helped me to dust myself off and get back on despite the harsh things he said at other times.

Shortly after John and Stephen ended their horse training that evening it began to rain. Lynx was not feeling well and Naomi decided to keep at her homework so I set the table for two and lit a couple of candles. For dinner I prepared the beef and potatoes with barley that Stephen liked so much - simmering it much of the day in the crockpot. I delivered a plate to Lynx in bed and some to Naomi at the kitchen table where she was doing homework. When Stephen came in from work out at the barn he washed up and we ate by ourselves at the dining table. When it was time for Bible reading we discussed Hebrews 2:1 through 18 then we watched some television but decided to go to bed fairly early. Since the rain had started up again I added a really large log to keep the fire going until morning, then headed for a rendezvous in my Lord Tyrant's bed. I reminded myself how lucky we were to be snug in a warm bed while listening to the rain outside. So we thanked God at the end of our session for our many blessings, then I rubbed his back until he fell asleep. Good night Stephen. Good night God.

I had plans to have lunch at my mother's house and Stephen had plans to get his hair cut then head down to Jack and Guillo's Spaghetti Western restaurant in Old Town, San Diego. It was November 15th and we were getting along really well. A friend, Dwayne Thomas, let Stephen know about the annual event. Stephen enjoyed the company of a few special friends relishing the marvelous food of Jack and Guillo. I left my mother's house after a good visit with the usual talk of politics, family and the upcoming holidays. About 3 p.m., I decided to take a short nap thinking Stephen would join me under the covers as soon as he came in. I was jarred awake by Stephen's booming voice demanding to know what the heck I was doing "being a lazy bum in bed at almost 4 p.m.!" I bolted out of bed and ran out to help him at the barn with a horse. So much for my thoughts about a quick snuggle. All was not lost though as much of our evening he was delightfully friendly. We became acutely aware of the electrical sparks between us which created the perfect chemistry and led to a great finale.

For the next few days Stephen was even more sexually motivated than normal, which was manifested in his teasing me and actually brushing up against me, which was very rare. He related sexy jokes and then he put one of my earrings in the pierced skin of his cock. When he was a young man he heard that if a guy pierces the skin of his cock near the head and tied a horsehair loop around it going through the piercing that his lover would experience a better climax. The piercing was not obvious. I did not even notice it until he showed me. And you know how much time I spent in close contact with his manhood. He was forward thinking at an early age. These days he just played games with it by lacing up a horsehair loop made of three horsetail hairs he braided or, as in this instance, putting on one of my earrings for fun. So far as I was concerned, his fancy cock was just part of our games. Unfortunately, the only time Stephen could maintain an erection during intercourse was if I faced away from him while I "rode the pony". I had so much to be grateful for but it caused me great sadness that he always lost interest at the idea of completing his orgasm while inside me - except orally. He maintained magnificently that way.

His favorite lunch consisted of a sandwich made a very specific way. We put mayonnaise on one slice and Grey Poupon on the other slice of Oroweat's Winter Wheat Master's Blend bread. Two slices of cheese (provolone or Swiss) were placed on top of the mayo slice followed by two slices of liverwurst and two slices of red onion. The Grey Poupon slice was then placed on top. He insisted that if the order of creation was changed the sandwich would be ruined.

After chores where completed the next Saturday, Stephen and I watched the *Lawrence Welk Show* then *Matlock* on television as I darned two more pairs of his wool socks. Then, when a movie came on, I continued my work on sorting his lifetime collection of photos. I came across an old photo album that Aline had started in the mid-1960s but never finished. I thought it would be a nice gesture to complete the unfinished project so I set aside photos from that time, specifically 1965 to 1968, as I came across them to consider placing in her album. Eventually I would send four boxes of Aline's photos and some books in Polish to her brother in England. I noted with interest several photos of Aline and Stephen with Tyrone Power and other celebrities. Dumped in bags and boxes in various closets and cupboards, Stephen's photos felt like a lost treasure. I wanted to honor Stephen and his history. I was plagued by the thought of those photos lying wasted and unappreciated so I became serious in my efforts to organize them. I also discovered a few large envelopes, a couple of flat boxes and some notebooks full of loose newspaper clippings about Stephen's movies and career. I found the clippings fascinating and promised myself to get around to sorting those as well. Much of the time Stephen seemed disinterested but once in a while he looked over and would talk about someone or some time that the photos illustrated. He really became animated when the photos were of his horses or his champion red Angus cattle. Horse and ranch photos were his favorites. Oh yes, as well as those of his pickup trucks. He was his ranching father's son and ranching was in his veins.

CHAPTER 33
ACADEMY OF BODYBUILDING AWARDS

We were to attend the Academy of Bodybuilding Awards in Redondo Beach, California on November 20th. By 12:20 p.m. we were on our way. We filled the jeep with gasoline, purchased batteries for the camera, ordered a Subway tuna sandwich and headed north. Stephen was in a pretty decent mood as we arrived at the Holiday Inn Crowne Plaza on Harbor Drive. We checked into our room and he rested while I got ready. I knew how much he hated when my hair turned out sort of frizzy so I tried to tame it down. Then we enjoyed a private little interlude when he roused long enough to request one. Then it was back to prepping myself again. With my ranch style working hands, quick pretty nails are a partial solution in fancy surroundings. Well, not even Hercules could budge the lid off the glue bottle so I poked a hole in the side of the plastic bottle and finished gluing the acrylic nails in place. Stephen zipped me up and we left for the event.

We enjoyed seeing the Grimeks, the Warners, Don Peters, Clint Walker, Glenn Sumbe, George and Tuesday Coates, Lou and Carla Ferrigno, Charlie and Marge Moss, George and Gerrie Eiferman, and Jack and Elaine LaLanne. I felt pretty in the fancy little cocktail dress I had worn stuffed into my pants and covered with my jacket back in New York City. Now, at least, there was no need to hide it and I was ready to enjoy an evening on the arm of my arrestingly handsome husband. Stephen never quite ignored me but if I wanted his arm I had to take it, if I wanted his hand I had to reach for it and he never once glanced at me when I took either. Maybe no one noticed that stuff but me.

If the organizers had not expected "the legends of bodybuilding" to stand together for endless photos I think it would have been a tolerable event for Stephen. We found it weird and insulting that the organizers included in the assemblage of legends a whole hoard of people we did not feel belonged, including Eddie Sylvestre - who in our opinion was the perfect description of slime ball. When Eddie slipped up behind and put his hand on Stephen's shoulder to pose for a photo I thought Stephen would explode! I cringed when I was certain Stephen was about to punch Eddie, but he thought better of it. I pitied Eddie's wife, who seemed a perfectly nice lady. The endless barrage of photos ended, as did all hope of having a nice evening, when Stephen abruptly stormed off after Eddie pulled his classless move and tried to appear as his friend. Stephen was angry and ready to leave right then and there but he had promised Frank Stallone that he would sign some posters. He did enjoy speaking with Frank for quite a while but for him the event had soured.

On our drive back from Redondo Beach, he shared that one time his friend, Don Peters, had offered to hook Stephen up with his wife (they were apparently still married but separated at the time). Stephen then admitted that he had likewise offered his Sandra to a friend but had withdrawn the proposition because the thought of this other guy with his Sandra drove him crazy. He went on and on about how he first met her, dated her (she was seventeen at the time), felt about her and then called and asked her to marry him. They married and moved to New York where he was acting in *Kismet*. They later bought a station wagon and moved to Florida where he bought a gym. Sometime later Stephen said he decided he wanted to travel alone and Sandra, who according to him never disagreed with him about anything, said, "If that's what you want." So he filed for divorce.

They continued to live together (and sleep together) after Stephen filed for divorce until he sold the gym and moved to California. He said he drove her across the country, carried her bags to the door of her parents' house, set the bags down and then left. He astonished me by admitting that he later returned and dated her! He conceded that Sandra's father did not like him dating her now that they were divorced. He then announced that he could have Sandra back anytime he wanted - that she would leave any husband for him in a split second.

When we arrived home we found the house in perfect condition. The kids were in school but the doors were all locked, the heater and lights were all off, the counters and bathrooms were clean, the dogs and cats fed and a load of laundry completed - even Stephen's shirts were folded the special way he preferred.

A DAY IN THE LIFE

November 23, 1994
Wednesday
69 degrees

A better day. Some of his gloom has lifted. Had a talk with him to ascertain the source of his depressions. He seemed to know exactly the first time the depression descended on him. He said the first time was in his Aunt's house as a boy, when she was showing Steve pictures of his Dad and talking about family. All of a sudden Steve says he felt all alone in the world. So it suddenly became painfully, vividly clear in Steve's Aunt's house - he was missing the family he was born to know and be part of. Apparently his mother didn't associate with either family much, then moved clear to Oakland, California, Steve said he never was a happy person, an "up person".

The End.

Thanksgiving Day went well. My brother David and his wife Joanne are vegetarian so it fell on me to prepare all the meat dishes. Stephen and I arrived at my brother's home with Lynx and Naomi at 1:15 p.m. as agreed upon. We brought with us the turkey, dressing, gravy and three homemade pies (apple, pumpkin and mince). Gathered for the feast was David, Joanne, their three children (Nate, Zack and Vania), the four of us, my mother and my aunt Hilda. Stephen was in a warm and friendly mood - just like our early days. I am sure we appeared to be the same loving couple we were at Christmas last year.

Two days after Thanksgiving it dawned dark and rainy. We had a really great early morning session after which we snuggled and chatted. I asked Stephen about preparing a last will and testament. He said that he had an odd feeling that if he wrote a will it would somehow invite death to his door. Knowing I could not use logic against such nebulous feelings, I tried another approach. I inquired as to what he wanted to have happen in the event of his death. Did he want the government or his cousins to inherit his estate? He replied with an emphatic, "NO!" I said nothing more at the time.

I knew, when Stephen was finished training whichever horse he was working with that morning, he would want to watch football while I served him lunch at his recliner. After the football game (he was a Charger fan) while Stephen went out to feed the horses their evening meal, I built a nice fire. I have always loved rainy days. The kids were visiting their dad, which happened less often than in the past, so we had the house to ourselves. I served my dearest Lord Tyrant a delicious menu of sexual delights. He fell asleep in his recliner with a big smile on his face.

With Lou and Carla Ferrigno at the
Bodybuilding Awards at Redondo Beach, Nov 1994

CHAPTER 34
DECEMBER AND THE SOUTHERN CALIFORNIA MOTION PICTURE COUNCIL AWARDS

We did our Power Walk but skipped our work out with weights because we needed to leave by 7:38 a.m. for the Southern California Motion Picture Council Awards in Studio City. It was held in a place called the Sportsman's Lodge which was appropriately landscaped with pine trees, meandering walkways, ponds and bridges. Nice enough that we were willing to just stay outside and enjoy the ambiance of the lodge. We had been informed it was to be a small event so we were not exactly prepared to walk into the Empire Room and find tons of people. Many of the women were wearing opulent gowns with sequins, satin and feathers. Our seats were at a table that was front and center of the semi-chaotic awards show.

An error on the part of Bea Beyer, who somehow lost our tickets, caused the help to refuse to serve Stephen and me any lunch despite the fact that he was the guest of honor! I hustled into the kitchen, confronted the cook and took care of that silly mistake. I was concerned that Stephen was about to heave our table with nine already served lunch plates either onto the laps of the other table guests or onto the floor. You do not refuse to serve Hercules his lunch!

After lunch Bea Beyer added insult to injury by doing a hatchet job on Stephen's introduction and bio. When Stephen made his appearance on stage, he was more than merely fit - he looked strong, handsome and virile as hell. And every lady in the place felt it. One other tidbit from the award show caught my attention. There were written and verbal references to a club known as the Ebell Hollenbeck, an organization for women actors and hoofers (dancers) that my grandmother, Kathryn Engelhorn, once belonged to back in the 1920s and 30s. My father's mother was on stage in Denver, then San Diego and Hollywood. Anyway, I was surprised to discover that the club was still active and had representatives at this particular awards show.

On our way home we stopped at a Burger King in Escondido because they were advertising ninety-nine cent Whoppers. Even though we were both tired I was surprised that great sex was still possible when we finally hit the sack. No VCR skin flicks, just me in the dark with him. Afterwards we said a slightly fuzzy prayer, at least on my part. Good night Stephen. Good night God.

The next morning we began a "work project day" on the ranch. Lynx cleaned paddocks for a couple of hours, Naomi worked on the pool and I scrubbed out water barrels for the horses until Stephen asked me to help pull fence with the truck. Horses like to lean on fences and rub along them which ultimately caused the fence to lean out. We would attach one end of a chain to the trailer hitch of the truck and the other end would be attached to the nearest fence post. Then I would slowly drive the truck until the chain was taut. Stephen would signal me to move the truck further while he gauged how much to pull the fence before signaling me with a whistle to stop. You had to pull it just slightly further than you wanted so it would snap upright once free of the chain. Stephen could get really impatient if things did not happen with absolute perfection. Then we would move on to the next fence area that needed straightening.

Work went unusually well so Stephen gave me a pat on the head (which amused me) and offered to take Naomi and I to the bargain matinee of *The Professional*. Lynx was invited by his friend Allen to the Will Rogers Follies at the new Center for the Arts in Escondido. He was initially reluctant to go but Stephen talked him into accepting the invitation. Later, when asked he said it was really awesome and tried hard to get us to go. Stephen was of the mindset, however, that we could not afford the tickets. I have since learned that Stephen's attitude regarding spending money is quite common among those who are retired due to an innate fear of outliving their money.

The next day we were expecting Troy Bertelsen to arrive at the ranch. Stephen had agreed to let Troy come for a brief two day visit as long as he brought with him a few pairs of the Wigwam wool socks that Stephen preferred. We could not find any in the local stores. Prior to the advent of the world-wide-web, finding and purchasing such specialty items was not easy. Stephen and I had purchased two pairs of Wigwam socks (Stephen referred to them as stockings) in Bozeman, Montana while we were there. Since Troy lived in Bozeman he was the perfect person to call upon to purchase and deliver a few pairs. Then too, Stephen had come up with a list of ranch chores he could have Troy do for him. Troy was a good worker and good with horses. It was a win-win situation.

Knowing Troy was coming, I did some extra shopping to feed our guest well, then I put diesel in the truck and went to the Post Office to pick up our mail (Stephen's mail for the most part since the only mail I received was from the IRS). When I returned home I found Stephen trimming the hooves of his goat named Daisy. Goats need their hooves trimmed a few times a year unless the animal is wearing them down by walking or climbing on rough surfaces like rock. Daisy was Stephen's retired milking doe. The fact that he kept and cared for her despite retirement spoke volumes to me, an animal lover since birth. Later that evening, Troy called to explain that he could not come after all which meant a shift in our plans and no new stockings for my dearest Lord Tyrant's feet.

It was December 10, which happened to be a Saturday, and the house was extremely chilly. Stephen went out early to feed the horses hay and grain but shortly thereafter returned, slipped back under the covers and put his icy cold feet on me to warm them. After my initial squeak of shock I was more than willing to help his feet get toasty again. I started by briskly rubbing his cold tootsies between my hands then massaged my way up his muscular legs. He caught his breath and gave me full reign.

Eventually we had to get up of course. After we escorted the kids over to their friends' homes to spend the weekend, we went to visit and have lunch with my mother before heading up to San Pedro in Los Angeles. Tom Lincir had invited us to a yacht party at birth 29. Since Stephen wanted to visit with another of the invited guests about a business idea he had, he decided we would go. On board the yacht, the guests visited and then started serving themselves once the feast was presented. We had learned that when food is first offered is the perfect time for Mr. and Mrs. Reeves to slip away for a romantic interlude. Most guests at an event jump in line when food is proffered to the crowd. So we sneaked off, found private quarters and initiated yet another yacht. Naturally that was the best part of the little voyage for us.

Having satisfied one appetite we quietly rejoined our host and his significant other at their table. The food was marvelous. Stephen left my side after a plate full of dinner to speak with a man I was not familiar with. By 9:30 p.m., many of the guests, including Stephen and I, were ready to call it a night but the captain had his orders so we were out a lot longer than we would have liked. While we were sitting at the table, our hostess sat down and invited us to spend the night at their house. When Stephen declined she put her hand on his thigh and tried to change his mind. Feline instincts aroused, I was about to take action when Stephen preempted me by standing up and stating firmly that we had other plans. Our good friends, Charlie and Marge Moss, were expecting us to spend the night at their home. Poor Charlie and Marge were kept waiting for us until 11:40 p.m. due to the late return to the dock. They were very gracious nonetheless. That night there was a 3.4 earthquake pretty much right under us there at the Moss' home. We were so tired we both slept right through it! We were surprised when the next morning Charlie told us about the small shaker. He and Marge were great hosts and fed us a delicious breakfast after which we headed for home.

When we arrived back at the ranch it quickly became business as usual. For the moment, however, life was good. Stephen had a tradition that his Christmas tree had to be put up and the house decorated on December 15th each year. Stephen hired a day worker to help spiff up the grounds and the ranch was looking really pretty good. John and Stephen worked the horses regularly. Sugarfoot was turning out to be a really good mount and Stephen had no regrets about having obtained her. Traveling Man was doing particularly well in his groundwork and, while not of our breeding stock, he could easily be a very nice work or riding horse. Torrey, who had an eye infection, was now much better. Stephen said that John was pleased with Rocky on the trail, so all was well as far as the horses and training was concerned.

Christmas Day 1994 went really well. I was prepared mentally for Stephen's unique attitude about gifts he received. He did not want the illuminating light I bought for his horse painting. He changed his mind about the cologne I had, pursuant to his instructions, bought him and decided he wanted one called Stetson Sierra. The Dockers pants I gave him were the right size but turned out to be the wrong shade of gray. He told me to return all three gifts. This time I toughened up and was not so hurt by his attitude.

I was grateful to Stephen for allowing my extended family (mother, aunt Hilda, brothers and their families) to congregate and celebrate Christmas in his home. He even paid for the lion's share of our meal. We took photos, laughed, gorged ourselves on all the food and told stories. We had a really lovely Christmas celebration with the fire in the fireplace crackling and the house warm and appropriately decorated. No more Christmas alone for Stephen.

New Year's Eve day had some really wobbly moments. Stephen changed his mind, again, and declared that he wanted a different bottle of cologne instead of the replacement Stetson Sierra he had asked for. He rarely wore cologne and never used deodorant (he said if you eat right you will not smell offensive). All of us at the ranch disagreed with his position on the matter but could hardly say so. Now he said that the X-rated video I bought him for our after-hours had to be returned as he did not like the scenarios depicted or two of the female participants. I did not mention the X-rated video when I spoke of our Christmas gifts before as it was given to Stephen in private, not at the family gift exchange. He made a remark again about exchanging me for a different woman. His words made me feel hollow, lonely and unbearably sad, and reminded me that in his heart everything was exchangeable, replaceable. After exchanging everything except myself, I found some solace in going for a horse ride, me on Torrey and my love on Sugar, up over the hill and down toward Pauma Valley.

For New Year's Eve we rented a three-hour video, the one called *Texas*, which I believe was written by Stephen's friend, James A. Michener. We ate a little apple pie a la mode and watched the movie while I stoked two fires, one in the man in the recliner next to me and the other in the fireplace. Our pets were our only company. We had two sessions - one just before midnight and the other just after. Happy New Year!

Christmas 1994
Stephen, Deborah, Naomi and Lynx

Family Christmas at the Ranch 1994
Back Row (left to right): Sue, cousin Jack, Stephen, Lynx, Pete and Lin, his wife
Front Row (left to right): Naomi, Amanda, Deborah and Aunt Hilda

CHAPTER 35
1995 BEGINS

The first of January of 1995 found Stephen in a very good mood. Our walk and workout went really well during which he laughed and teased me. When we rested afterwards I gave him his customary warm-up and when he gazed at me I saw that warmth I valued so much. I knew from experience it would not last but I reveled in it while it was there. For now he was everything I could hope for and he behaved as if I was everything he wanted.

When he made his New Year's resolution it was, as expected, regarding our "sexual study". He announced that I was to "bring him off" at least once a day for all of 1995. I have to admit I found his resolution amusing. Thus far in our relationship we had participated in planned and agreed-upon sensual stimulation a minimum of three times a day. Scientific Stephen had decided his experiment was going sufficiently well enough to schedule an ejaculation once a day, minimum. Many were the days he had experienced multiple orgasms but now we had an official decree by my dearest Lord Tyrant.

My journal for January 2, 1995, states that, among other things, we participated in sexual contact five times that day: three times in bed (morning, noon and night), once during our workout in the gym and once on the hallway floor (Stephen liked the mirrors in the hallway). He was in a particularly potent state that day. He was quite fiery in his role of master to my usual sex slave.

Instead of doing our walk the next morning we went directly to the workout as it was bucketing rain. The back patio and the walled arena had turned into ponds. Since working outside was not possible we went through a wooden box, brought by Stephen from storage in the barn, containing his mother's things. She had saved pretty much every Christmas, birthday and Mother's Day card Stephen had ever given her. We found a blue leather jewelry box, containing a few pieces of her jewelry, which I adopted as my own and still keep my jewelry in, and a small flat box of old photos and negatives. There was also a large envelope of articles and clippings about Stephen and his career. I was really interested in sorting through the photos and newspaper items about Stephen.

January 8 was the second anniversary of our first real contact, our first real talk. Although we officially met in 1973, we never spoke more than a passing "good morning" until January 8, 1993. We spoke that day as two adults who felt a mutual flicker of interest. Now, two years later, we stayed home and watched the Chargers play the Miami Dolphins. I kept the fire raging in both the fireplace and my man. I had made lasagna the night before so it would taste extra good this day. We also ate salad and French bread then his favorite apple pie (with a chunk of cheddar cheese for him). I served him a mixed pair of light and dark beers. Stephen was in a good mood, our horses were healthy, our cats and dogs spent much of the day keeping us company and all was quietly right at the Reeves ranch.

CHAPTER 36
"SO-CALLED WIFE";
FAILURE TO LAUNCH

Near the middle of January Stephen suggested we get married on Valentine's Day, February 14th because it fell on the right side of the moon and his astrological sign. Those two factors counted in his plans. Obviously I had no objections but I cautioned myself with the thought, "I will believe it five days after it has happened."

When I am building a fire, I tend to worry about all the little critters that hideout in the bark and in the little crevices of the logs. I have never discovered a way to get all of them to vacate the logs before I put them on the fire. It is possible to scoop some of them up as they make a dash to escape the heat. One evening we were watching *My So-Called Life* on the television. As Stephen observed me capture some little life as it ran from the fire he chuckled and said, "There is my so-called wife saving the world." From than evening onward he often referred to me as his "so-called wife".

Not long after that, Naomi came to me with a concern over her father describing me as nothing but a whore. In fact, he told both Naomi and Lynx that I was actually lower than a whore. When I spoke to Stephen about what Larry had said, his response touched me. He smiled, gazed into my eyes and said, "I love you." Nothing else seemed to matter after that.

After dinner that evening I asked Stephen if he would someday take Naomi and I to an El Torito restaurant for their special deal. We had all seen their advertisements on the television and had spoken of how good their meals looked. Stephen said that I would not be able to finish such a large meal and would therefore undoubtedly want to take some of it home in a "doggy bag" like the low-class person I was. That comment was just starting to sting when he added, "No one with any class takes food home from a restaurant except Chinese food as then, it is expected." He finished by saying, "You are too low-class to even realize how bad you look!" I was angry with his verdict about my classless behavior and felt (not for the first time) that his own current behavior was the pot calling the kettle black. He snapped at me a few more times that evening but I held my tongue while noticing he was lost to me again. If he did not want to take us to the El Torito restaurant I wish he had just said so!

Although I expected his foul mood to continue for a few days, the next morning he was in a marvelous mood. We had long, slow sex and talked. Then for no apparent reason he decided to make me a toasted bagel for breakfast. I teased him, "Hey, what did you do with last night's Stephen?" He just grinned and answered, "Got myself a new attitude!" He spoke to me of wishing he had met me when he was eighteen. He said he needed me then so he could have had adventurous sex as a young man. He said if I had been there in his early life we could have corresponded while he was overseas and that I could have been waiting for him, loving him. I replied, "And you would have loved and cherished me beyond belief!" He agreed. It was the most loving way to begin our day. Remember that I was not even born until Stephen was well into his twenty-fifth year.

On Tuesday, January 17, Stephen ordered my wedding ring and paid extra to have its delivery expedited. I was pleased, particularly since he did not behave resentful about the cost. That meant everything to me. Stephen asked me if I wanted to use the ring as an engagement ring instead of wedding ring. He offered to have a band made for me for a wedding ring. I told him that I would very much like to use his mother's wedding ring. It was decided then - Goldie's wedding ring would be mine when we married. I was walking on cloud nine.

We spent part of the day working on the details of a prenuptial agreement, which sounds negative but was not at all. The prenup was the first step in insuring that the debts and liabilities from my marriage to Larry could not and would not adversely affect Stephen or his estate. We were particularly concerned about past due federal and state income taxes. He further surprised me by deciding to set the record straight. He had read my journal entries about Larry telling the kids that I was a whore and my muses that I was more a mistress than a whore. Stephen looked me straight in the eyes and stated with finality that I was neither a whore nor a mistress. He explained that a mistress was supported to provide sex and nothing else. He then noted that I kept house, cooked, helped with ranch work, office work and a host of other duties in his life. He surprised me by speaking of my services as having considerable value. I could not have been more pleased. Surely this day had been perfect.

January 21, was Stephen's sixty-ninth birthday so after a special wake-up call and the usual Saturday morning chores, we drove up to a quaint restaurant located on Palomar Mountain and enjoyed mugs of hot chocolate while looking out at the freshly fallen snow. Next we drove over to the Ranchita property. We were in the midst of a rare wet year here in California. Thirty-four counties had been declared disaster areas so we were naturally concerned about possible erosion damage. Fortunately, when we arrived at the Ranchita property the only erosion we found was in the same areas and no worse than that which had occurred the year before. As we walked around inspecting the property we also started making plans for the future. We wanted to erect horse corrals and build a weekend cabin on the five acre property. We returned to the ranch but left shortly after to go see a movie we had seen advertisements for called *Legends of the Fall*. It was so good that we ended up forgoing our usual sensual escapade in the theater. When the movie was over we enjoyed a prime rib dinner at the Fireside Restaurant. When bedtime came I set the scene by wearing my sexy, deep purple teddy and black stockings, lighting two candles, adjusting the mirror, and curling hair as I knew he would prefer it. Happy birthday my Sweet Lord Tyrant!

In late January Stephen became very agitated when he misplaced his very nice prescription sunglasses. As a part of my search I decided to check the tack room. I imagined that when coming in out of the sun to work on leather or buckles he could easily have absentmindedly set his glasses down somewhere in there. Although I did not find his sunglasses I did discover another wooden storage box. I pulled it out far enough to look inside and was excited to spy a whole new treasure trove. Inside was a host of Goldie's mementos including linens, photos and Stephen's childhood wood burning projects.

The day my much anticipated ring arrived I was particularly excited. I had been slathering my rough ranch hands with moisturizer for three days to help them become more feminine in honor of my coming treasure. We went together to pick up the ring at the FedEx office in San Marcos; California. When I am excited I tend to become chatty so I tried real hard to hold my tongue on the way there. Once we had the ring and were back in the Jeep I paused and asked Stephen, "Before I open the box will you tell me why you want to marry me?" He seemed unprepared for my question so I shelved my disappointment and said, "It is okay Stephen, you think on it and then tell me." I placed the unopened package on the backseat of the Jeep.

Two hours later all Stephen could come up with was, "I think you are a nice person and you have not had much in life, I could give you something." I wanted more than a marriage based on obligation. He then admitted to me that although he had married Sandra because he loved her, he could only remember feeling love for me one time - when we reclined together on the patio at Casa De Zorro in Borrego Springs while listening to music near the pool. He admitted that as the mother of two children I was too much of a liability - that I involved him in a responsibility he resented.

Days later we finally spoke of the ending of our latest engagement. Stephen said if we were married he would have to purchase medical insurance for me to keep from being wiped out in the case of a major medical problem. He said he thought it would cost him approximately $250 per month. He also said as my husband he would be responsible for any medical emergencies of the children as well. It always came down to money.

CHAPTER 37
VALENTINE'S DAY PROPOSAL

February 4, was a lovely day so we decided to go riding that morning with Stephen on Rocky and me on Torrey. While getting the horses ready for the ride, Stephen talked about how he once rode a superb horse around the Egyptian pyramids at night accompanied by a beautiful woman who rode like the wind. He described how the pyramids looked in the moonlight at midnight. I can only dream!

Rocky was still in training but he did well enough to please Stephen. He liked to crash through bushes for some reason which we both found amusing. Torrey made me feel like a better rider as he was smooth and cooperative whereas Monty was a combination of headstrong and easily spooked. It was a good ride for all four of us as the horses always liked to get out on the trail.

Later that day, George Helmer came for a meeting about the Steve Reeves International Society. He was one of the really nice fans - full of enthusiasm and he seemed quite honest. The meeting lasted about an hour and a half. Later, when Stephen was not exactly enthused about the whole thing, I pointed out that if it did not cost him anything and had a possibility of bringing in some money eventually, why not pursue it? I liked George and I liked the idea of reminding fans about Stephen's uniqueness and great example. I could sense that Stephen liked George. I was pretty sure, given enough time, Stephen would come around to realizing what George offered was more positive than negative. Stephen and I spent a quiet evening watching *Carousel*. I realized that many of the songs in the musical were ones my Mother used to sing when I was growing up. Now I finally knew where she learned them. We enjoyed a very pleasant evening.

Another morning, we went for a ride in order to continue both Sugarfoot's and my training. Near the end of our ride, as we were crossing a small waterway, Sugarfoot sidestepped and then backed slightly to avoid mud and the shallow but moving water. By doing so she entangled both her tail and her hind legs in partially submerged loops of double strand barbed wire that was hidden by some brush. A broken fence-line was the culprit. Stephen summoned me to come back, so I turned Torrey, slipped off him and went to Sugar. She was trembling with fear. As I held her bridle he carefully dismounted. Sugarfoot would have reared and bolted, ripping her legs to shreds if it was not for the quiet, authoritative and calming tone of Stephen's voice. He stroked her flank as he moved to check out the damage and scope of the problem. He was dismayed at just how much barbed wire there was tangling her long tail and legs. He instructed me to hold her still and stroke her neck. I watched as Stephen ran his hands down her left hind leg and grasp the first loop of wire. He bent the wire away from her leg and then worked it methodically back and forth until it broke. Wire by wire he removed each strand first from her legs then from her tail. By the time she was finally free her trembling had subsided but her nerves had produced an abundance of lathered sweat. We guided both horses to a level area away from the water and the wire then remounted for the short ride home.

Once home we checked Sugar over with great care and were thankful to find that her wounds were limited to minor cuts. I was very impressed with Stephen's ability to calm such a green horse. His abilities prevented what otherwise could have been certain disaster. We doctored her wounds, carefully groomed her and gave her an extra treat of molasses with her grain, and then Stephen gave her an antibiotic injection. While I unsaddled and then groomed Torrey, Stephen drove the Jeep back to the barbed wire trap and removed it so no other animal would be ensnared or injured.

The next day, my dearest Lord Tyrant worked out on the ranch like a hired hand trying to impress a new boss man. He did horse chores, loaded decomposed granite, filled in huge indentations in pastures so the irrigation pipes would lay level again among other tasks. Later, while he was doing shovel work on the road, our neighbor, Tom, who was doing some nearby clean-up with his skip loader, accidentally sent a huge fifteen foot, 500 pound piece of timber flying straight at Stephen. The timber clipped Stephen's shin as he leapt out of the way. We were blessed that Stephen was neither severely injured nor, as he put it, "knocked to kingdom come". After taking care of his shin wound, I went back to work in the yard. I am never more content than when I am kneeling in rich, prepared soil with my hands nurturing soft young plants. It also allowed me to keep an eye on whatever my man was doing while enabling me to be close, but not too close, when he was feeling crabby, I did, however, stay within hollering distance in case he needed me for something.

On Valentine's Day we suddenly meshed very well again. I do not remember what my Valentine card to him said but I am sure it was a perfectly nice card. However, his card to me was wonderful. By now I knew him well enough to know he never bought a card without reading it. So I knew that the sentiments expressed inside the card had to be close enough to what he wanted to say otherwise he would not buy it. Knowing that made it all that much sweeter. It was a poem called, "What is a Sweetheart?" A bit later, as I worked in the kitchen, Stephen came in, took my hand, stood very close to me and then said, "Will you marry me?" He produced the ring, and, as I accepted, he placed the ring on my left hand's ring finger! Now that is quite a way to do up a Valentine's Day. He then took me to the Acapulco Restaurant in Escondido for lunch. We had come full circle yet again. The struggles that Stephen seemed to go through could leave me dizzy but for his own reasons (and this time I held my tongue and did not ask) he had decided he wanted me to be his wife.

CHAPTER 38
RANCHITA PLANS;
NO MORE TIERA DEL SOL

Sometime later we went out to the Ranchita property to stake out the specific area we had chosen to build our weekend cabin. We spent a good afternoon together getting the measurements and markers ready for our friend Larry Herman who does dozer work. We planned to have Larry prepare the building pad and also create a wide swath around the entire perimeter of the property just inside the fence line. We also asked Larry to doze out a water collection point at the bottom of our back hill. Our idea was to create a pond to serve as a watering hole for local wildlife and for our horses once the front fence and gate were installed. We were also planning to stock the Ranchita property with either Texas Longhorn cattle or American bison (buffalo).

We spoke often of our plans and dreams for the Ranchita place. It was a rather perfect location due to sharing the back fence line with the Warner Ranch. There is a gate on the back fence which allowed access to the Warner Ranch's thousands of acres. Stephen had obtained permission from the foreman of the Warner Ranch for us to ride their cattle range. As a part of the bargain, Stephen, a former cattle rancher, had agreed to keep an eye out for cattle in distress or downed fencing. This wonderful, seemingly endless ranch, unfettered by fences and gates (which was a growing problem in Valley Center), was rather perfect for Stephen and me. During our return trip to Valley Center we discussed the Jaguar needing new shocks. Stephen was trying to remember when he last had new ones installed and I said, "Well it must have been more than two years ago because it was before my time with you." Stephen replied "Haven't you always been here with me?" That felt really nice and warm.

I took the income tax receipts and information to our CPA, Dave Edwards, on March 20th. I meticulously organized the receipts in each category and thoroughly listed every allowable deduction and applicable expense. Dave Edwards had been Stephen's accountant for years, and still does my taxes to this day.

A DAY IN THE LIFE

March 21, 1995
Tuesday
Lots of rain

Our first session was at 5:01 a.m. when Mr. Steve Reeves woke up like some 20-year-old with a striking resemblance to a stud in season.

Another long, unending rain shower that got down to a falling mist for our walk. So I changed my clothes before taking Naomi to school. Came back and instead of getting to work on some project I jumped into bed with Stephen who had waited for me. We snuggled and later had a session.

Worked for two hours on fan mail - whew, only $10 in all that mail. The rest want and expect free autographed 8x10s I guess. What is this Knoxville? Fans are a strange lot, who else would expect something for nothing.

Let's see - we ate lunch after that. Had session number 3 at 2:30 p.m. because at 3:15 p.m. I had to leave to go get Naomi.

Steve has been charming all day - no cuts, no pokes, no coolness - lots of warmth and laughs. Had session number 4 at 9:10 p.m. in Stephen's recliner on impulse. Had session number 5 at 11:35 p.m. when we went to bed. A really good one too.

Oh I forgot, got a call from New York City, Roger Van Ostrand who wants Steve to consider a part in a James Garner movie of the week. Stephen said, "No thanks."

The End.

In late March Stephen had an appointment with a real estate broker named Al Dart who was coming to our ranch to make an offer on Stephen's property in Boulevard, California. When Mr. Dart arrived Stephen was still out at the barn so I welcomed him and we visited for a while. I learned that he had known some of the people from the Campo and Boulevard areas that Stephen knew years ago, such as Ed Roberts, John Wayne's double, Slim Talbert, and a man named Homer Morehouse. I also discovered that he also knew my uncle Harold Engelhorn (who was the doctor of Campo). Mr. Dart said when he was a boy he was taken to my uncle Harold for some serious ailment. While there his heart suddenly stopped but uncle Harold was able to revive and stabilize him. It is a small world. When Stephen came in from the barn, Mr. Dart presented his client's offer on the part of Stephen's Boulevard property that he still held the title to. Stephen countered. Mr. Dart left a bit later to take the offer to his client. A short time later a deal was struck and the property sold. No more Tiera Del Sol for us.

The next morning, we went on a ride. Both horses did fine until suddenly, while trotting up the last hill at a really brisk rate, Rocky startled at a small rivulet going across the dirt road and went down on his knees. Stephen never even came close to falling or losing his seat despite not only the major stumble and fall but also the tremendous jerking and lurching as Rocky jumped back to his feet. It was super impressive! I was so relieved to see he was all right. That was Steve Reeves folks, legend of the Silver Screen.

CHAPTER 39
ANOTHER HOLLYWOOD COLLECTORS SHOW

On April 1, we attended another Hollywood Collectors Show at the Beverly Garland Hotel. The crowd this time was quite nice, not too pushy or overwhelming, and generally very pleasant. For the second time I saw Ron Libonatti there. As a young boy, Ron had been a resident in Larry's and my home at Ahern Ranches back in 1973 or 74. He had been placed with us as a result of his having a less than adequate parent, none of it was Ron's fault or responsibility. After we visited briefly I had to get back to business but it warmed my heart to see him again, a grown man. This show was one of the Ray Courts events that were our favorite to take part in. After we closed for the day we had an arrangement to have dinner with Stephen's old and dear friend, Steve Ferry. They met back in the mid-1950's while doing the off Broadway play *Kismet* in New York. Apparently they had only seen each other a couple of times in the last thirty years or so. I found Steve Ferry to be a really nice man who seemed a bit tired at the moment. He ruminated over two ruined marriages but was obviously well pleased with his three children. We chatted over dinner then went our separate ways.

As it had been an exhausting day, when we retired to our hotel room I served up the sensual part of our evening early so Stephen could get some sleep. I put on a midnight blue sexy bra and panties, black stockings (never pantyhose, which my dearest Lord Tyrant was convinced were invented by someone who hated sex) and long black lace gloves. Right in the middle of our erotic escapade some idiot started pounding on our hotel room door despite my having remembered to hang the "DO NOT DISTURB" sign. Needless to say, it was annoying; however, much to my surprise Stephen did not become upset. Afterwards I showered and rolled my hair for tomorrow's curls then inventoried our supply of photos and accounted for the money received that day. Before I slipped under the covers to say my prayers I found Stephen's foot and kissed his big toe. Then off to the land of nod I went.

Stephen enjoyed the final day of the show and was more than content with the amount of economic success as well. After closing shop I drove us back to Valley Center. We arrived home to find the horses fed, the house clean and even the dishes done. Lynx and Naomi made me proud.

It was April and part of me was wondering if Stephen was going to kiss me sometime this year. Up to that point in time he had given me those dry little pecks one gives in an offhand way, but no actual kiss. I loved his kisses. On April 4, however, he surprised me by focusing our session that day on pleasuring me. His ministrations were so refined that I felt as if I was flying around the rafters overhead. As the children were home at the time I hardly let out a squeak - which was not an easy task under the circumstances!

It has been said that complicated people have complicated relationships. I would have preferred to thrive in an environment that was a bit less complicated. There were periods when there was a very special bond between Stephen and me. I had learned, however, that the bond always faded as he withdrew his emotions and slipped into one of his bouts of depression. When we were in the midst of a trough, I reminded myself that his warmth would eventually return, and it always did. In this memoir I have chosen to skim over the depths to which he would sometimes fall. I am determined to focus on the good times I had with my dearest Lord Tyrant.

CHAPTER 40
TRIP TO AUSTIN, TEXAS

During one of our close, affectionate periods we made reservations for a trip to Austin, Texas. For some reason Stephen was really excited about that anticipated trip. He spoke with enthusiasm of having meals out and going to nightclubs which surprised the heck out of me. Never before had he taken me, or even offered to take me, to a nightclub. Perhaps he was remembering some fond yesterdays of his own. Nonetheless I was really thrilled to be going to Austin. I had never been to Texas and was looking forward to the opportunity to become familiar with Austin and the surrounding towns. The next day we went to a travel agency in Escondido to purchase our airline tickets which, because of the "Friends Fly Free" program then being promoted by Southwest Airlines, only cost Stephen $378.00 for our round-trip. To celebrate he treated me to a ninety-nine cent Whopper at Burger King.

On Sunday, April 9, Stephen woke me with a request, rather a demand, for a full-fledged session and so the morning began. After the horses were fed and tended to, we watched the television program *Sunday Morning* on CBS while eating homemade versions of Egg McMuffins. When Stephen asked for my assistance with fence realigning and repairing I smiled and thought, but did not say, "My love we could have it all. This is real life." The area of fence to be repaired demanded the attention of two persons - one to drive the truck and the other to handle the realigning and capping of the rails to the posts. Chains were attached from the truck to each post, one by one, and I was given the easier job of driving forward or backing up at Stephen's direction until the post was upright. Then Stephen would replace the rail and bolt it to the post. Sometimes he had to cut one of the metal rails with a hacksaw in order to custom fit it.

After lunch and our customary nap we separated and turned our attention to our own end of the day agendas. I reviewed with Naomi the feed and watering routine which she would be responsible for while we were in Texas. Later that evening, while Stephen and I were watching the movie *The Ten Commandments* on television, we received a call from Richard and Francesca Harrison. They called in order to discuss an Italian pension Richard and Stephen were each to receive. As a prerequisite to receiving the pension, the men needed to open an account with an Italian bank. Richard and Francesca mentioned that they intended to travel to Italy in July or August so that Richard could open his bank account. Stephen decided that he would arrange his schedule so that he could go with them.

We were busy for the next two days preparing the ranch for our absence. Then, finally, Texas here we come! Our trip to Austin, Texas was an exceptionally nice period of time in our relationship. For whatever reason, Stephen was even-tempered and cheerful on this vacation, like he had been when we went to Montana. We had no business to attend to or fan obligations to deal with. The Austin area was so beautiful and it was easy to relax and enjoy oneself. We rented a Chevy Corsica and stayed at the Days Inn South for fifty-nine dollars a night.

Stephen called his old friends, Terry and Jan Todd, who taught at the University of Texas in Austin. They were the type of warm, friendly, intelligent people you are glad to have as friends. Terry was teaching a class when we arrived at the university that evening. After the class ended at 9 p.m. they took us out for dinner and we were fascinated listening to them describe what interesting lives they lived. They also knew Stephen's friend, James A. Michener, who we would also visit while in Texas.

The next day we toured the areas of Aquarena Springs and Fredericksburg. We loved the atmosphere of the area and enjoyed having lunch while we were there. We also visited Burnett, Marble Falls, Spicewood and Bee Cave before heading back to Austin. We enjoyed the rolling hills, herds of cattle, the rivers, rock formations and the interesting Texan penchant for constructing grand entrances to their properties (whether the property held a grand estate or only a rusted single wide mobile home). My fondest memory, however, was the discovery of all the fantastic wildflowers. A wonderful place.

After yet another day touring the Willow City loop and surrounding areas, we enjoyed dinner with Jan and Terry at a Spanish hacienda styled restaurant. Later, with the aid of a mirror provided by the Days Inn South, and me all done up in black garters with black stockings and long lace gloves, Stephen experienced his second explosion at the motel. It was his third orgasm in Texas since we had put one of the scenic areas we passed through to great good use. We needed to initiate certain parts of Texas, said Stephen. Afterwards, while we lay recuperating in bed, he glanced at me and noted, "You're kind of pretty today." I replied, "Why thank you." He was not one to gush.

We began April 14, our third full day in Texas, with Jan and Terry. Our first stop was to Gregory Gymnasium at the University of Texas, including quite a tour of its library which Jan and Terry had invested a tremendous amount of their time and expertise in developing. After the tour we ate lunch at Black's Barbeque in Lockhart that had been open since 1932. It was very casual in that you stood in line to order prime rib, pork loin or some sort of spicy sausage. The aroma of the various cooked meats made the place smell wonderful and caused our stomachs to grumble. Each meal is served on brown paper. You sit at long tables where the knives to cut the meat are quite literally chained. It was an excellent, delicious experience that Terry and Jan provided.

After lunch, Stephen and I went to visit his old friend, James A. Michener, the internationally acclaimed author. Mr. Michener lived in a very interesting home full of reminders of his late wife, who he clearly missed. He was in fragile health but was ever so pleased to see Stephen. I believe he was eighty-six years old at that time. He spent three days a week in dialysis but his mind was marvelously sharp. His live-in caregiver put an "L" on his left slipper to help with the small details that can frustrate extraordinary minds. His writing place in his home faced a large window which looked out onto an emerald green, large garden with shade trees and flowers. While Stephen and Mr. Michener visited and swapped stories I was free to explore a bit. It was a memorable end to a wonderful vacation in Texas.

CHAPTER 41
CRITICISMS;
DOZER WORK OUT AT RANCHITA

The warm glow which our relationship had enjoyed in Texas vanished about thirty minutes before we arrived home. A black cloud seemed to envelop Stephen for a period of time whenever we returned from a trip. Out of the blue he decided he needed to remind me about Sandra. He reminisced about how she caught his eye back in 1954 while at the beach with friends. He described how he thought her the prettiest girl he had ever seen. He spoke about her in wistful almost reverent tones then, glancing at me, he changed the subject by noting that I should have started applying sunblock when I was in my late twenties rather than my early forties. Point of order: there was no sunblock on the market until I was much, much older than my twenties. Stephen then slid into a criticism of how I spoiled my children by buying them soft drinks when I purchased them food at Burger King, "if he wasn't there to keep things reasonable." And on and on his demeaning sentiments went, quite certain I had been raised by illiterate swine and that I was raising some sort of like offspring. Oh well, the trip had been remarkably positive for days and we already knew that homecomings could be hard on Stephen. He remained despondent for about five days then seemed to decide life was not as dark and gloomy as he had been conjecturing.

A few days later we went out to the Ranchita property to witness Larry Herman work magic with his bulldozer, grading and creating the building pad for our future weekend place. After creating the perfect pad, Larry turned his bulldozer to clear a perimeter around the edge of the five acre parcel. We watched with interest and fascination, picnicked and made plans for our future weekends out there. There were few things Stephen loved more than watching dozer work. The contouring and restructuring of raw land was fascinating to him. While Stephen and I were sitting together in the dirt watching Larry's ballet with the dozer, I spotted a severely damaged horned toad. I realized the dozer had almost severed his hindquarters. I asked Stephen if we had an axe or a shovel in the truck. When he asked why I suddenly needed one, I showed him the poor horned toad. He did not have either tool that day so glancing around I found two fair sized rocks to use in helping end the poor creature's misery. I gently laid him on top of one rock and, saying a rushed prayer and apology under my breath, then I crushed the poor little creature with three quick hard blows from the second rock. Sick at heart, shaking and crying I jumped up and started toward Stephen. He admonished me not to cry. He seemed almost shocked that I would lament over the incident. "But it's hard for me to kill, it's really hard!" I explained. He responded by saying, "But you're not Jesus Christ!" I am still not quite sure what he meant by that. He sighed, gave me the briefest of hugs then shook his head as he turned his attention back to watching Larry work. Later he expressed real surprise at that part of my character which in turn astonished me since I had told him many times that I cannot bear to watch a mortally wounded creature suffer.

CHAPTER 42
STEPHEN'S
LAST WILL AND TESTAMENT

Sometime later Stephen requested that I act as scribe as he outlined the terms of his last will and testament. Despite being encouraged by others to utilize a revocable living trust as the foundation to his estate plan, Stephen of course decided, being the self-made Western rancher that he was, that he was not wasting good money to have some lawyer prepare legal documents directing what he wanted to have happen when he died. He knew what he wanted and he had his late wife Aline's last will and testament to use as a general guide. At his request I sat and transcribed everything as he dictated his intentions.

His last will and testament made specific bequests to certain individuals. He wanted his best friend Dave Morris to receive his pickup truck and horse trailer, which he considered the best of all the specific bequests. At my suggestion, Stephen left Troy Bertelsen his 1994 Jeep Grand Cherokee. We both thought Troy seemed like a nice young man who had weathered a bad divorce and was struggling somewhat. When he came from Montana to visit the ranch he always drove an unreliable vehicle. We could not think of anyone who could use the Jeep more. Stephen rarely paid much attention to my suggestions and later I would sincerely regret that I had made this one. Stephen decided that his Jaguar should go to George Helmer in consideration of George's dedication to the Steve Reeves International Society, which he was now hoping would bring in additional income. I knew that sometimes Stephen took people's efforts on his behalf for granted so I was happy that Stephen was being considerate of George. The newly formed Steve Reeves International Society was to receive Stephen's photo and newspaper clipping collection. At first that caused a knot in my stomach because I was spending countless hours sorting, filing, mounting and loving all the photos, articles and memorabilia. It was my labor of love he was giving away and it caused me no small amount of pain. I comforted myself with the thought that in all probability I would die before Stephen and therefore no longer care. When Stephen and I later reviewed the draft of his Will I had a chance to express my feelings regarding the photographs and articles. He ultimately decided that I could keep all personal photos and request to have copies of the professional photos, the articles and the clippings that I had assembled and or gathered. Finally, Stephen included a charitable bequest of $50,000 to Guide Dogs for the Blind.

The rest of his estate was to go to me if he predeceased me. Stephen was concerned that I would blow the entire estate in a single year so he included provisions that mandated his estate was to be distributed to me at the rate of $50,000 per year. It stung a bit that he did not trust me; however, Stephen was providing my children and me with future security which was a huge, totally unexpected gift and I understood that I was in no position to quibble. Stephen signed his Will on June 2, 1995, which was a big hurdle for him, an ordeal of sorts, because he held the superstition that once he signed the Will, he might die. It was his first (and his last) will and testament ever so for him it was quite a milestone.

Shortly thereafter he undermined the feeling of security he had given me by making it very clear that the Will was only in effect until he was inclined to change or destroy it. He reminded me on a regular basis that I had better keep on his good side. As the years progressed, with the exception of Dave Morris, everyone given a gift in his will found themselves in danger of losing their bequest. Every time Troy would cancel a scheduled trip down to the ranch for a visit Stephen would rant and rave about removing him from his will. When George wanted to put some photo of Stephen or a product that Stephen did not like in the Steve Reeves International Society's magazine, Stephen would threaten to change his will. Likewise, when George wanted to have meetings more often than Stephen desired, out came the threats. A couple years later, Stephen decided to sell his Jaguar to George Helmer. I voiced my objection to this decision. How could he sell that special car to the very person he had bequeathed it to in his Will? To Stephen there was an ironic humor in having George buy what would be his anyway.

CHAPTER 43
SOLO TRIP TO ROME

Most of the time Stephen's humor was wonderful with plays on words so clever it delighted me. He knew more jokes than anyone else I ever met and he shared them generously. He enjoyed telling me risqué jokes so that I could pretend shock and then laugh with him. He once admitted that I was the first wife he felt comfortable revealing his nasty and sexually adventurous side to. I had no problem with that.

June 3rd was departure day for my Stephen. We went to town at 9:45 a.m. and enjoyed breakfast at Carrow's restaurant. When we returned to the ranch, I undressed down to my red satin panties and bra and then went into the bedroom to satisfy my man. That mission accomplished we then finished our last minute preparations for the trip to the airport and Stephen's departure for Rome via Paris. We left the ranch and about 3:40 p.m. and headed to Denny's restaurant. At that time, Denny's was advertising a $5.99 prime rib dinner. After a very pleasant meal with a friendly and humorous Stephen, I drove us to the airport. We arrived in plenty of time for Stephen's flight which was scheduled to leave at 7 p.m. I was dressed in a hot pink blouse, semi-short multicolored skirt, black stockings and heels. If Stephen was going to be looking at any woman's legs in the airport they were going to be mine. He gave me a good-bye hug and said, "I'll miss you." And then he turned and left. I watched as his plane taxied out of sight. I drove home to the ranch and began my first real separation from Stephen, at least for any length of time. The house felt strange without his presence.

Four days later Stephen arrived home safely having succeeded in opening a bank account in Italy in which to receive his movie industry related pension. And I thanked God. About a week after Stephen returned from Italy he offered to buy me a puppy of my own choosing for my birthday. Originally, I think Rommel was supposed to be for me but I had no desire to own a Rottweiler. My favorite breed had always been Alaskan Malamutes which are infamous chicken chasers (I know from personal experience), so they were out, but I also adored German Shepherds. We found a local ad for German Shepherd puppies and contacted the owner. I selected one of the puppies whose coloring was less common. My pup was sort of sand colored with black ticking on the end of each hair. My son's favorite movie at that time was *Dune* and with my pup's sand coloring it was an appropriate name. So Dune it was. Although the Rottweilers, Zorro and Rommel, were allowed in the house, Dune was not because Stephen said his tail was a disaster waiting to happen. So I spent my free time on the back patio, in the backyard or anywhere out on the ranch with Dune (except when we were working horses). He was the delight of my days.

On June 13, Stephen and I began work on his new book. I jotted down his ideas and knowledge on bodybuilding and fitness in general as he paced around the room dictating them to me. I knew I would learn a lot from the Master. I really loved working with Stephen anytime he was in a good mood so this day was particularly exciting. The following day was my forty-fourth birthday. When my brother David called to wish me a Happy Birthday he naturally asked what was happening with our marriage plans. I told him there would not be a wedding and he wanted to know why. I gave him a brief explanation about the problems brought about by Larry's back taxes and other financial concerns. He said, "What does that have to do with whether or not Steve marries you? Money is never a reason not to marry the woman you love!" He said a lot more too but then he is my big brother and thinks that I am a catch.

CHAPTER 44
NICKNAMES AND IRRITATIONS

Periodically Stephen would come up with a new to me nickname. I had been his Wildflower because he identified me as his hippie woman who loved all the plants and animals. He was not entirely thrilled that I loved everything in nature from spiders to elephants, from the clouds to the rocks and every plant that grows. Then I became his Pumpkin-head. That one, he said was because I was his Pumpkin and I gave him "head". He rather delighted in referring to me as Pumpkin-head when we were out in public because while we knew its real meaning, no one else did. My dearest Lord Tyrant often referred to me as his Palomino which made perfect sense given his background as a horseman and my long blonde hair.

Near the end of June I continued my work on Stephen's private snapshot collection. I had separated the photos according to the year and event and then bound each stack with rubber bands. Now I planned to take one stack at a time and trim the edges of the photographs so they would fit into albums. I bought four big albums with some of the monthly household budget money so I could start mounting Stephen's history. I was thoroughly enjoying this undertaking. And Stephen was really pleased.

After a sensual session one afternoon in late July, as we were lying in bed together being lazy and chatting, Stephen turned and said to me, "Isn't it nice to be desired!" And I responded, "Of course it's nice to be desired. I never knew what it was to not be desired until you became my mate." We were an odd yet matched pair. He was so virile, so sexually active and driven. I was the private masseuse and sex slave who specialized in the art of pleasing Steve Reeves.

I was perplexed and somewhat disheartened to find that Stephen found fault with my gardening. No one had ever criticized me in that regards before. I thought that perhaps from a rancher's perspective my gardening held little to no value because it produced nothing he considered of value. I landscaped areas that from my perspective were neglected and needed to be brought more in-line with the beauty of the home we lived in. I felt the yard needed some garden areas as accents near the front doorway and in the half-circle area which lay on the other side of the driveway. Stephen felt I wasted too much time and energy gardening. It was not a matter of wasting his money as I obtained free clippings from neighbors and transplanted native plants which I found in the back-country beyond the groves that surrounded the ranch. I hauled native rocks down from the nearby hills to make basins and accents for my gardens. Once Dune was old enough he enjoyed acting as my guardian on these excursions into the hills.

It also irritated my Lord Tyrant that I drank diet Squirt. He wanted me to drink water, milk and juice. My personal preference for diet Squirt caused him no small amount of distress. I was never a strict health enthusiast before I met Stephen. All things considered, diet Squirt seemed to me to be such a bland sort of sin. Stephen chose at a very early age to treat his body with near reverence.

My weight was next on the list of irritants for Stephen that July. Six months earlier he had told me that I was too fat to have wedding photos taken. At the time I was five feet seven inches and weighed 123 pounds. I had in the meantime lost six pounds so at the moment I only weighed 117 pounds. Now he said I was too skinny. After two and a half years of working out under Stephen's tutelage, I was in excellent condition but my butt, calves and biceps were not the perfect shape that he preferred. I muscled out in long slender fashion which probably had a lot more to do with how God created me than with how Stephen designed my workouts.

CHAPTER 45
ONE PROHIBITED SEXUAL FAVOR; SOLO TRIP TO VEGAS

The morning of July 30th we had a really great session after our Sunday feed and water routine. I was really in the mood and having a great time until Stephen unexpectedly said he was going to get a woman who would deny him nothing. His announcement made little sense to me as there were only two sex acts I refused to be part of - a threesome and jamming my tongue somewhere I did not want it to go. My Lord Tyrant never pushed me on the threesome part but hated being denied the second. We allowed each other considerable latitude in our fantasies. That is what fantasies are about. Stephen wanted what he wanted, how he wanted it and he wanted it now. Apparently this morning was one of those times when he was toying with the idea of finding a new woman who was more to his liking.

Two days later I found myself watching the home movie of Stephen's marriage to Sandra Smith. That was quite an experience! They were so incredibly beautiful together - so young, so full of life and endless possibilities. It may seem odd, but as much as I loved this sometimes difficult man, when watching the two of them at their wedding I could not help but wish they had never parted. I felt real regret that their love had not kept them together. No wonder I like some of those killer country-western songs of lament.

August arrived hot and dry as is usual for our Southern Californian locale. Stephen was out of sorts and voiced his usual list of complaints about how I had disappointed him or cost him. He ranted on about how he had a much better life before I came into his home and that he had lost his freedom to come and go at will. He told me, "I don't see anyone banging on the door to take you away. Go ahead, find someone who wants you." He also complained that after yet another year of working out that I was in worse shape than when I started. He scolded that if I just worked harder on my thrust exercises I would have a real butt like other women. In my heart I knew I just needed to wait out his depression, but it was discouraging.

Stephen had an upcoming Las Vegas appearance on the calendar. Realizing that Las Vegas would be populated with younger women with real butts, I informed him that I would be staying at the ranch with my kids so he could pursue his dream girl. I had come to the conclusion that this particular sex-slave needed a new Master and a new love. I wanted someone who did not constantly compare me with women half my age, and I told him as much. On August 11, Stephen put on a big effort to make amends. If he was dependent on good behavior for sexual favors from me it would be different but, with rare exception, he enjoyed his three or more interludes every day whether he was being nice or not. So when he reached out and touched my arm I knew that it was Stephen trying to please me. And yes, I let him know how much I appreciated the gesture.

On August 14, Naomi and I made apple pies using apples from trees on the ranch. Naomi did well with the crust and showed a definite talent with baking. Lynx passed the written portion of his driving permit's test that day which was another milestone. Stephen was in a rare good mood. He joked a few times then commented on how the children were growing up, referencing Lynx getting a license soon and Naomi helping to bake pies. We enjoyed one of the apple pies after dinner - he with his usual chunk of cheddar. Once the children had retired to their rooms for the night he commented on my decision to start wearing underwear and one of his large t-shirts to bed lately. I told him I had no intention of letting his eyes see me naked since he found me so physically out of shape. He fell silent at that.

The ranch had two older Acacia trees that had toppled over during the last winter's storms. Their seedlings were growing like weeds all over the place - standing from three inches to three feet tall - so I took the time to pot as many as I could. A year or so later I would run an ad in the local paper to sell the small trees. I noted in my journal entries for August 24 that Stephen gave me a peck on the forehead. Almost of more importance, knowing he would be in Las Vegas on Lynx's birthday, and knowing how much Lynx needed new clothes for school, Stephen gave Lynx fifty dollars as his birthday gift. We were sure to thank him more than once.

During one of our intimate episodes, Stephen declared what a good slave master he was. I responded with, "I still need a new Master." His upcoming trip to Las Vegas was partially to scout out possible new sex-slave candidates. One that was younger, firmer, and sans children and ex-husbands. We both knew that. When Stephen left on August 29, I packed a letter in his gear releasing him from all fidelity to me. When Stephen returned from Las Vegas a few days later, the first order of business was to update him on conditions at the ranch in general and the horses in particular. After he shared some of what he did and who he saw while in Las Vegas, I asked whether he had sex with anyone while he was in Vegas. His answer surprised and pleased me. He said that he had not been with anyone at all. I believed him.

CHAPTER 46
TRIPS TO WYOMING AND WASHINGTON STATE

I agreed to accompany Stephen to the Morgan Horse Show in Wyoming, which was to be held on September 8th through the 10th, and also to an Oktoberfest in Leavenworth, Washington scheduled for October 8th through the 11th. While we were out of town Lynx and Naomi would manage the ranch - which was no picnic. We were placing considerable responsibility onto the shoulders of two young adults. In addition to getting themselves up and ready for school there were morning ranch chores which had to be handled. After school they had to take care of their homework, deal with more ranch chores and duties, then find themselves something to eat.

September found us back in an up period so far as life on the ranch was concerned. Dave Morris came one day to work on our horses. Stephen asked me take on the task of catching and corralling Rocky and Monty while he helped Dave with something at the cross ties in the barn's breezeway. I was always happy when Dave visited the ranch. I could hear them talking and laughing as I brought Rocky in to be worked on and thanked God under my breath for bringing Dave into Stephen's life. Then I went to catch Monty and place him in a nearby holding corral to wait his turn. When Stephen said he would handle the remaining horses, I returned to the ranch house wishing I could be a fly on the wall out there by those cross ties so I could listen to what they spoke of. Part of me was curious as to what caused their laughter. They shared the private camaraderie of old friends who had spent years in each other's company. As fellow horse ranchers their bond was strong.

A few days later we found ourselves at the San Diego airport waiting for our flight to Wyoming for the Morgan Horse Show. I excused myself, went in to use the restroom and while there removed my underwear as a surprise for my dearest Lord Tyrant to discover sometime later. During a brief layover at the Las Vegas airport, Stephen and I both took time to use a restroom on the plane. Stephen returned to his aisle seat first so I had to slide past him in order to return to mine. As I was gliding over Stephen in his seat he ran his hand up my inner thigh and, instead of encountering the expected panties, he touched my exposed heat. His face was priceless! For the remainder of the flight he sat there with a bemused look on his face. Although we were comfortable having an escapade anywhere we could reasonably get away with it, this particular flight failed to provide a proper opportunity. So we made up for the delayed climax once we reached our suite at the Virginian Lodge in Jackson Hole accompanied by claps of thunder as a storm raged outside.

The next day at the horse show we saw a particularly beautiful palomino named Gold Sovereign who we later discovered was a descendent of one of Stephen's horses from his Oregon ranch days. Gold Soverign's lineage included Dickie's Pride, S R's Duchess, High Pass Duke, Princess Sonfield and Long Hill Justin!!! While at the show, Stephen ran into Mr. and Mrs. Painter, the couple he bought Sugarfoot from. The Painters owned a beautiful black Morgan which was definitely one of the very best being offered at the auction. During our return home we both commented on how pleased we were to have discovered the palomino and met the Painters.

On September 20, David Gest called to invite Stephen to a benefit show in New York City which was being held in December. I was excited at the prospect of attending the event but I knew Stephen was not likely to want to make an appearance. Rather than think about it, I kept myself busy planning Naomi's fifteenth birthday party which we had agreed to celebrate on Friday, the 22nd of September.

October arrived with its usual hot, gusty (what is commonly referred to as "Santa Ana") weather and Stephen was endlessly busy out in the heat and dust. His main focus was finishing his repairs and alterations on the older Miley horse trailer. He would alternate scraping and puttying the roof of the horse trailer with doing other ranch chores. Up the ladder he would go, scrape and putty, and then down the ladder keeping busy doing another ranch chore while he waited for the putty to dry. I kept wishing the unrelenting sun would go behind a fat cloud layer and give him some respite from the heat. I also kept up a schedule of hydration offerings, knowing that was about all he would allow me to do for him. An earlier offer to hold an umbrella to shade him was the cause of considerable ridicule.

On October 7, we left the ranch and headed for Washington State where it was much cooler and greener. We flew into Seattle then drove a rental to Roy, Washington to check out some of the gaited Morgans owned by Bill and Leah Heib. They kept a young black stallion named Dynamite that Stephen wanted to view. We were duly impressed with Dynamite but Stephen was concerned that he would not be gaited under saddle. If the single-footing gait is not really pronounced while the horse moves naturally around their enclosure then the horse is unlikely to continue that gait (which is what we were breeding for) while saddled and ridden. The good news was Dynamite had admirable withers (the highest point on a horse's back, just behind their neck). This was a major breeding requirement for us as our Sugarfoot was a bit too low in that department. Dynamite appeared a bit high-strung or perhaps a little flighty which was not what we wanted in a mount to be ridden by Stephen. I was a relieved when Stephen decided to pass on Dynamite. Leah and Bill were warm and very pleasant people. I have found that many of God's best are horse people. That evening we ate at a Denny's restaurant near Bellview and spent the night at a Days Inn in Everett, Washington. We were both unusually restless after our bedtime sensual pleasure and prayers but eventually drifted off to sleep.

The autumn drive from Everett to Leavenworth was enchanting. The combination of a heavy forest and a powerful flowing river sprinkled with various rock formations created a perfect contrast. We were enthralled. Our impression of Leavenworth was so positive that we decided to look at property there for a possible summer home. Downtown Leavenworth was designed and built with a German/Bavarian motif. What a charming place to hold an annual Oktoberfest. There was music, art, marvelous foods and cheerful, enthusiastic crowds full of good humor. We stayed at the Der Ritterhoff Hotel. Before we left home, Stephen had noted that our first night in Leavenworth would land on a full moon so I brought my black fishnet stockings, the black garter and a lacy top that was perfect for both of us. The top hid enough of my flaws to allow me to relax yet showed enough to cause Stephen's imagination to ignite his libido. I also packed one red candle and two sticks of incense in order to create the atmosphere he preferred. We enjoyed a very nice end to a beautiful day in Leavenworth. The next morning we went to breakfast in the Edelweiss Hotel Restaurant where I was mistaken for a local resident. First the waitress then two patrons thought I was someone they knew. Stephen and I thought it very interesting and sort of wished the person I resembled would show up so we could decide if we agreed with the locals.

We made appointments to view a number of properties in the outlying areas where homes on acreage were available. We had a few hours to kill before our first home tour so we went for a drive to Plain and Lake Wenatchee then back down Tumwater Canyon to Leavenworth. After lunch we enjoyed a short romantic interlude in the jacuzzi at the Der Ritterhoff and then prepared to meet our real estate agent, Jay. He showed us four homes which sat on more than an acre where horses could be kept. We had also specified that we were looking for a nice but not large home of either log or chalet styling with direct access for horse riding from the property to nearby trails or parkland. We did not find anything we would buy but Jay could not have been more helpful.

We ate dinner that evening at Andre's Keller on Front Street. Keller is German for cellar so down we went into a basement so full of atmosphere that we instantly loved the place. Music was provided by two friendly, talented musicians, one playing the violin and the other played her accordion. The Bavarian music caused chills of pleasure in me and I was quite surprised. My father's ancestors came to America from the outskirts of Mannheim, Germany so perhaps I was enjoying some innate visceral recognition of the music? Since that day I have read a study that suggests that is exactly what happened.

We decided to use the Jacuzzi again upon our return to the hotel. Finding ourselves alone in the forty-eight degree weather that evening, we turned off the area lights and had ourselves a "siren calling the mesmerized sailor" session there in the warm, bubbly waters of the Jacuzzi. I guarantee Stephen slept soundly that night! Up early the next morning we packed and checked out. Heading back to Seattle we drove again through the wondrous mountain terrain that treats travelers to numerous waterfalls very close to the road. We detoured briefly to visit the small town of Roslyn where the television program *Northern Exposure* was filmed. We stopped to have hot chocolate for me and coffee for him in the Roslyn Cafe, which was featured in the program. We both enjoyed the old-style wooden buildings and unique atmosphere. We boarded our Southwest Airlines flight from Seattle at 3:10 p.m. and zoomed towards San Diego, arriving there at 6:30 p.m. We returned home to find the kids fine, the animals all fed and watered and the dishes done. Looking back, I consider our trip to Leavenworth, Washington to be one of our best trips ever.

CHAPTER 47
PALM SPRINGS; NEW BOOK; RAIN

By the middle of October that year, Stephen had disappeared into a fog of depression. He found fault with everything Lynx said or did and much of my character and personality. There was legitimate tension due to Lynx having obtained his driver's license and, as can be expected, pestering us to allow him to drive my Buick anywhere and everywhere he could drum up a reason to go. Although Stephen had, in the goodness of his heart, agreed to pay for his car insurance until Lynx landed a job there was that added stress. Fortunately, Lynx searched for and found a job pretty quickly.

Two good things happened that third week of October. Stephen finished his horse trailer repair project and he crafted new feeders for the horse corrals that we purchased and planned to erect on the property in Ranchita. That old Miley horse trailer was looking good; all the body and rooftop work looked really top-notch. I was proud of him and relieved that he was no longer up on top of that ladder. Stephen seemed to relax and the dark cloud that had enveloped him dissipated.

On October 27, after we completed our usual Friday morning routine we left the ranch and headed for Palm Springs. Richard Harrison, one of Stephen's old friends, was running for mayor of Palm Springs and had requested Stephen to make a personal appearance at one of his campaign events. Steve first met Richard in Italy when they were in their twenties. We arrived in Palm Springs early and found Richard and Francesca's home. We visited with them for a while, ate a snack, put our few things in a spare room, and then changed into our evening clothes. At Stephen's request I wore my red dress with polka dots. It is a bit short but Stephen did admit (for the very first time) that he wanted to show me off. Stephen wore a blue sports shirt and slacks. We left for The Racquet Club at 4:50 p.m. and arrived at the evening's gathering at precisely the right time. Linda Christian, an actress that was in *Athena*, Stephen's second movie, was also present at the event. She had to be in her late sixties but she looked fantastic. It was an easy public appearance and at 7:15 p.m. we all left together and enjoyed a delightful dinner. Afterwards, at the Harrisons home, we retired to our room. For some reason, Francesca had opened a door between their bedroom and ours so we only had a partial partition and little privacy. I returned from the bathroom to find Stephen sitting perfectly at ease in his undershorts on the bed. I asked Stephen to close his eyes while I changed into my lingerie but noticed him peaking a few times. Stephen had a good time and I enjoyed him having a good time. At one point Stephen said, "You don't have to hide yourself from me anymore - you are looking good now, in good shape." We spent a slightly restless night because we were hot and unaccustomed to the city's nocturnal noises.

At 10 a.m. on November 4, which was a Saturday, we had an interview scheduled with John Little who was co-author, along with Bob Wolf, on the book by Stephen that would come to be called *Building the Classic Physique - The Natural Way*. George Helmer accompanied John down from where ever it was that John lived. No one ever realized just how stressed Stephen felt about meetings, interviews and cameras. Everyone seemed to think that somehow their questions or their photos would not be a problem for Stephen but all of them were wrong, particularly about being photographed. On our vacations he was really unhappy with me if I pulled the camera out and requested he be in a photo. Sometimes I ventured to ask despite knowing how he would react - there were times when I just had to take a picture of my love. His reluctance and anger over being recorded photographically seemed to increase as he grew older. He did not seem as averse to having his picture taken as long as friends, such as George and Tuesday, were around him. Those are my favorite photos of Stephen because he appears relaxed and happy.

Eventually George Helmer learned to recognize Stephen's stressors and behaved in such a way that Stephen grew more relaxed around him. There were times that Stephen even looked forward to their talks. When this evolved, I recognized that Stephen had finally accepted George as a friend rather than just a business associate. It was unfortunate that George and his wife, CJ, lived so far away. I would love to have been able to invite them to social gatherings so we could further deepen that friendship.

Well it was November, which always heralded the beginning of our rainy season, so we were dealing with flooding. The living room and bedroom hallway had water damage. Our roof leaked so I set out pans, bowls then later buckets to catch the dripping rain and to enable us to sleep through the night without worrying about the problem. The most problematic area was where the rain ran down the living room wall. The paintings had to be removed and the books taken out of the built-in bookshelves. I developed a way to redirect much of the water running down the wall by thumb tacking black plastic bags, which had been cut open and taped together, to the place where the ceiling met the wall. The black plastic was fashioned into a makeshift funnel with a large bucket at the bottom to catch the rain.

Whenever we anticipated any significant downpours we had to corral the most important horses and lead them into their stalls. Over the years, different horses were granted this privilege in inclement weather, but Monty, who was our eldest horse, was always kept comfortable and dry. Stephen and I often had to siphon out the rainwater in the cross tie area in front of the barn. We also shoveled channels to drain the two most flooded areas of the corrals near the north end of the barn and the small corral at the south end of the barn. We did not want any horse to be forced to stand in water.

Front Row, left to right: Sheila (friend of my mother's), Hilda, Tommy, Naomi, Deborah, Audrey

Back Row, left to right: David (with little Zack), Joanne, Stephen

CHAPTER 48
A MISERABLE THANKSGIVING; FAILURE TO LAUNCH, AGAIN

As November continued, my Lord Tyrant fell again into the pit he had trouble climbing out of. The full moon fell on the seventh day of November, which was usually his favorite day for a "special session" as he called it, but he was bitterly angry at the world and would not respond to my loving touches. Most of the time, his depression impacted him emotionally but not physically. That was not the case this time.

November 11 arrived and I could sense Stephen coming back to us. A fan by the name of Angie Angiuano, who we had never met, was scheduled to come for a visit to the ranch. On a whim he had sent Stephen a replica of an antique black powder pistol with accessories. Stephen decided, as a thank you, to invite this fan to our home. I do not remember asking Stephen to extend the invitation so it must have been his own idea. He scheduled a two hour block of time for the visit thinking he could stand anyone for that long. It turned out that we both really liked Angie. For me to like someone was not at all surprising but for Steve Reeves to like someone was much more unusual. So Angie Angiuano came to lunch and Stephen's mood did nothing but improve.

A few days later, Stephen again raised the subject of becoming married. He said he wanted to get married before the end of the year so he could claim us as deductions on his income tax returns. I would believe it five days after the ceremony and only if there was photographic evidence.

A DAY IN THE LIFE

November 20, 1995
Monday
76 degrees

During our walk this morning I reintroduced the subject of getting married in the near future. I had dropped the subject after Stephen had canceled our June 12th wedding date and he suggested later that maybe we should marry in October when we went to see and experience Leavenworth, Washington in all its fall colors. We went to Leavenworth but he never mentioned any wedding so neither did I. He had recently mentioned something about being able to claim the children on his taxes if he marries me even at the end of the year. At the time, (this morning) I mentioned marrying real soon, Stephen was shockingly interested. He asked about getting married on the 23rd of December. He asked what I wanted to serve and who I thought to invite. When he started to add people to my list and agreed to most of my ideas. I was delighted and I just about floated home. Stephen seemed to be looking forward to our wedding, helping to plan it. I did shut off my joy at one point to wonder just how long he would support the plan before he got negative about the whole affair. But off and on all day Stephen and I brought up the idea and made lists.

Felt loving and lovely. Stephen brought up the idea that perhaps if we didn't marry on December 23rd, then how about on his birthday January 21st? But largely he kept us focused on a Holiday Party, at which we would surprise the guests by getting married.

We both thought it would be a lot of fun and a lovely way to get married.

The End.

On November 21, Stephen asked me to call the minister of Gray's Chapel (just down the road on Cool Valley Road). We had heard he not only performed marriage services there but also at the location of the couple's choice. I, in turn, reminded him to call Jack Stevens (the attorney in Del Mar), to prepare a prenuptial to protect Stephen's assets from the back taxes and other outstanding debts of my prior marriage. Stephen also wanted legal protection from any liabilities caused by my children while they were still minors. And so it went that day - our usual ranch chores and personal pursuits plus the warming buzz as we spoke of and planned our surprise wedding. Just before heading for bed that evening, while finishing watching a holiday movie, I asked whether Stephen would prefer getting married on December 23rd or January 21st. He selected December 23rd.

About the time we completed our evening preparations for bed, Stephen complained he was developing a headache. I strongly suspected it was related to setting in stone, so to speak, "the date" but I just sighed to myself and offered to go get him a cold compress, which he accepted. When I returned, I placed the cold compress on his forehead, kissed his big toe then slipped under the covers to rub his back while I said my prayers. He said he was done with his. Good night Stephen, I love you. Good Night God, we love you.

Our plans continued the next day. We spoke about which business made the least expensive cold cuts tray, where to buy the napkins, invitations and other wedding materials. By that afternoon our guest list had climbed to sixty-eight. Stephen's tone was more and more chipped and impatient as the day wore on so I decided it would be a good idea to take a break. As we snuggled together in bed, he suggested that I rent a wedding dress. I respectfully declined his offer. Wearing a white wedding dress (the symbol of purity and virginity) seemed inappropriate given my age and the fact that I had shortly before finished a robust act of fellatio. So I let him know I would wear something nice but not expensive, and thanked him again.

As Stephen's mood continued to deteriorate, everyone in the house tried to walk on eggs so as to avoid being the cause of the explosion we could all sense was coming. I finally decided to take the bull by the horns and said, "Stephen, I can see how upset you have become about our plans - marrying me was not supposed to be a prison sentence and you're behaving like a condemned man. Forget the wedding if you are once again reluctant to marry me." His response was, "I need to sleep on it." In my mind I screamed, "Son of a Bitch!" That was not the answer I needed from him but how could I say no? The end result was predictable - no wedding again. Sometime the next evening, when he still had not made up his mind, I told him I was not going to plan for a wedding and the subject was dropped. For the life of me I never could understand why he would periodically become enthused about getting married and then shut down.

On Thanksgiving Day, November 23rd, Lynx and Naomi were off visiting their father. Stephen and I took the turkey and dressing to Aunt Hilda's for our holiday feast. Only my mother, my aunt, a neighbor and Stephen and I were present. Somehow I spoke when spoken to and put forkfuls of food into my mouth. I do not know how Stephen could behave as if everything was fine for I could hardly bring myself to participate. Then at long last we left the gathering and were swallowed up by the dark as we drove away. It was one miserable Thanksgiving.

CHAPTER 49
NEW YORK EVENT

December 1st found us traveling to New York and then Connecticut. David Gest and company had us flying first class, which was particularly generous. A limousine was waiting for us when we arrived at JFK. A host of loud, pushy fans and photographers had also gathered which we found to be overwhelming. As the limo threaded its way through traffic the driver disclosed that he was originally from Yugoslavia and had been, when he was a young boy, an extra in *The White Warrior*, one of Stephen's movies. He described in detail the town where the movie was filmed. After hearing all the little bits of information the driver remembered about the locale and details of the production of the movie, Stephen was quite convinced that he was really there. Listening to the driver relate his story brought back warm memories for Stephen as well. The limo driver was a really nice man. Stephen seemed to think so too. He delivered us to the Hyatt Regency in Greenwich, Connecticut which was really something with its center arboretum of trees, vines and a babbling brook. Everywhere we looked we saw faces of people from movies, stage, music and television. I was not great at knowing their names but had that warm, familiar feeling developed from all the years of seeing them in different venues. It is remarkable how certain actors can seem like old friends even though you are obviously only familiar with the characters they have played.

The main event was scheduled for the evening of the following day and held at the New York Hilton and Towers so we had plenty of time to relax and rest. At the appointed time we were whisked away in another limo and eventually joined a long line of other limousines near the large entryway. Police lines held back the throng of fans and paparazzi. As each limo delivered its celebrities and honored guests a cry of recognition went up from that crowd amid a myriad of bright flashes of cameras capturing the moment. This was definitely not my world but I was not going to let that daunt me. When Stephen stepped out of our limo the crowd apparently included enough Steve Reeves fans for him to be instantly recognized. I heard someone shout, "It's Steve Reeves, Hercules, look - over here!" Then he turned and gave me his hand as I exited the limo. I heard others in that mass calling out his name. He turned and with me on his arm moved toward the doorway. He even paused to wave to fans a couple of times.

It was exciting to enter the crush of people in the foyer. Robert Wagner was the designated Master of Ceremonies and was busy greeting people but when Stephen stopped to say hello Robert turned in obvious delight and gave Stephen a bear hug. Robert's wife, Jill St. John, and I were then introduced. She was taller than I thought she would be but just as beautiful. Stephen and Robert had been roommates in their earliest New York City days when they had both been trying to break into acting. As time pressed on they later lost touch. Robert and Jill introduced Ann Rutherford to us and we then moved on.

Our assigned seats could not have been better: third row right next to the inside aisle. Don Murray and his wife, Elizabeth, were seated next to us. Stella Stevens and her husband sat in front of us while Jill St. John and Robert Wagner sat behind us (except when he was acting as the MC of course). The evening's entertainment was incredible and left me speechless. There were approximately 215 celebrities in attendance with awards going to many. One of the first awards went to Gene Autry. Being in the company of such famous stars as Kirk Douglas, Ray Charles, Paula Abdul, Whitney Houston, Jane Powell, Stephanie Powers, Michael

Bolton, Juliet Mills, Tyne Daly and Douglas Fairbanks Jr., among others, was wonderful. Stephen and I had a lovely evening full of Hollywood magic.

We had enjoyed our usual intimate episode prior to the event. When we returned to our hotel room we savored another full session. While my mouth was devoting its full time and attention to his manhood, he asked me, "What would have made this evening perfect for you?" Without missing a beat I answered, "If you loved me." To which he whispered, "How do you know I don't love you?" As my mouth was full at the time, I did not answer him.

December 4th dawned sleepily there in Connecticut. Stephen was not in the mood for socializing until much later in the day so we relaxed in our room until it was time to attend a gallery opening of Anthony Quinn's artwork. The evening before, we were paired with Don Murray and his wife, Elizabeth, on the return trip from the big event back to our hotel. We both agreed that if Don and Elizabeth were living near us, back home, we would definitely add them to our little circle of friends. They were awfully nice people - horse oriented too, which was the icing on the cake. This evening we were paired in the limousine with Douglas Fairbanks Jr. and his wife, Vera. We chose to sit with them for the art gallery's dinner as well. Douglas was a tease and it was obvious that he loved his Vera dearly. She was a bright and compassionate woman and I found it truly a pleasure to become better acquainted with both of them. They were quite a pair. I was tempted to mention that Douglas Fairbanks Sr. (his father) and Cecil B DeMille had acted as witnesses to my grandparents' wedding (George Engelhorn and Kathryn Jenkins) back in 1905, at Elitch Gardens near Denver. But it did not seem the time or the place and I did not want to risk adversely affecting Stephen's good mood.

One other person that caught my eye that evening was Jan Sterling. She was in the *Topper* television series. Stephen had made an occasional appearance on that show and had become somewhat acquainted with Jan as a result. When she took the time to stop by and speak with Stephen I could see he was favorably impressed. To me, she was the most beautiful woman there. It was as if time had forgotten to touch her face. Fortunately for me Stephen was, as always, mindful of her age. Although some men at the gathering paid me a bit of flattering attention, I felt like a dishrag next to the crown jewels with Jan Sterling sitting next to me. I was not jealous, I was in awe. Stephen and Jan spoke for a while and although she had to be near his age, she was amazing even up close.

Anthony Quinn, his wife and their young daughter put in an appearance since the evening's event was all about him. The love Anthony had for his wife and child was obvious. I felt a touch wistful. His artwork was interesting and the company very entertaining. We shared the limousine ride back to the hotel with Susan Blakely and her husband along with Franco Nero who Stephen knew from years before. Mr. Nero shared stories about making movies in Russia, which seems to have been a real nightmare. Once at the hotel we said our goodbyes and headed to our room. By that time, Stephen and I were more than ready for a little private time before a good night's sleep to prepare us for our travel day returning us home to Valley Center. When we arrived at the ranch it was to find that Lynx and Naomi had kept everything going in good shape. They even prepared a meal (spaghetti with meat sauce, garlic bread and a fruit salad) to welcome us home! As far as I was concerned, they were the best welcoming committee ever.

CHAPTER 50
VISIONS OF A DREAM LIFE;
YEAR END

On December 18, Stephen shared with me his vision of a dream life as he had imagined it before we met. His vision included traveling throughout the Western states, breeding single-footing Morgans and finding a summer home in a cooler, forested area where he could ride all summer on either park land or a designated trail area. He also wanted to build a cabin or casita (little house) on the Ranchita parcel in addition to corrals and shelters for his horses. He asked me about what my idea of a dream life had been before we met. I admitted that my vision of a dream life had not included another man in my life as relationships take so much sacrifice and compromise to remain viable. I imagined living with my children in a small cottage in Valley Center, working at either the San Diego Wild Animal Park or the San Diego Zoo and spending my free time planting gardens in the yard. There would be music and the scent of something baking drifting out of the window and a dependable vehicle sitting in the driveway. I would have a couple of dogs and a couple of cats and my birds. In my dream, I led a peaceful and simple life.

Our life together did not quite match either of our pre-relationship dream life visions. We did travel the western United States, we were breeding the special gaited Morgan horses and we continued to hunt for a summer home in either Montana or a cooler area of California. As far as Ranchita plans went, we did erect corrals and shelters for our horses to use on weekend trips out there. Of what I had hoped to have in my dream life I was raising my kids in a lovely adobe home on a ranch in Valley Center and I did have my dog, Dune, two cats plus Mr. Shivers down by the garage. After our first few months together Stephen announced that he did not want music playing in the house or car but sometimes I could smell my pies baking. However, I never, in my wildest dreams, ever thought I would find myself in a relationship with Steve Reeves.

CHAPTER 51
1996 BEGINS;
I MAKE A PROPOSAL

We celebrated our third anniversary on January 8, 1996. Stephen had not been in a good mood since some time before Christmas. His struggle with depression was often hard to live with but this prolonged lack of spontaneous humor and pleasure in life was verging on alarming. Stephen said I took away his freedom to travel, that I looked in worse physical shape than when we began his training of my body and that his life had been better before I came into it. So on the twelfth of January I presented Stephen with a proposition. I offered to supply my services to Stephen in the home, office and on the ranch as an employee (minus the sex). I proposed to move out to the groom's quarters provided he installed a phone line so he could reach me when needed and so I could keep in touch with Lynx and SkyHorse who would remain in the far end of his house until they were emancipated.

He seemed intrigued with my offer but, predictably, he was not happy about the "no sex" clause. As far as that was concerned I told him this new arrangement would allow him to focus his attention on finding new sexual partners and he was guaranteed he would not be living alone on the ranch ever again. In anticipation of his acceptance of my proposal, I spent time cleaning, organizing and making the groom's quarters my little personal space. However, by mid-January, Stephen's mood returned to normal and our relationship fell back into our regular routine. Although my proposal was not accepted, at least at this time, I did enjoy using the groom's quarters as an occasional place of respite.

Our January closed shortly after a first ever dinner at Roland and Virginia Essmaker's home in San Marcos, California. Stephen believed that Roland Essmaker was the first Mr. America ever. He acknowledged that there was controversy but he was thoroughly convinced that Roland held the original title. He and his wife were gracious hosts with a mixture of interests. Roland enjoyed hand-carving marvelously clever and beautiful things out of wood. Virginia was an avid gardener. So we each found a common interest. Even though Stephen and I were at a very hard place in our so-called marriage he still introduced me as his wife, Deborah Reeves, everywhere we went. I was warmed by the obvious love between Roland and Virginia. From that point on we thought of the Roland and Virginia as valued friends.

CHAPTER 52
VALENTINE'S DAY; BIRTHDAYS; POEMS

On February 1, a new interest entered Stephen's life in the form of Jackie Farmer who was an avid fan of single-footing Morgan horse, which was Stephen's biggest passion (outside of sex). Apparently Jackie was anxiously engaged in drumming up interest in the specialized gait of these rare horses and Stephen was more than happy to jump on the bandwagon regarding starting either a newsletter or a single-footing horse club. You may remember that Stephen said he hated telephones and always had either the children or me answer all incoming calls without bothering him if at all possible. However, we were instructed to find him where ever he was on the ranch if she called. With our relationship on the rocks, I was understandably curious about what Jackie looked like and her age. Stephen told me that Jackie was single and lived in Warrens, Wisconsin. I suggested that if she turned out to be young and pretty that he should consider asking her out. When he seemed surprised, I continued, "This coming August I have an Engelhorn family reunion being held not far from Warrens, Wisconsin. We could consider attending the reunion and you could visit Jackie. Maybe she will have a horse for sale by then and you could arrange to view her horses so you can check her out." He was clearly interested but it was only February and August was a long way off.

You can imagine my total surprise when Stephen was really nice to me on Valentine's Day. Whenever he was in a good mood he could be delightful and I had become conditioned not to read anything else into it. He took me out for dinner and even offered me a scoop of ice cream from Baskin Robbins afterwards. Then he selected an X-rated rental for later. We had a really nice session in our afterhours but my favorite thing about the whole day was that he treated me as if he enjoyed my company. It felt like the spring's sunshine after a long winter.

The evening of February 23rd we went out to celebrate three birthdays: George Coates' 60th, Stephen's 70th and Roland Essmaker's 80th. It was our first of what would become a yearly tradition celebrating all the birthdays together, even though Stephen's was on January 21 and Roland's sometime in early March. Anyway, the little party was ruined for me when Stephen became abrasive and rude to me in front of everyone. Tuesday's compassion helped a lot when she tracked me to the restroom to try to cheer me up. I was moved that she was so warm and considerate of my feelings. I never forget a kindness and I added her and George to my prayer list that night. Now, many, many years later, they are still on my list even though I have not seen them since the day of Stephen's memorial service.

On March 1, I copied down poems Stephen had written during his life and recorded them in my journal. They are as follows:

Proposal written by Stephen to Aline in the spring of 1963:

Spring is here, spring has sprung
Let's get married while we're young

We'll be married by the moon
On the twenty-third of June

Don't ask me if I love you, Don't ask the reason why
You'll find that the years to come will give you your reply

I'll try to make you happy, I'll try to make you gay
I want to make up for all those years when you forgot how to play

We'll walk hand-in-hand together along the paths of life
You'll be my true companion, my pardner and my wife.

Advertisement for Morgans written by Stephen in the local paper:

If you want a horse that's a pleasure to ride, with pep in his step and pride in his stride, ride a High Pass Morgan.

Poem written by Stephen contemplating the possibility of death someday:

When my days on earth are over, with my faithful dogs by my side
I will ride through knee deep clover on a horse called "Classic Pride"

They have been my true companions, along mountain trails and rivers wide
My friends will look at me with envy, when we cross the Great Divide

Poem entitled "*Full Moon and You*" written by Stephen to me in the spring of 1993:

It was the time, it was the place
The full moon shining on your face

A soft breeze blowing your golden hair
It was a night beyond compare

I gently kissed you on the lips
You answered passionately with your hips

As I gazed at the stars shining bright above,
I pondered; is it passion or is it love?

As you walked away into the night
I felt that life was good, all was right

Love, Steve

Poem entitled "*Rainbow's End*" written by Stephen to me also in the spring of 1993:

You are the rainbow in the storm of my life. My heart was lonely before you walked beside me, took my hand and showed me the way.

You filled my heart with joy and happiness, and made the sound of music echo through a house that has not heard it in many years.

You showed me tenderness, passion and love. For all this I thank you, and the Man high above.

Love, Steve

Poem entitled *Deborah* written by Stephen to me in the spring of 1994:

Marry me, marry me soon
On the twenty-first of June

The summer sails will light up the clear blue sky
The majestic snowcapped Tetons will stand like sentinels proud and high

The near full moon will shine brightly, lighting up the darkness of the night
As we walk hand in hand together, we hear night birds taking flight

The wind blowing softly through the trees and making ripples on the lake
There are the sights and sounds that only God can make

If you want to make me happy and enjoy my way of life
And if you truly love me, I want you to be my wife

S.R.

On March 11, Stephen was in one of his better moods. He was not a man who gave out compliments and it was not a special occasion so I was surprised to hear him say, "I do not need a bedtime story." You may well remember that I read him sexual stories pretty often at bedtime. His next words floored me, "I have you, my real live fantasy." Then he quoted his version of an old musical song, "Pardon me Miss but I've never done this with a real-life fantasy."

CHAPTER 53
STEPHEN FULFILLS A PROMISE

March 29th found us in Studio City for another celebrity signing show but our first order of business was to meet with Bob Wolff, John Little and George Helmer regarding the final selection of photographs for Stephen's nearly completed book *Building the Classic Physique*. That was a big milestone and the meeting went well. All three gentlemen are intelligent, friendly beings who seemed to genuinely like and respect Stephen. I never felt a bad vibe off of any of them back then.

On April 10, Stephen and I went to Beaumont, California to look at a mare that was for sale. On our way there we were chatting away when Stephen tried to point out some sight to me. Turned out I was supposed to look at a man near the roadside. I said, "Oh, I wasn't looking for a man" to which Stephen teased, "Well you better not be!" After seeing the mare and deciding (after riding her) that she was not for us, on our way home Stephen stopped off at the Chrysler dealership in Temecula in order to compare their prices and selection with the San Diego and Escondido dealers. We were in the market for a Chrysler Concorde. Well they had one that was Candy Apple Red in the model we liked with the more powerful engine and fancier interior. We test drove it and then Stephen bought it for me! I was really not thinking we would be taking a new car home. I was in total shock and disbelief.

On May 8th Stephen bought Lynx a car, a 1986 Burgundy Nissan Maxima. Naomi, Lynx and I were amazed and grateful. Some ten days later Stephen and I were excited to receive delivery of two horses we had purchased from other states. A breeding mare, Mount Hope SweetHawk, was delivered from Illinois and a particularly impressive four-year-old seal brown (almost black) gaited stallion named Zee Beam came from Nebraska. The beginning of our new gaited Morgan breeding program was now really underway.

CHAPTER 54
FUN BREEDING ZEE TO HOPE

On May 24th, we had an extremely unusual, but not unheard of ice storm in Valley Center. The storm delivered an onslaught of hail mingled with some snow flurries and caught everyone in Valley Center off guard. It also destroyed most of the strawberry, melon, lettuce, bean and squash crop at a popular educational farm known as Bell Gardens (established by Mr. Bell, the founder of Taco Bell).

It was the end of May and our routine continued to include some sort of ranch work after our morning routine of Power Walk and workout followed by our brief rest. We were busy this day putting up new feeders in different pastures. The work entailed Stephen lifting the feeder up against the fence rails, me jamming my weight against the feeder to hold it in place while he scrambled over to the other side of the fence, drilled holes through the rails and then bolted it in place. While we worked we discussed Stephen's upcoming trip to Montana with Dave Morris. He casually mentioned he would miss me! It was not a first but pleasure washed over me when he said it.

Later that day, our neighbor and local sheriff, Jim McClain, an owner and lover of Morgan horses, came over to help with the breeding of Zee Beam to Hope, our new mare. The breeding process was complicated (which surprised me). Prior to the actual act, the mare must be exposed to the stallion in order to move her into an estrous cycle. Mares are not continually ready and willing to be bred - they need to come into their cycle. I assumed, however, that once the mare was ready we would breed her by introducing a stallion to the pasture where the mare was held and let nature take its course. I was a bit naïve, I suppose, but I am a naturalist at heart. After Hope (the mare) "came in" the process involved our wrapping her tail, placing her in the breeding chute and then bringing Zee (the stallion) in. As Zee approached I was to pull Hope's wrapped tail out of the way just as he reared up to mount her. It was a very interesting experience, to say the least. I asked what would happen if we let Zee into a pasture where an in-season mare was and Stephen said we would be risking the mare getting hurt and the stallion damaged. He also needed to be able to record the timing of the breeding which he could not easily do if the mare and stallion bred at will. The ranch was Stephen's domain and he was the master of his territory.

We had not experienced a truly awful day together in quite some time. Stephen was uncharacteristically calm and balanced. I relished every day that dawned while this situation was true. It was not in Stephen's nature to utter passionate, loving words but on this one night, just as he was about to drift off to sleep, he suddenly said with crystal clarity, "I'll never let you go!" I turned to look into his eyes but he was sound asleep. Early in our relationship he would, on rare occasion, say such things to my face or while holding me tightly.

CHAPTER 55
SOLO TRIP TO MONTANA

I am a firm believer in sending my man off on any overnight journey with something to remember. So I made sure that our interlude on the morning of Thursday, June 6th, was something special. Then my dearest Lord Tyrant gave me a quick goodbye hug, jumped into his truck and left for Montana. As his truck rumbled down the dirt driveway I whispered a couple more farewell prayers then turned and went into the house to call and let Dave know that Stephen was on his way.

As always, when Stephen left on a trip, my goal was to care for the ranch with great energy and love. I kept everything in good order and decided to accomplish one of the hardest of projects as my gift to Stephen upon his return home. Our Hot Walker (a horse exercise machine that resembles a huge four legged spider) was in desperate need of attention. Four horses can be attached to the Hot Walker which, once turned on, leads the horses around rather like a carousel of living horses. Depending on the goal, the Hot Walker can be set for a slow walk or a more vigorous trot. Our Hot Walker was once painted red but now was totally rusted. I decided to repaint it top to bottom with blue and white rust stopping paint. Climbing up the ladder and brushing on paint with one hand while hanging on for dear life with the other hand was quite a challenge. I do not handle heights well so I was busy muttering little prayers to God like, "Please God, hold off on any earthquakes until I'm back on the ground!"

Shortly before Stephen returned, I managed to finish painting the Hot Walker. Stephen had a policy of not calling home while on one of his trips. For some reason, however, he called the night before he was to return and the sound of his voice lit the fire in me. What a silly sap I remained! The last leg of Stephen's trip home was really bad because Cajon Pass had a chemical spill of some sort which shut down Interstate 15 just south of Victorville, California. Stephen and Dave sat gridlocked on the freeway for three solid hours with three horses baking in a metal horse trailer. One of the horses was a two week old filly who was really desperate to nurse (and the mare was in need of relief of an overload of milk in her udders). Stephen and Dave could not let them out on the side of the freeway to relieve them but once on the ranch everyone felt so much better. I drove Dave home while Stephen kept watch on our new horses. There was Brendalee and her filly (whom we named Belle Starr) plus a chestnut mare named Carmen. When I returned to the ranch Stephen talked a blue-streak about their trip. He had a lot to share and I was his avid listener. After about three hours he walked up and gave me a kiss, I mean a real one, and said, "I like the colors you painted the Hot Walker." That was my first kiss from Stephen in nine months.

CHAPTER 56
FRECKLES

On June 13th, Stephen sent me to the file cabinet in the closet of Lynx's room for some DMV records as he had decided to sell his 1990 Dodge pickup. While looking for those DMV records I came across a set of divorce papers. I remembered he told me early on that although he had filed for divorce in 1977 he opted to terminate the proceedings when Aline became suicidal. As I read the actual divorce papers, however, I realized that the divorce decree was entered on November 24. 1976. In California there is a six month delay between entry of the decree and the final judgment of divorce in order to give the parties time to "cool off" and confirm their desire to divorce. Stephen had the decree reversed on May 3, 1977 (just days before the running of the six month statutory period). Wow. I was surprised. I am not sure it actually made a difference but it did make me think.

Later that summer we were standing in line, waiting our turn to serve ourselves at a fundraising barbecue being held at the fire department in Shelter Valley (also known as Earthquake Valley). We went on occasion to the fundraiser held in Ranchita and less often to the one promoted in Shelter Valley. Stephen, who was in a pretty good mood that day, turned to me with a distinct expression of distaste on his face and quietly indicated a woman further up our line. When I did not understand what he was trying to convey, he whispered, "I cannot stand freckles on a woman, they are really yuck!" I was surprised to say the least since there I stood in all my freckled glory. At the time I had freckles scattered on my face, my chest and my legs. Did he not realize that every year I would be decorated more and more, first with freckles and then age spots? Sure made me feel like a lump of fecal material! Today, in my early sixties, I am top to bottom, front to back, age spots. With my coloring, fair skin, green eyes and blonde hair I have never thought I would end up anything else. Worse, my body is now more the shape of a potato than an alluring sex slave. You have no idea how many times I have been glad that Stephen cannot see me now.

During that summer, Hope, Zee Beam, Carmen, Brendalee and Belle Starr were added to our herd of original five horses (Torrey, Sugarfoot, Traveler, Monty and Rocky). The best breeding mare to realize Stephen's plan of producing really good gaited Morgans was Brendalee. She was what would be called our foundation mare. Carmen, Hope and Sugarfoot had their good points but Brendalee held the best of all characteristics. Her filly, Belle Starr, was not related to Zee so eventually would be bred to him as well. We were waiting to observe Bell's gait, but it seemed to me the ranch was going particularly well despite Stephen's current dark attitude. I was thinking at the time that the origins of Stephen's depressions were partially unrelated to outside factors. The cloud of depression would approach and set the stage, and then something or someone would set it off. More often than not I was the culprit. We were extremely busy with all the training, grooming and exercising of the horses. For me, a horse lover, it seemed an exciting, hopeful time.

In an effort to alleviate some of Stephen's stressors I planted eight trees along a bare section of our fence line. I first dug the trees up from the eucalyptus grove down by the pond. There had been substantial change in our neighborhood during the last few years. Until recently there had been a green, pleasant buffer zone in the form of citrus groves all around the south and east sides of the ranch. But now the orange grove had been subdivided and houses built on the numerous lots. One such home in full view from the kitchen and dining room windows of the ranch was an eyesore with an unkempt yard. So, by relocating some of the trees, I was hoping to create a blind to block some of the ugliness. I was well aware that our changing neighborhood was really upsetting to Stephen. He verbalized his anger about the changes frequently. When we are young it is easier to welcome so-called progress. As we age, however, many of us find the inevitable replacement of the familiar surroundings with foreign people, circumstances and change a source of alienation.

CHAPTER 57
SIXTH ANNUAL MONTANA GAITED HORSE CELEBRATION

It was not until Stephen and I boarded a flight from San Diego to Salt Lake City, Utah on July 24th, that his mood actually lifted. He suddenly emerged from his dark place and I was so pleased! Once we landed we rented a Corolla from Alamo and drove to Riverton, Wyoming where we stayed at a Days Inn. Our purpose behind the trip was to attend the Sixth Annual Montana Gaited Horse Celebration in Bozeman. The next morning we drove eight hours and visited two ranches during our journey. The first was the Barrett's place near Pavilion, Wyoming where we saw the most beautiful bay colt named Sirus. The Barrett family was very welcoming and justifiably proud of their Sirus. Then on we went to Dell, Montana to view a friend's stock. Dorothea Hilgrin was an old friend of Stephen's and we liked each other immediately. Her stud, Sharthunder, was a good-looking mount that we had previously seen perform in Boundurant, Wyoming. I would have liked to visit with Dorothea longer but Stephen was anxious to get to Bozeman. We arrived at Mike and Iliana Delaney's home and were enveloped in their warm welcome. Their guest room rivaled the best accommodations that any fancy hotel provides. They not only supplied us with a wonderful room in their home and food from their kitchen but also offered one of their vehicles to use. Their generosity was not lost on us. Stephen was his affable, charming self and I was thrilled to be enjoying his company again.

We tracked down the first day's event, the Trail Trials, which took place out in the wooded hills with creeks, logs, boulders and other natural obstacles. In addition to running the obstacle course like trail, the horses were required to stand still while the rider dismounts, drops the reins to the ground, retrieves and puts on a yellow raingear slicker from a saddle bag and then remounts. During the trail ride, each horse had to deal with such things as sharing the trail with backpackers and mountain bikers, going over small noisy bridges, crossing through water and coming upon an animal skin hanging near the trail. It was a timed event and hard to observe because of the natural distances and terrain but we enjoyed what we were able to see.

The next day we went to watch the Riding Trials event that was held in the fairground arena. We found the Peruvian Passos and the Paso Finos too unnatural and affected for our taste. Their gait and total manner was painful to watch as they have been schooled in an artificial mode of movement. We preferred the Tennessee Walkers, Fox Trotters, Morgans and Quarter Horses as we found their movements much more fluid. We never understood why some trainers require their mounts to "bend at the poll" (which means for the horse to keep their nose tucked in so the poor animal must keep looking forward in an odd upward angle). It is an unnatural condition for a horse who should be allowed to keep his or her head high. For dinner that night we had reservations at the Oasis in Manhattan, Montana. It was a very special place with great quality beef and I was pleased to be having an extra nice dinner with Stephen, Mike, Iliana and Troy who also lived in the Bozeman area.

At one point Stephen rose from our table with his napkin to his mouth. At the look of almost pain in his eyes, my mind tried to fathom the source. Perhaps he had bit his lip or the inside of his cheek, or maybe he bit a bone fragment and cracked a tooth? I stood and whispered to him directions to the men's room. I always noted such things upon entering a restaurant. Minutes passed agonizingly slow and I felt flushed with worry when he did not return. Mike Delaney, who was sitting opposite me, read the look of concern on my face and quietly left to check on Stephen. "Bless him Lord 10,000 times!" I said under my breath. He returned in a few moments saying, "Steve seems okay but is emptying his stomach." After another couple of minutes Mike went to do a double check on Stephen. When he returned he informed me that, "He seems to be breathing normally." I was reassured but felt uneasy as another minute and then another passed with no Stephen. Then Mike and Troy both stood up and went to check a third time. A few minutes later, Iliana saw Mike leave the restroom and head for the front desk. She and I panicked at the thought that he was calling for a doctor but he retrieved a glass of water from the hostess and headed back to the restroom.

After what may have been only four or five minutes but seemed like forever, Mike and Troy returned to the table announcing that Stephen would soon follow. They said he had something (probably prime rib) caught in his throat. The bit of food was not blocking his airway but took an interminable amount of time to decide whether to go down or come up. Drinking water did not solve the problem. Troy tried the Heimlich Maneuver to no avail. Eventually the object in question decided to get out of harm's way. Sure enough my dearest Lord Tyrant soon reappeared much to my relief. My hands were trembling and my voice refused to produce anything but some strange, squeaky sound so I just silently thanked God over and over. As Stephen sat down he half-jokingly said to me, "Well, you just about lost me!" Once my voice returned, I thanked Mike and Troy for going to Stephen's aid.

As table conversation returned to normal, I could feel I was about to lose my composure. I blinked back tears over and over, tried swallowing the lump of emotion that was stuck in my throat but soon my cloth napkin was thoroughly wet. The ever vigilant Mike passed his napkin across the table to me. I stood and left for the restroom where I could privately let go my failed attempt at self-control. My relief was too raw to allow me to take part in eating and talking with friends for a while. This time it was Iliana who came to make sure I was okay. I touched up the eyeliner that had washed away and returned with her to the table. I stared down at my plate and realized I had only taken three or four bites of my delicious steak. I saw that Troy was just about done with his prime rib and that Mike and Iliana were almost done with their shared dinner. While Stephen had eaten quite a chunk out of his dinner, he opted to take the rest home.

We spent the night before our return flight home in a motel in Salt Lake City. Much to our surprise, we found a porno magazine sitting under the telephone book in our room. Once found it could not be ignored so as we climbed into bed I tossed the magazine his way and, like the idiot I can sometimes be, said, "Here, get inspired." The combination of my loving his body and him imagining himself with one or more of the girls portrayed in that magazine worked out so well for him that he wanted a similar visual aid almost every time from then on.

CHAPTER 58
ANOTHER WHAT IF

We were lying in bed one night in early August when Stephen brought up another one of his "what-if" scenarios. He said, "What if we had met back when you lived in Oregon? Then we would have had our ranch there and be raising cattle, Morgans and a couple of our own kids." I loved it when Stephen fantasized this way even though it was an impossible circumstance. The next day, while we were working side-by-side outside, I wondered to myself whether he and Aline had ever worked on projects together. I worked up the nerve to ask and his answer was a terse and unemotional, "No."

CHAPTER 59
THE 50ᵀᴴ ANNIVERSARY OF THE MR. AMERICA CONTEST

September began and we fell back into a school routine with Naomi. On September 9th, Stephen became agitated at the prospect of our upcoming trip back east for an appearance he had agreed to at the 50th Anniversary of the Mr. America Contest being held in Fairfax, Virginia. Stephen had been hoping his new book *Building the Classic Physique (The Natural Way)* would be printed in time for that event. The reality that it would not be was just another stressor that adversely affected his mood. Stephen questioned people's motives for wanting him to attend the Mr. America contest. He became negative toward George Helmer and someone new to us, Fairfax Hackley (he liked to be called "Hack"). I knew Stephen's negativity would pass but in the meantime I brought some of his ire on myself by defending George and this perfectly nice Mr. Hackley. According to Stephen pretty much anything good these men did was for their own personal gain. I knew that it was the gray cloud of depression looming over him that was causing his stress.

By the time we reached the United Airlines departure gate at San Diego International on September 12th, Stephen was in an improved mood. When we arrived in Fairfax, our welcome, by Mr. Hackley and his friend Rick, was particularly nice and our accommodations were phenomenal. While we were at the dinner party later that evening of about ten people (including Dave Chapman, "Hack" and "Mrs. Hack"), the Secret Service suddenly came in, did a quick search then former President Bush was escorted into the restaurant. It felt surreal. Stephen was his charming self and seemed over any reservations he had about coming to Virginia. I had never been to either Virginia or Washington DC so for me this whole trip was particularly interesting.

We toured the White House on September 13th. We were disappointed that George Helmer did not arrive in time to join us for the tour. We both loved history and our country so the visit to the White House and environs was particularly enjoyable for us. We had a dinner appointment with George Helmer and his friend, Dave Dowling. George had gone to a lot of trouble and expense to be with us on this trip then missed the White House tour so in private I put a little pressure on Stephen to cover the dinner expense. He felt I was being way too generous with his money but he did finally agree. We were meeting Dave Dowling for the first time and he struck me as being one of the more sensible fans of Steve Reeves. He did not come across as pushy or the least bit fanatical. Like George, he seemed willing to work on selling the Steve Reeves International Society's products with little or no economic benefits for himself. I for one could not see what was in it for him but he seemed quite the gentleman. Looking back I find that I was right - he is a gentleman and a good friend to this day. We enjoyed a good dinner but I made the mistake of suggesting we have dessert which irritated the heck out of Stephen. Most of what I remember about that evening is Stephen being upset with me.

Stephen was not really happy until the next day when, just prior to the scheduled Mr. America contest, like magic five boxes arrived containing his just finished book *Building the Classic Physique*. Our plan was to sell them at the event. Although we had no time to give the books a thorough examination a cursory look pleased even Stephen. Such happenings made a world of difference in the quality of my life. In addition to selling numerous copies of the book, George and Dave Dowling were able to set up shop right next to our display table and sell some of their Steve Reeves International Society products. George provided a well thought-out display and Dave came across as a genuinely friendly man who graciously donated his time and energies to promote the products.

The Mr. America contest itself was ruined for us by the obvious steroid use among many of the contestants. The appearance of their physiques, the unnatural vein and artery systems and the size of what used to be their sex organs made the use of steroids blatant. The contestants we thought demonstrated the best in natural body building were not able, as a result, to compete well against the steroid users. The Steve Reeves Award was the only honor which we thought was given to the proper contestant - and that only because Stephen and George were the judges who selected the winner!

We skipped the after-hours get together held at a restaurant so we could retire early to our hotel room. We had developed the habit of indulging in more than the usual private interludes during our away trips. Stephen decided that he wanted to partake of five separate sessions on this particular day. I thought four was plenty but he was rather insistent. Fortunately, he responded well to the hotel's pay-per-view, softened version of an X-rated movie so the fifth session was well worth it.

At the White House on September 13, 1996

CHAPTER 60
GLIMPSES OF THE FUTURE;
LOSS OF A FAVORITE HORSE

October arrived and we were home one evening making plans for our future. We called our planning session "Glimpses of the Future". One of those glimpses showed Stephen and I writing a few books. The two titles he liked for his were: *Trouble Rides a Fast Horse* and *The Day of the Rope*. His were quite obviously Western in time period, location and subject matter. I hoped to write a book for children and another one that would be about Stephen (from inside his skin so to speak). To my surprise and delight, he readily agreed to allow me write such a book. I played with possible titles to the book about Stephen: *Living Legend* or *Legends Never Die*. He approved both titles. Stephen frequently referred to my journals as part of his legacy. During the planning session we enjoyed noticing how we both favored rather dramatic titles. Another glimpse showed us buying a summer place. We envisioned spending our summers in a home nestled in a pine forest or meadow in the mountains near a river where we could ride forever in a cooler clime. Stephen always wanted a horse named High Pass Hercules or High Pass Power Walker to ride at our summer home. He also always wanted to name a ranch Belle Moray (I am not certain of the spelling as he only spoke the name to me). He fancied being "Reeves of Belle Moray".

That fall we had to call our vet to come take a look at Brendalee, our best mare. She was colicky and we hoped he could help her. Our vet, Matt Matthews, did not seem overly concerned. After he injected her with a drug called Butte she seemed to recover. In spite of our hopes and our fervent prayers, however, and despite walking her and doing everything the vet and Stephen's experience told us to try, she went down the next morning and could not get up. We called the vet again, this time to come and put our Brendalee down. We hoped that the vet would come quickly as death by colic is horrifically slow and painful. Poor Brendalee, she was in such horrible pain. With her filly, Belle Starr, in the next paddock, she started thrashing around in terrible pain. She bloodied the whole side of her head in her agonized, uncontrollable thrashing. I ran to the house to get my gun, tears running down my cheeks as I tried to imagine exactly where on her poor battered head to place the gun in order to help her out of her tortured state. I returned a moment later with my 9mm Kurz pistol held with purposeful dread in my hand. I prayed nonstop as I headed to her paddock. Just then Stephen came back and shouted "Wait!" as Matt Matthews had just arrived at the ranch. I was so relieved! The vet expertly put her down. Knowing my crying would only add to Stephen's own anguish I turned and hurried back to the house. We had lost our best mare before we could even obtain one offspring between her and our beautiful Zee. Her filly, Belle Starr, had just lost her mother. She was comforted by our mare, Carmen, who stayed by her side for a month or so afterwards.

Stephen took the loss really hard. He had such high hopes for breeding Brendalee with our stallion and starting his own new line of single-footing Morgans. He had just watched a very bloody end to his most important dream. We had purchased her already in-foal with Belle Starr. Stephen had made detailed plans and arrangements with the breeder to delay bringing Brendalee to the ranch until the foal was born and old enough to bear the burden of long distance travel. Stephen had told me that Brendalee was even better when he saw her in person than the pictures he had seen. When he and Dave brought her finally to the ranch he was like a little boy, giddy with the prospect of his dream coming to fruition. Now she was gone and so it appeared was the dream.

CHAPTER 61
WILDFIRE

In the early hours of October 19 the largest firestorm in Valley Center's history up to that time started down the hill in the Rincon Indian reservation. We were unaware of the impending disaster headed in our direction. Lynx called me from where he was in San Marcos, California, worried as he had heard on the news that the fire was climbing the ridge just east of the ranch. As I talked with Lynx on the telephone I went to the front door (which faced east). When I opened the door and saw the nightmare approaching I said, "My God it's coming close!" I hung up the phone, went directly to Stephen and said, "Stephen, the fire is really close! I'm afraid!"

He became angry, at the situation probably but it felt like at me. In an emergency I am generally really hard to rattle until the danger is past. What I saw out that doorway was overwhelming. Stephen strode with purpose to the front lawn and turned on the sprinklers which I will say, in my ignorance, seemed about as useful as trying to put out a house fire with a squirt gun. The recessed sprinkler valve tops were really hard to see in the dark so I brought a flashlight to help. Except the high winds kept blowing leaves into the sunken valve box obscuring our view. The job was made even more difficult since half of the valve tops were buried by gopher dirt which filled the sprinkler control box on one side. Together we desperately dug out the gopher dirt in order to enable him to attach the long metal pronged apparatus to the top of the valves. Stephen was yelling at me the whole time. He cursed the damned gophers who refilled the control box periodically. As the sprinklers finally started I dashed for the house in order to wake Naomi up and get her into evacuation mode. Naomi, upon waking, was understandably terrified to find her once dark bedroom now bright from the flames of the wildfire that had crested the ridge to the east of the ranch. The fire crews and news reporters later estimated that when the wind-driven flames hit the top of the ridge they were blown at least 250 feet high. A catastrophe of unimaginable devastation was headed our way.

Naomi followed directions well even under such dire circumstances. With tears streaming down her face she dressed then filled one bag with priority items from her room then another with priority items from Lynx's room that she felt he would value. She did a great job of the fastest packing job of her life. Certain that the fire was about to engulf us, she begged me to jump in the car and leave. However, considering every remaining moment to be precious, I insisted we focus on saving whatever we could. Naomi had called her longtime boyfriend, Tommy Davis, who lived in Escondido to come and help us. When he arrived, he stuffed his car with whatever priority items he could. I was amazed that the fire had not yet overrun us. We worked like Trojans who had gone mad. Looking back, it seems like the fire had slowed down in order to enjoy devouring the wild lands, edges of the groves and all the creek beds between us and the ridge to the east.

Stephen was out in the barn and pasture areas with the horses. I rarely saw him as we loaded everything we thought he valued into the cars. Then Lynx arrived in Stephen's borrowed pickup from San Marcos where he had gone to meet his girlfriend, Nicole Lyons, who had just returned from her trip back east. The four of us, Naomi, Tommy, Lynx and me, pitched in saving articles of value, desperately trying to evaluate what to leave and what to save. We knew no matter how many items of worth we managed to save there would later be regret at what was left behind.

I periodically sent one of the boys to check on Stephen to make sure he was safe and ask if he needed help with the horses. He always declined. Then Lynx reported that the front line of the fire was burning all the trees, brush and wooden fences at north side of the ranch. Lynx and Tommy grabbed armloads of bath towels which they soaked in water, in the bathtub or the swimming pool, I do not honestly know which. Using the drenched, heavy towels the two boys beat down random fires created by hot ash blown by the wind as the inferno crept toward the back of our home and the propane tank. The grass, weeds, shrubs, trees and even the tall prickly pear cactus were burning as the wind drove the wildfire from the north pasture and ranch land to the western side of the ranch. My heart sank when I saw the fire coming up close and personal just beyond the backyard fence. Tommy and Lynx, with soot smeared faces and blackened teeth, returned from beating the fire back and I told them, "Be ready at a moment's notice to leave with Naomi and the cats and get to safety!"

In the midst of the maelstrom, with burning leaves and embers whipping all around us, people started showing up with offers to help. Members of a horse rescue group from Bonita, California asked if we needed help evacuating animals. Terry, from Terry's Hay and Grain where we bought our horse and chicken feed, showed up to offer assistance as did the local sheriff, Jim McClain, who had bred his mare to our stallion. We were so full of gratitude that all these wonderful people, some of them complete strangers, would risk so much to offer us help. During all of this chaos, with wind and fire and debris all around us and hounded by the unearthly screams and wails a firestorm is known for, Stephen had been patiently moving horses from paddock to pasture and then from pasture to pasture as the firestorm swept through. Then a change in the direction of the wind caused the fire to alter its course. He single-handedly kept the horses out of harm's way so they did not need to be evacuated. Controlling and transferring terrified horses from place to place in the midst of a firestorm was a Herculean task.

Once the immediate danger was past I went outside to discover the extent of the damage but found it was too dark to ascertain much of anything. I walked midway into the northeastern pasture and could see from the light of the small fires dotting the lower pastures that the wooden perimeter fence was gone. The iron gates had been left open to allow the horses to move between pastures. I decided to close the gates before the horses discovered that they could escape through the gaps in the fencing. Stephen had already taken most of our horses to the open field in front of our barn but I did not want to lose the few that remained in these pastures.

Stephen joined me out there sitting on a low adobe wall in the turnaround area of our driveway. The sky was still dark but the light from the remaining fires allowed us to sit there and observe the fire crews and a single bulldozer (turned out it was our friend Larry Herman on that dozer) slowly moving in and out of the flames and the granite boulders on the hills north of us. We sat there, stunned, exhausted and relieved to have been spared, as we watched the wildfire devour brush and trees up around where Larry's dozer was hard at work. Larry was risking his life for people and animals he would never meet.

As we sat there on that adobe retaining wall we could see areas where the fire was still very hot and active. We watched as it consumed our neighbor's home on the rise to the southeast of the ranch. The firestorm had reached the Cuff's home despite it being surrounded by orange groves. When we heard the explosion of their propane tank I prayed that they were already gone and safe. In 1973 and 1974, when I lived and worked with Larry as house parents at Ahern Ranches down the hill from the Cuff residence, Mrs. Cuff would call to warn us whenever she saw a cougar moving through their orange groves toward our place on Little Quail Run. As soon as she called we would usher our boys indoors. Now their home lit up the hillsides as it burned to the ground.

When dawn finally arrived, we jumped into the Jeep and surveyed the damage in our immediate locale. We later were able to observe the magnitude of the destruction caused by the firestorm by watching the news on our local television station. We learned that there had been several fires raging at the same time in San Diego

County and that countless homes had been destroyed. Three of our neighbors lost everything - their homes, outbuildings, absolutely everything. Several of our neighbors had fire damage to their outbuildings or garages. Everyone lost trees, crops, irrigation equipment and the like. Four people died in the Valley Center fire including one lady who was consumed by the firestorm after she loaded her horses into a trailer and attempted to drive to safety. She had driven off the road and into a ravine during the blinding chaos caused by the firestorm. Her body was found where she had burned to death trying to climb out of the ravine. We thanked God over and over for sustaining us during a very dangerous and difficult night and asked Him to bless and comfort our neighbors who had lost so much.

CHAPTER 62
ACADEMY OF CINEMA AWARDS;
WORLD BODYBUILDING CHAMPIONSHIP

A week and a half later we enjoyed a wonderful stay at the Westin Bonaventure Hotel in Los Angeles while attending the Academy of Cinema Awards on November 2. We were provided with a complimentary room and meals for all the events. David Gest was always generous and gracious toward us. Some months later Stephen started declining such invitations but this particular awards show was very enjoyable. We arrived in plenty of time to relax and unpack in our room. I even had time to press Stephen's shirt and tuxedo pants. Once we were dressed and ready, we left for the dinner and show. We were able to somehow avoid most of the paparazzi and went to find our assigned seats at table 120. When we were unable to find the table after a diligent search, misinformed hotel staff told us there was no such table number. My Lord Tyrant was understandably irritated at this disclosure. Before Stephen could erupt, however, I spotted it, a small round table for four situated in a place of honor right up next to the stage. Wow! Our food was great and the entertainment superb. I tried to keep a personal written record of the names of the entertainers and those who won awards but I was way too impressed to keep up. My list included: Virginia Gray, Dina Merrill, Gregory Peck, Elizabeth Taylor, Kirk Douglas, Jane Russell, Janice Paige, Rhonda Fleming, Douglas Fairbanks Jr., Marjorie Lord, Steve Reeves, Virginia Mayo, Burt Reynolds, Richard Dreyfus, Susan Lucci, former Pres. Gerald Ford, Laurence Fishburne, Janet Leigh, Michael Bolton, Cliff Robertson, CeCe Wymans, Tristan Roberts, Julia McGinnis, Little Anthony and the Imperials, the Chieftains, Paul Jackson Jr., Tony Bennett and the incomparable Bob Hope. We had such a good time and were very pleased to have been invited to the event. When we returned to our room we enjoyed a good, long after-hours session without the aid of video movies or girlie magazines. Our session made the end to a perfect night. Then we said our prayers and I rubbed his back until he drifted off to the land of nod. Good night Stephen. Sure had a wonderful time, God. Good night.

On November 7th we flew into Rome. The purported purpose for the trip was to attend a number of events that Stephen had agreed to make an appearance at. However, Stephen's real reason for accepting the invitations was so he could handle some personal business at the bank in Rome at which he maintained an account. The various appearances had been arranged by our good friend, Giuseppe Alletto. Just as our plane landed at the airport in Rome, a drenching downpour hit. Stephen and I were relieved and happy to see Giuseppe waiting for us with his driver standing by. After a three hour drive south along the western seaboard of Italy we arrived at our destination, the beautiful, quaint town of Battapaglia. A television camera crew interviewed Stephen upon our arrival at the staging area for the next day's event. Everyone at the staging areas was warm and friendly. I was presented with a beautiful bouquet. We were so exhausted and gritty it was hard to fully appreciate all the accolades. After a brief respite we were whisked off for dinner in the far-off hills. We did stop at one point along the way to tour a cave. Not just any cave but the Cave of Spartacus which was appropriate as Steve Reeves had once played his role as the Son of Spartacus. The cave with its various rooms, walkways and amazing formations was both fascinating and spectacular. After the tour we were treated to a very nice dinner at a restaurant called Spartacus during which Stephen was given a giant beer stein to add to his collection. There was live music and we enjoyed the company of our host and his companions. We returned to our hotel room in Battapaglia very late and exhausted. Despite our weariness, however, we enjoyed a rather special session - our first for this trip. We always enjoyed celebrating our "firsts".

The following day Stephen was scheduled to make an appearance at a local theater where the movie *The Last Days of Pompeii* was playing. After Stephen was introduced he fielded questions from the audience and signed autographs. When the crowd became overly enthusiastic (i.e. unruly) the bodyguards stepped in to protect Stephen. One of the assigned bodyguards shoved me away from Stephen at one point. I complained to him in English and shoved him right back. The bodyguard weighed in the neighborhood of three hundred pounds and was built like a brick wall. I nearly lost my footing and went down when he turned and propelled me again away from Stephen. One of the promoters observed the altercation and intervened. The muscle man profusely apologized to me in Italian. Although I did not understand a word he was saying it was obvious from the tone of his voice and the look on his face that he was mortified by his error in judgment. Knowing my English was as lost on him as his Italian was on me, I was hoping my outstretched hand, and my tone and expression would stop the onslaught of self-recriminations he was showering on me. I was then allowed to join my dearest Lord Tyrant. Stephen and I had one thing in common at these events - we abhorred crowds, pushy photographers and all the hoopla that was part and parcel with his appearance. Since the airline tickets, ground transportation, meals and lodging were expenses covered by the promoters in exchange for Stephen's personal appearances the nuisance was considered a small price to pay to accomplish Stephen's business at his bank.

I would have dearly loved to meander among some of the wonderful historic places and stroll along a Mediterranean beach, but that had already been done by Stephen years ago with others, including Aline. So it held little interest for Stephen now, with me. Our personal escorts, Mauro and Philippe, did take us off the main road and drive us along the scenic western coastline at one point in time which I greatly appreciated. They could not have been more accommodating. During the drive both Stephen and I could not help but chuckle at the comedy occurring in the front seat. For reasons we never understood and were afraid to ask, Mauro and Philippe had brought with them a number of cell phones. There were two or three stashed in the glove box and a couple more in the middle console of the car. At any given time one or more of the cell phones would ring. Watching the two men struggle to determine which cell phone was ringing and then juggle the phones between them while driving, as Italians do, lickity split down a serpentine coastal road, was nothing short of comic relief. Although, I have to admit, there were times when the ongoing comedy felt like it might turn into a tragedy as we sped pell mell along the edge of that narrow, winding scenic byway.

On November 9, we attended the main event: the World Bodybuilding Championship. The bright note of the event for me was seeing a familiar face, Raymond Mialon, whom we met and stayed with in the south of France in June of 1993. I looked for his wife, Brigitte, but never spotted her. They were a very nice couple but we unfortunately never had the opportunity to meet and visit with them while in Italy this time. The contest had a disappointing number of steroid abusers despite competition rules to the contrary. There were competitors from eighteen or nineteen different countries. Afterwards we snuck out the back entrance under guard to a waiting car. A few paparazzi were not fooled despite our carefully planned exit strategy but we survived.

The next day we were taken to Rome by our escorts and now friends, Philippe and Mauro. They were relaxing to be around and full of information. The hotel Stephen was accustomed to staying at while in Rome was unavailable so they dropped us off at one close by but unfamiliar to Stephen. The first thing we discovered once we were safely ensconced in our hotel room was that the toilet honked loudly after every flush. Stephen demonstrated a simple trick that worked like a charm to silence the toilet - just turn on other faucets first. The following day Stephen was able to accomplish his bank business while I relaxed in our hotel room feeling under the weather. Afternoon television in Rome that day included an American Western with Brian Keith dubbed in Italian. I was not feeling well but seeing Brian Keith riding a horse as a cowboy while speaking Italian was pretty amusing. By the time Stephen returned to our room I was feeling much better. Now that all his obligations and goals were completed, Stephen was able to relax and he felt much better. After a quick nap, we meandered along the streets of Rome and ultimately decided to have dinner at a restaurant not far from our hotel. We laughed and enjoyed a wonderful meal together. Between the first and the second courses of our dinner, Stephen reached under the tablecloth and put his hand on my thigh just above my stockings. The tablecloth hid his game from everyone so he decided to use the Braille method to determine which panties I was wearing. By the time we returned to our room we were both ready for a culmination episode. It was a very nice way to end our stay in Rome. While we were not looking forward to the long flight ahead of us, we were glad to be going home tomorrow.

Our trip home the next day ended up almost being a nightmare. We had arranged with Lynx to pick us up at Lindbergh Field, the San Diego international airport, upon our arrival. However, one of our flights was canceled and then, when we were mere minutes from arrival in San Diego, our plane was re-routed to Los Angeles due to a thick pea soup fog which had closed the airport. Unfortunately, Stephen did not believe in cell phones so there was no way for us to let Lynx know what had happened. At LAX they herded us onto a bus and we were subjected to a three hour drive down an extremely foggy and gridlocked Interstate 5. With all the delays it took us over thirty-one hours to travel from Rome to San Diego. When we were finally delivered unceremoniously to Lindbergh Field in San Diego we were beyond exhausted. While en route from LAX, Stephen kept telling me Lynx would not be there when we finally arrived in San Diego. He was certain that Lynx had either crashed our Jeep Grand Cherokee or was drunk partying somewhere and had forgotten all about us. So when I saw our Jeep, still in pristine condition, and Lynx standing there waiting for us at the curb where the bus had parked in order to offload its weary passengers at 5:30 in the morning, tears of relief began to fall.

CHAPTER 63
A CHRISTMAS SEPARATION

The ranch house was plagued by a leaky roof. Trouble first appeared along the seam between the back roof and the covered patio area then later indoors in the living room, front entry and the hall leading to the master bedroom. We had to do something. Roofers had given us an estimate of $2,700 to handle all the repairs so we decided to save money and do it ourselves. Around the middle of November, Lynx, Stephen, Tommy and I began by repairing the patio roofing. Lynx and Tommy did the majority of the work. Up on the roof, Lynx carefully removed each roofing tile one by one and then handed them to Stephen who was at the top of the ladder. Stephen handed each one to me and I in turn gave each to Tommy who stacked them on pallets. Once the deteriorated areas were cleared, Lynx swept the dirt and debris off. The exposed cracks were then filled with roofing tar by Tommy and Lynx. Next, roofing paper was tacked down and then the tiles brought back up and gently replaced. It was a lot of work.

On November 21, Stephen announced that we would host our first ever holiday party on December 21. I was so excited I could hardly wait. In early December, we were informed by Gerrie Eiferman that her husband, George, had undergone two valves and one bypass surgery. We immediately went into prayer mode: holding hands with the children and praying each night for poor George. It was so hard to imagine gregarious, strong, funny George Eiferman seriously ill at a hospital in Hawaii. Gerrie's call caused us to reflect over and over again just how fragile and mortal even the strongest of us still are.

Stephen bought himself a gelding named Ranger for Christmas in early December. The Morgan gelding was delivered direct from a Montana ranch. Stephen was well pleased with Ranger which was all important to me. While Stephen worked and familiarized himself with Ranger, I concentrated on building small rock walls on the west hillside of our burnt-bare ranchland in order to help thwart massive erosion during the upcoming rainy season. I planted seeds by the thousands and formed many piles of long branches from all the burnt trees and brush. I knew the piles would also serve as a place of shelter for the small creatures that had survived our October firestorm.

I had intended to place one of my "A Day in the Life" sections here but to cover this next event took nearly fifty pages in my journal and I decided that no one could possibly want to wade through all that. So instead I am recording here only the briefest of accounts of what happened from December 20th through New Year's Eve. The consequences of what happened echoed through the rest of our time together.

On December 20th, Stephen became upset when Lynx decided to drive his girlfriend, Nicole, to school. Lynx had been sick the day before so Stephen demanded an explanation from me. Stephen felt that I should have forbidden Lynx to take Nicole to school. Lynx was eighteen years of age and working full time so from my perspective it was just a young man wanting to drive his new car to pick up his girlfriend and take her to school. Without any word of explanation Stephen packed his bag and suddenly left the ranch. As he left, I called out my usual, "Go with God!" He apparently did not quite hear me so he reopened the door and demanded to know what the hell I had just said. I replied, "All I said was go with God." He realized the truth of my words, mumbled, "Oh" and then went back out and headed for the Jeep.

At the time I fully expected that he would drive somewhere and return once he had cooled off. He had never just taken off before. I was wrong. I spent four-and-a-half days not knowing if he was physically all right or if something had befallen him somewhere. I never suspected that he would just walk out and stay gone on purpose. It seemed so unbelievably out of character. I realized he was Steve Reeves, Hercules to many, but to me he was my dearest Lord Tyrant and seventy years old. Men with ill intent could bring down a seventy year old Hercules. I kept thinking anyone can be mugged. Why else is he still gone, why else has he not called? So I just kept praying that he was okay.

As Stephen had packed up and stomped off on December 20th, I needed to call all the guests who had been invited to attend our first holiday party which had been scheduled for the very next day, December 21, and politely cancel the party. I did not record in my journal what sort of excuse I gave each of the invited guests. I had conflicting instincts screaming at me. One voice told me Stephen had to be hurt or waylaid - why else had I not heard anything - and that I needed to do something. Then the other voice kept telling me he would never forgive me for calling the police to find him, to make sure he was alive and well. I admit that I was afraid of just how angry that would make him. There were certain things he would never forgive and I was always particularly careful not to tread there. Then the first voice in me would start in again with, "But what if he went in to buy some of his chocolate milk and while he stood out by the Jeep to drink it (he almost never ate or drank inside that Jeep), he was mugged?" Round and round I would go. It just did not seem reasonable or rational that Stephen had disappeared without a trace over a disagreement about Lynx driving Nicole to school. All I could do was pray that God would keep him safe.

I had fifteen dollars in my purse when he left. I put five dollars in the gas tank and hoarded the rest. My children were mostly spending their holidays with their boyfriend or girlfriend's families. They did check in on me but I was careful to reassure them that everything was fine. Friends called and I lied about the situation. How could I say anything to anyone about what had happened? It did not make any sense to me so how could I expect anyone else to understand? I was on some level ashamed of what had transpired. I had to spend a pre-Christmas evening at my mother's house, where George and Tuesday were also planning to be, and try to get through the evening without falling apart although my heart was in my throat. When asked, I had to honestly say I did not know where he was, why he was gone or when he was coming home. My kind sister-in-law, Joanne, secreted a twenty dollar bill into my purse which I found later. Thank God for Joanne. My urgent prayers that God keep Stephen safe now ended with me muttering that if he was just fine I was going to kill him!

Stephen returned late in the afternoon on Christmas day. His arrival on the ranch was such a relief to me that when I saw the Jeep from the kitchen window my knees buckled. I watched in disbelief as he parked the Jeep over by the barn and then saddled Torrey for a ride! To say the least, I was shocked that he had no intention of coming in to see me, speak to me or tell me what had happened. I walked on wobbly legs out to the barn to speak with him but soon realized he was in his righteous indignation mode. The first thing he said to me was, "You drove me out of my own home!" That was his entire explanation. I was stunned and angry too. Then off he rode for a Christmas afternoon trail ride on Torrey. I was in a weird state - nearly overcome with relief followed by shock and anger. I did not think the knots in my stomach would ever go away. This wound in our relationship never fully healed.

CHAPTER 64
1997 BEGINS

January, February and March of 1997 were somber months. I kept to my expected routine and did what was required, including daily sexual interludes, but something was missing. Even though we later mended our relationship somewhat, things would never be the same between us. We planned to observe Stephen's seventy-first birthday on February 23rd at the now annual joint celebration with the Coates and Essmakers at the Fireside Restaurant in Escondido. However, on January 21, which was his actual birthday, my goal was to pay tribute to my dearest Lord Tyrant in a more personal manner. So we began his day with a special intimate session then I suggested we go for a trail ride, me on Torrey and he on Sugar or Ranger. He chose Sugar this time. As we saddled our horses I told him I desired to make him one of his favorite dinner menus and that he could choose from pot roast, stuffed cabbage or lasagna. He decided on the pot roast so as soon as we returned from our ride I headed indoors to start the meat. Stephen preferred his pot roast to be so tender it would fall apart.

The ride was not as enjoyable as it could have been due to the ongoing strain between us due to his decision in December to punish me by abandoning ship. I made Stephen's lunch and started the preliminary prep on that evening's meal. After our usual nap, as per his instructions I set up the VCR and an X-rated movie in order to indulge his sexual appetite. However, he decided to forego the video until later in the evening and requested just a "warm up then tongue service" without culmination. I did as requested even though it sounded more like a command than a request. Afterwards we completed our afternoon and then evening chores. I had arranged for Lynx and Naomi to be elsewhere for the evening so we ate his birthday dinner alone. After dinner we sat in the living room and watched a show on television. I kept my hands busy altering another of Stephen's shirts that his mother Goldie had made for him decades before. The kids returned one at a time, checked in with us and then departed to their rooms. When the show was over Stephen and I retired to the bedroom to have the promised session with his X-rated movie. He enjoyed a good explosion. Afterwards I said, "Happy Birthday Stephen, I hope you sleep well." That was the most I could manage as I rubbed his back then turned to say my own prayers. Good night God.

On February 23, we met Roland Essmaker (who was turning eighty-one years old), his wife, Virginia, and George Coates (who was turning sixty-one years old) and his wife, Tuesday, who was turning a mere thirty-seven years old, at the Fireside Restaurant as agreed. It was reassuringly normal and relaxed to be with the four of them. Stephen's and my relationship was stretched so tight that it seemed our old relationship was a million miles behind us. Gathering with these four special friends brought back so many great memories of times spent in their company. There was much camaraderie, funny stories told and memories shared. The evening's celebration was very nostalgic and momentarily lifted the heavy weight of sadness I had been struggling with. Stephen behaved the way he usually did in company - warm and funny and full of witty asides. It was Stephen being Stephen at his best - just not the one at home these past few months. After dinner, as we exited the restaurant, we were all upset to discover that some careless soul had backed into George and Tuesday's car. Whoever had caused the damage was long gone. We were quiet in the car on our way home. I do not know what Stephen was thinking but I was full of that wishful kind of regret for all that we had lost.

Stephen and George Helmer held meetings at the ranch with John Little and Bob Wolff, the publishers of Stephen's new book. I liked all three men as I have said before but naturally felt more comfortable around George as he seemed so dedicated to promoting Stephen and had become quite a good friend to both of us. On March 9th a Steve Blechman of Twin labs (and also connected somehow to Muscle and Fitness magazine) was at the ranch for yet another meeting that also included George and Bob Wolff. George was arranging everything regarding the Steve Reeves International Society's supplement line of products. George had been doing a lot of research and contact work on behalf of the fan club and Stephen. As I recall, Twin Labs was the contractor hired to handle the production of the supplements.

CHAPTER 65
CONCERN FOR THE FUTURE;
A DISPUTED FULL BODY MASSAGE

I believe it was around this time that I felt comfortable enough with George, who was by profession some sort of financial auditor, to confide a concern I had. I have never been any sort of financial whiz and I did not know anyone else to ask about my anxiety. According to Stephen's last will and testament I was to receive the bulk of his estate in trust with the understanding that I would receive $50,000 per year, no more and no less. With all the monthly expenses of the ranch in general, and the deferred maintenance concerns in particular, my fear was in not knowing whether I would be able to maintain the ranch and cover all my living expenses on $50,000 per year. I asked George if he would be willing to mull it over and assist me in determining whether the ranch would need to be sold if Stephen were to die. George never got back to me on that question. Each time he came for a meeting at the ranch I thought he would take me aside and offer me some guidance. He never did. I reassured myself that I was much more likely to die and leave Stephen than the other way around. Stephen always said he planned to live to one hundred years of age whereas I had no interest in living past the age of seventy-five. I have always hoped that God will take me home while I am still relatively young. During my time with Stephen I always considered George to be our friend, not just Stephen's fan. There was a moment back in 1996, during one of George and Stephen's meetings at the Ranch, when George witnessed Stephen being rather autocratic towards me. When Stephen stood up from the table and left to get something in the other room George said to me, "I see how things really are." Silly me I thought I saw a touch of compassion in his eyes. So while I knew he was Stephen's fan and loved Stephen, I thought he also now understood that Stephen could sometimes be a very difficult and unappreciative mate.

Some years later, shortly before Stephen died, George started treating me as though I was some awful enemy. I just could not determine what had changed, what had happened, to make him all of a sudden treat me so differently. It is always bewildering when you think of someone as a friend and then later discover that they are not. During all the court proceedings involving Stephen's estate George felt like the enemy. His deposition certainly did not paint me in any sort of positive role in Stephen's life. I kept thinking he should know better. Then one day, after attending a hearing at the probate court settling Stephen's estate, he spoke to me in the parking lot and the mystery was solved. He admitted that when I had asked him if receiving $50,000 per year would be enough to live on all he could think of was, "Hell, I wish someone would leave me $50,000 per year." I finally understood the cause of his alienation. I guess he was estranged from me way back then but I never felt it until Stephen was in the hospital, a day or so before he died.

Now back to 1997. I was twenty-five years younger than my dearest Lord Tyrant. There is no doubt that difference in age and experience caused a good deal of our difficulties and stresses. Stephen felt that I was disloyal to him if I did not chime in when he was upset at someone and condemning them. Most of the time I would give no comment and just hope that after venting his frustrations or anger that he would calm down. Sometimes though I would mention why I thought the person suffering his wrath might have done whatever it was that bothered him.

On occasion Stephen would say, "I'm not looking for anyone new but if I was I would look for someone younger and prettier than you." There were times when I was sorely tempted to retort with some hurtful barb. I was guilty once of saying something totally unforgivable to him. It will bother me forever since all these years later it still plagues me that I could have ever responded so hatefully. Stephen, like most people, enjoyed a good massage. At one event a beautiful woman masseuse offered him a full body massage. My hackles were raised the instant I heard the offer. When Stephen did not decline her overture I decided that I needed to discuss it with him in private. When we were alone I asked what he would be wearing during a full body massage. He said, "Nothing, but I will have a towel over my privates." I asked how large a towel and he replied, "The towel covers my butt pretty much. When I turn over I fix it so comes up between my legs to cover my cock and balls." He demonstrated with his hands coverage about the size of a large bandage. In shock and without conscious thought the next thing out of my mouth was, "If you let that woman give you a full body massage, I'll cut it off!" We all know what "it" was. I could not believe I had uttered such an awful threat and I regretted it a fraction of a second after I said it (and ever since). Of course I apologized profusely. I tried to explain that I would never consider having a member of the opposite sex perform what to my provincial brain is a sensual act, whether or not it is physically beneficial. Unfortunately, once you have said something you truly regret there is no retracting it.

There were common grounds between Stephen and I that we discovered as time went by. He and I both absolutely loved horses and dogs. Before I came to the Ranch I had owned only two mares, two geldings and one rescued quarter horse colt that had been headed for the slaughterhouse with his mother. I could not save his mother but I did bring him to the group home Larry and I operated in Hermiston Oregon. The boys under our care liked the horses a lot. Stephen had owned horses pretty much all of his adult life. We both enjoyed some, but not all, country music, anything by the Three Tenors and most show tunes from classic musicals. Stephen was not as keen on classic and soft rock as I was but then he loved a lot more Opera than I did. We valued the American rural areas with mountains, valleys and rivers. We both refused to ever again live anywhere except out in the country. We both enjoyed going to the movies a lot during our early years but almost never later. There were several television programs and shows we favored during our years together including Charles Kuralt, CBS's *Sunday Morning*, *Nash Bridges*, *Picket Fences*, *Matlock*, *Dr. Quinn*, *JAG*, *Missing Persons*, *60 Minutes*, and *Becker* (who we all agreed was a lot like Stephen). We also sometimes watched *Colombo*, *Christy*, *Dave's World* and any Westerns available. Stephen also enjoyed watching the *Lawrence Welk* show. It was not exactly a favorite of mine but my habit of doing some sort of project while watching television in the evenings meant I could focus a bit more on the project when something I found less interesting was on. To this day I cannot think of the *Lawrence Welk* show without an instant image of Stephen in his recliner, with me next to him in mine while I darned another hole or pulled the stickers out of his wool stockings, coming to mind. We appreciated the English language. Stephen and I enjoyed plays on words, word origins, interesting phrasing, creating our own words and the like. We maintained long lists of Western phrases and Western terms. Taking short trips to places like Shelter Valley, California and cataloging the names of all its Western themed roads and streets was something we relished. As you have learned, we loved having sexual escapades during adventurous times and in interesting, unusual places. We had considerable fun being somewhat naughty. As long as we did not hurt or embarrass anyone we felt our interludes were a bonus part of our relationship. Later, as Stephen developed a dependency on porn to become aroused, I was treated more as a facilitator than a motivator.

CHAPTER 66
A LITTLE THAW;
A BIT OF HEALING

The terrible coldness which had settled in between us at long last started to melt when April arrived. We found ourselves at five a.m. one Sunday in mid-April enjoying our first session of the day. The dawn heralded in a beautiful sun filled day. We slipped back under the covers and dozed off again when Stephen returned from his horse feeding routine. A bit later we watched our favorite CBS *Sunday Morning* on the television while we enjoyed a delicious breakfast of golden hash browns and English muffins with the eggs, ham and a slice of cheddar in the middle.

Stephen and I took advantage of the warm weather (which had dried out most of the slippery slopes) and went for a trail ride. Stephen was in an affable mood, which was always a blessing, and my blues had retired for the moment. I was on Torrey and Stephen rode Rocky. Both horses were a little antsy after not being ridden for a few days but they were not unmanageable. We enjoyed a delightful ride and the sunshine on our backs felt delicious. Here and there were small creeks to cross but the rains had brought fresh greenery up out of the earth and it was wonderful to be on the trail. Sometimes, on the trail ride down toward Pauma Valley, a thick cottony blanket of clouds would cover the whole valley. This ride was one of those times. The panorama appeared otherworldly and I felt blessed to be a witness. Out of consideration for me, which was a pleasant surprise and greatly appreciated, Stephen strived to avoid the more hazardous drop off areas on the trail. The recent rains made it very difficult to ascertain where the earth was stable. I knew if I was not along on this ride Stephen would have rode much faster and not taken the easier, safer routes. This day turned out to be one of those turnaround moments that I had almost given up hoping for.

Stephen regularly received Muscular Development and Iron Man type magazines in the mail. All well and good except I did not approve of all the girlie pinup photos included in the magazines. When I said as much, Stephen replied, "I don't look at them, I just read the articles." Typical male - where have we all heard that before? The next such magazine that arrived in the mail had over fifteen pages in a row of color pinup photos in the usual array of provocative poses so I tore that whole section out. Stephen was predictably perturbed and told me, "Instead of being upset and ripping that section out you should study all those photos and try harder to become like them." He offered this advice knowing full well that I had spent the last four-and-a-half years working out five days a week under his tutelage in the gym. I was forty-seven years old and even Steve Reeves could not transform my body into a centerfold. So right then I decided to quit trying. I did continue to do Power Walks with Stephen five days a week but when he headed for the gym I turned my attention to my ranch chores. I cannot tell you what a relief it was to relieve myself of the pressure of trying to chase his dream woman's body. It had seemed so possible when we first began but I finally realized, even if he did not, that it was an unrealistic goal.

In June I decided to get to work on an eyesore out on the corner of the ranch property. If you approached the ranch via Little Quail Run before reaching the entryway you had to pass along the outside edge of the property near the upper horse training arena. This critical area of the ranch, the part that visitors first observed, had never received any tender loving care. There was a broken wire fence line, bits and pieces of irrigation trash scattered all over and a dirt slope covered with weeds and riddled with rabbit and squirrel burrows. In retrospect, I was not only trying to upgrade the property but also keep a little distance, physically speaking, between us. I began referring to this project as the Memorial Garden or sometimes just the Corner Garden. I considered it my tribute to our neighbors who had lost their homes in the Rincon fire of 1996. I was still haunted by the memories of the devastating wildfire that occurred on that terrible night in October.

When Stephen was in a good mode, he occasionally liked to tease me by saying, "When are you going to write your memoirs? You could call it 'My Life as a Sex Slave'." I never knew quite how to respond but I knew I had the material to write a hard-core, nonfiction eye-opener if I ever penned my experiences with Steve Reeves. His sexual appetites and preferences would likely astonish his friends and fans. In writing this book; however, I decided to obscure most of the details of our sexual escapades. I am certain a reader will be able to fill in the blanks so to speak.

A DAY IN THE LIFE

July 17, 1997

The 34th anniversary of my father drowning

Stephen was criticizing my mother this evening, saying, "Well her children sure all made bad choices in marriage! They each married the wrong person and had to get a divorce!"

My response was, "Well, lots of people's children don't pick the right marriage partner the first time. Look at all of us." Then I paused because it occurred to me that he might think himself exempt from that inclusion, so I quickly added, "Except maybe you." At which point he jumped right in and agreed saying, "That's right, I married the right one the first time - I just didn't know it then."

The End

August arrived and the weather was crispy hot, dry and windy. I was pleased to finish my outdoor chores early and return to the house to make Stephen's juice one morning. He was out in the pool doing his pool exercises with his weight belt on. At least the water was not frigid this time of year. He let Gem, our Abyssinian cat, in as he entered through the sliding glass doors down by the bedroom. Once he toweled himself dry it was time for stimulation session number two. I did not linger in the bed afterwards but kissed his big toe and went to work on his fan mail. There were a lot of requests and I could do everything except sign the photos, posters and books. After I completed my preparatory tasks, Stephen would come in and finish the orders relatively quickly. Gem was stretched out on the wide dining room windowsill enjoying the morning rays. Her daughter, Isis (who Stephen called Isaacs) was more inclined to snuggle with Stephen's dog Rommel than to keep me company. No figuring the kitty cat's taste.

Stephen came in while I was finishing up my work on his fan mail and spoke of the deal he had negotiated with John Little and George Helmer regarding the sale of Stephen's supplements being offered through the Steve Reeves International Society. They had agreed to split any profits three ways. The only impact the sales of Stephen's products ever had on my life was how they affected Stephen's mood. Stephen could sign his fan mail without my company so I left to start the laundry and defrost some meat for that night's dinner.. Then I turned my attention to my latest project of whitewashing the adobe interior walls along the hallways. The passage of time and Rommel's penchant for rubbing the walls as he passed through the hallway caused them to need more than Naomi's monthly scrubbing.

CHAPTER 67
ZEE THROWS HERCULES; THE WOUND THAT NEVER WOULD HEAL

The summer winds made the horses restless and a bit jittery so when Stephen went to work Ranger and Zee after his nap, I went not just to help but to keep an eye on his safety. I never let Stephen know my underlying purpose for being there, of course, as he would have thought me quite silly. That day Stephen decided to ride Zee in the smaller arena which was surrounded by high adobe walls. His selection of arena turned out to be a blessing as Zee reared, then bucked and dislodged my dearest Lord Tyrant sending him abruptly to the ground! My heart was in my mouth as I stepped forward to grab Zee's reins. Much to my surprise and relief, Stephen recovered with a nimble grace that belied his age. He said he was not hurt but being thrown off a stallion at any age is no laughing matter.

He re-mounted Zee and put him through his paces for about forty minutes in order to work the horse through his jitters. The walled arena was less windy than the large arena which was fenced with four-rail metal pole fencing. The next horse to be ridden was Ranger. His workout went without a hitch so Stephen instructed me to open the wooden gate to the small arena and then run and open the pole gate to the large arena. I did as instructed then ran back to the small arena and shut and latched its gate. I did not want the wind to slam the gate back and forth or break the hinges. I also knew the racket might disturb Ranger not far away in the large arena. Once Stephen was finished working the two horses we groomed each in turn and put them back in their respective pens. I then headed out to work in the Memorial Garden for an hour before coming back to fix dinner. When I returned to the house I discovered that Naomi and Tommy had already made dinner. I was so pleased. The Tostados with rice and a salad was delicious and so appreciated. I brought a tray of food to Stephen in the living room where he was watching *Lawrence Welk* on the television. Stephen loved Naomi and he really liked Tommy so he had no complaints that evening. A bit later I ran a bath in the Jacuzzi for Stephen. I knew his muscles and body could use the heat and ministrations of the Jacuzzi jets after being thrown by Zee. After the bath I rubbed him down with liniment before interlude number four for the day. Stephen was perfectly happy to culminate our evening with an explosion. We said our prayers and then I rubbed his back until he drifted off to sleep. Good night Stephen, Thank you God for saving Stephen's neck. Good night God.

For Labor Day we held a barbecue for friends and family at the ranch. The day was hot, sunny and cloudless. We had the ranch pretty well at its best in honor of our guests which included Virginia and Roland, George and Tuesday plus my mother and my Aunt Hilda. Naomi had Tom Davis as her guest and Lynx had Nicole Lyons as his. Lynx was in charge of barbecuing the chicken and hamburgers. Tom, who by then was like another son, pitched in wherever needed. I guess once you risk your life and limb helping to save your girlfriend's home from a dangerous wildfire you are deemed a member of the family from then on. George and Tuesday provided decadent desserts while Virginia brought a big pot of homemade pork and beans. The Coates also furnished some dark beer and light ale that George and Stephen liked to mix. We provided the rest of the side dishes including green salad, potato salad and Stephen's three bean salad. It was a wonderful day with great company. Roland went with Stephen out to check out the horses.

A few days later we were watching a commercial about some sort of skin care product and somehow the subject of our future came up. I said, "Well I figure I'll not be around for more than four more years, since you can't see yourself with a woman who has turned fifty." Stephen started to deny the truth of what I had said but then let that denial die on his lips. Although we tried to pretend we were doing fine there were private truths we hid from the world. The damage done to our relationship by his inexplicable disappearance last December still lingered.

Zee

Aunt Hilda's Birthday Party, August 23, 1997
Back Row (left to right): Hilda, Naomi, Tommy and George Coates
Front Row (left to right): Stephen, Deborah, and Audrey (Deborah's mother)

CHAPTER 68
FIRST WARNING SIGN;
CHANGE AND UPGRADES

The next day I went on a hike with Dune by my side in order to search for more rocks to use in my landscaping projects. On the return trip, while clambering down a ravine carrying two triple-layered plastic grocery bags full of the precious rocks I had pried from their resting places in the back country hills, I noticed something wrong with my left shoulder and arm. I had learned to ease the discomfort in my hands by creating a sturdy handle utilizing a thick, six inch long stick or branch slid through the handles of the plastic grocery bags. The pain I experienced in my shoulder and arm was the strangest combination of dull pain and a peculiar numbness followed by a sort of a tingling sensation sometimes. The first time I experienced this problem I shrugged it off. I was forty-seven years old and in terrific health after all. I started to pay closer attention, however, when the pain reoccurred more often over the next few months. I finally mentioned it to Stephen who knew a tremendous amount about the human body, its structures and nutrition needs. He did not have much to say, only that I was far too young to have a serious problem. He knew I was strong, active and that I was eating very healthfully ninety-five percent of the time. He assumed, as I did, that I had pinched a nerve or something. I tried to put the whole nuisance to the back of my mind. Little did I know at the time that this little inconvenience would fester and become, in a very real way, the ultimate cause of our separation just before Stephen died.

Like most people, especially seniors, Stephen disliked change. He preferred that the ranch be left as is so I had to be very cautious and diplomatic when broaching ideas about altering anything. I found the adobe walls and Italian tile floors absolutely beautiful. The sliding glass doors and other windows in the home were perfectly placed; however, the absence of drapes or other sound softening elements caused the dining room and hallways to have a harsh, echoing quality. I knew Stephen would not allow drapes in the common areas but I thought perhaps he would agree to having some of the hand woven small rugs and saddle blankets hung on the bare walls. I had long since discovered various woven treasures Stephen had accumulated over his travels. The residence was a beautiful hacienda style that Stephen had first designed utilizing sugar cubes on a board then made a reality in adobe. The woven rugs and the saddle blankets would serve a dual purpose - give color and style to the whitewashed interior walls while absorbing some of our living noises. When Stephen agreed with my idea I was delighted. I experimented with different positions on the walls and finally came up with a look that I liked and Stephen approved. The hollow echoing was not completely eliminated but those long forgotten rugs did help and were a perfect decoration for his hacienda. I positioned Southwestern terra-cotta pots in the small arched windows on each side of the fireplace. Stephen did not say anything when I placed the pots but I heard his grunt of agreement and turned to catch a smile.

I was hoping to purchase a new bedspread for the king-sized bed in the master bedroom. The current bedspread was at least twenty years old. Stephen allowed me to use it to finish making the bed only when we were leaving on a trip or when we had company. The rest of the time I was instructed to cover the bed with a simple flat sheet. I asked but Stephen would not budge. Above the bed was a bare wall which seemed awfully Spartan. Several months after we exchanged our private, personal vows in the Chapel of the Transfiguration near Moose, Wyoming, I asked my dearest Lord Tyrant if I could place a group of pretty autumn leaves in a scattered pattern on the wall above our bed. He said he would not mind that. After a couple of years the leaves lost their color and beautiful form. I requested and received permission to replace the leaves with a vibrant royal blue and white fabric with patterns woven into the border which I molded into a large fan shape. I suspect that Aline had purchased the fabric decades before in some exotic locale. I was pleased that Stephen approved of the finished project.

We worked well together on the ranch as he had been in a decent mood for some time. It was time for Dave Morris' regular appointment to work his Ferrier magic with the horses. By now he was one of my favorite people as his visits always brightened Stephen's spirits. While he trimmed the horses' hooves they talked and laughed and shared dirty jokes. I suspected I was sometimes the subject because they would fall silent and have a slightly guilty look on their faces when I approached. Good day or bad, sunny day or rain, Dave was always good for Stephen.

Then one day my contentment was temporarily squelched again. Stephen was not feeling well and I was looking for an opportunity to cheer him up so when he asked me to go get him a bowl of ice cream I did without hesitation. After I delivered the treat I knelt before his recliner, gave his knee a slight squeeze and said, "I'm happy to be able to do something for you." His look of repulsion was disturbing and hurtful.

CHAPTER 69
YEAR END

It was now over a year since the firestorm. We had rebuilt the wooden fences and I had planted new cactus on the western hillside. The piles of burnt branches and small rock walls I had worked so hard to erect had done a fair job of stopping any erosion. The burned areas no longer looked like moonscapes as all sorts of greenery had sprouted out of the blackened earth. Wildlife was returning to the ranch as well. All things considered, I think the past year had just about been the worst twelve months of my adult life and it was good to at least see the land recovering. One day I went to my Aunt Hilda's for lunch and our conversation turned to that old poem about children who are born on such and such a day of the week having certain characteristics. You know:

> Monday's child is fair of face
> Tuesday's child is full of grace
> Wednesday's child is full of woe
> Thursday's child has far to go
> Friday's child works hard for his living
> Saturday's child is loving and giving
> And the child that is born on the Sabbath day
> is bonny and bold and good and gay.

My aunt brought out her almanac to determine which day of the week each of us was born. The end result was the realization that Stephen and I were both born on a Thursday. As the poem predicted he certainly went far! On the other hand I still must have far to go.

For dinner one evening I prepared pork roast with baked potatoes and gravy, steamed artichokes and coleslaw. We offered Peach Melba (peaches, vanilla ice cream and a dab of strawberry jam) for dessert but the two young'uns were not interested. Once the children completed their chores and Naomi finished her homework they slipped off to their rooms. Stephen worked on a research project about horse lineage. He was investigating mares with the strongest single footing gait in their background. I worked on my current project, Stephen's family history, with particular emphasis on participation in either the Civil War or World War I. We worked side by side until he declared "Bedtime!" The appointed time for our special session was at hand. This episode started in the shower. We were squeaky clean when the water was finally turned off as we were in there a very long time. As it was obvious Stephen was totally aroused I did not tease him once on the bed. I just brought him off quickly. Sometimes I could be really merciful.

We celebrated Christmas that year with family and friends gathered at the ranch, as had become our general custom. I could not really throw myself into the holiday spirit the way I had in years past as the ghost of Christmas 1996 was still haunting me.

CHAPTER 70
1998 BEGINS

One day in early 1998 I went to the dentist for the replacement of a missing filling that was now causing me considerable pain. Stephen arranged for me to see his dentist, Dr. Ronald Adair, in Valley Center. Stephen had known Dr. Adair for quite a while and Stephen spoke of him not only as his dentist but also as his friend - one of those rare people he liked and respected. So there I was in Dr. Adair's office, mouth wide open and having some repair work done. While examining my mouth, Dr. Adair noticed a few other issues with my problematic, soft and crooked teeth. He called Stephen and informed him that I would have to come back for additional work. Apparently the astute Dr. Adair sensed my uncertainty on that point. After the filling was replaced I left to go home, appointment card shoved down in my purse where I figured it would never be used. I knew Stephen all too well. Later that evening, Stephen addressed the issue and stated that he would pay for one, and only one, more appointment. I was pleasantly surprised and made sure to thank him no less than twice since he often accused me of not being the least bit grateful for all I was given.

A week later I found myself again sitting in Dr. Adair's examination room. At one point, Dr. Adair inquired if I had ever considered having my teeth straightened. When my mouth was free to speak I shrugged and said that after a lifetime of crooked teeth I did not see any reason to worry about cosmetics now. When he admitted that he would like nothing more than to give me a pretty smile I told him it was entirely out of the question but thanks very much for the offer. Dr. Adair left the room shortly thereafter. When he reentered the examination room he said, with a slight air of satisfaction, "It's all set. We will begin by removing tooth number twenty-three here in the front in order to relieve the overcrowding." The look of disbelief on my face must have been obvious so he reassured me that he had cleared his intentions with Steve on the phone. When the reality of it all sank in I started to cry. I could not believe that my teeth were going to finally be straightened. A little voice in my head kept saying over and over again, "My Lord Tyrant will never forgive this expense!" I briefly considered refusing the offer but the thought came in a rush of bittersweet clarity that Stephen would not love me any more if I saved him this expense. So I accepted the kind offer.

Dr. Adair proceeded to explain to me his entire plan for my mouth which included, of course, installing braces. When Dr. Adair left the room (as dentists tend to do on a regular basis), in a very low voice I inquired of Christie, his dental assistant, "Will my braces interfere with my giving Stephen oral sex? Will the braces cut him?" Christie gets full credit for masking any shock she might have felt. Without any hesitation whatsoever she answered me - as if people asked her that question all the time, "No problem. It will not adversely affect your performance and he will not notice a difference." She was a total class act. I have often wondered how many people asked her about their sex life as it relates to dental procedures. For the record, she was a hundred percent right in her prediction.

CHAPTER 71
PASSING ON HIS TRAITS; ANOTHER WARNING SIGN

During one of our smoother periods in February, Stephen was talking to me about construction sites and told me that it was best to build on "cut" rather than "fill" earth. He also explained to me about compaction and drainage after which I said, "I wish I had all of your knowledge and information." To that, my dearest Lord Tyrant, with a mischievous glint in his eyes, responded, "You're getting it every time you swallow my cum!" A standing joke between us was his claim that whenever he experienced an orgasm he passed on everything from his strength, to a cure for most any disease, to youth (he claimed he was my personal fountain of youth) and knowledge. Since I went down on him (not always to culmination) three to five times a day, according to Stephen I should have become immune to all disease, developed the strength of an ox, been getting younger by the minute and attained a genius level intelligence quotient.

One day, while searching for some tax information that Stephen needed, I came across an old appraisal of a ring in the file cabinet in Lynx's room. I probably should not have read the appraisal as it clearly had nothing to do with my ring nor was it any of my business. Curiosity however got the better of me. The ring referenced in the appraisal had belonged to Aline and was valued at a mere $18,000 plus. Wow! Mine cost about a tenth of the price of Aline's ring so I guess I should not have felt quite so guilty about setting Stephen's pocketbook back a bit. Times had changed, I was not Aline and Stephen was retired. I found myself hoping that buying my ring in his present financial condition would not adversely affect his later years. That would make me feel awfully small hearted.

A week or so later, while climbing up into the upper branches of one of our naval orange trees to pick some of the sweet fruit, I felt a sudden tightening in my chest. I grasped the nearest large branch and tried to stay absolutely still while catching my breath and struggling to remain calm. I felt weak, dizzy and found myself praying, "Naomi still needs me, God, not now God, please!" Slowly the grip that something held on my chest started to ease. I waited until I could breathe almost normally then I relaxed my hold on the branch and said, "Thank you, God!" I turned and saw my forgotten, not yet full fruit basket down below. I proceeded to pull off oranges with a strangely weakened hand while shifting my other hand's steadying grasp from branch to branch. When I climbed back down to the ground I was out of breath and knew that I had just received a serious warning, a wake-up call God style. I related the episode to Stephen at lunch. He found it of little interest and I began to suspect he thought I was making it all up in order to obtain his sympathy. Since all I had were my suspicions I could not protest. I knew that the more I denied that my purpose was to get his attention the more pathetic I would seem. So I dropped it.

I was having an awful time one day trying to please Stephen during one of our trail rides. I knew he liked to micromanage my riding skills. I had become accustomed to that aspect of our riding together. However, this time he barked at me from the very beginning of the ride. His barrage of orders and frustrations included such things as:

"Go more to the left!"
"Stop going so fast!"
"Dammit speed up will you!"
"Stop using your reins that way!"
"What the hell are you doing now?"
"You're the worst rider I've ever tried to ride with!"

When we were on the last stretch of our ride he barked at me one last time saying, "Slow your horse down!" I was quite tired of being corrected, criticized and yelled at so I turned slightly in my saddle and said over my shoulder in a brisk, firm manner, "Get off of my back!" His attitude and orders had totally ruined our whole ride. I found myself wondering just how much better at riding all the other people who ever rode with him must be. I could not imagine anyone volunteering to go on a second ride with Stephen if he shouted at them every few minutes as he did with me. When we dismounted and unsaddled our horses, getting ready to groom them, Stephen came over and apologized. Then he said, "Hey, I'll take you out for lunch before we go to the dog show in Del Mar." I was so surprised. In an instant all my anger evaporated. Later, we each ate a ninety-nine cent Burger King Whopper and enjoyed a great time at that dog show. We both appreciated the lure trials best. I was amazed at how quickly he had been able to turn the spirit of the day around. As soon as he had apologized he transformed into the delightful, witty man that everyone loved, especially me.

CHAPTER 72
A PICTURE WINDOW FLASH

The next day found us back in our weekday routines. I took Naomi to the bus stop while he did groundwork with Carmen who was in foal. She could not be ridden but needed some exercise. Afterwards we both went for errands down the hill into Escondido: shopping at a Boney's natural health food market, then to Bank of America and finally back up the hill to the Post Office before heading home. I put away the groceries while Stephen made our sandwiches. At 2:30 we had an appointment for our second sensual session of the day. It was pretty spectacular, even without relying on videos or girlie magazines. Stephen had been in a great mood ever since yesterday's apology. Me too.

Stephen worked at least ten hours the following day. Now in his seventies, I felt an uneasy mixture of pride at his stamina and concern for his health and welfare. Although healthy as the proverbial horse, long hours working difficult tasks at the ranch in all sorts of weather seemed too much even for Hercules. On days like today, when he utilized the services of a day worker, Stephen worked extra hard. He slaved side-by-side with the laborer most of the day then continued on his own after the helper left. They worked for hours trimming and removing the ice plant where it had overgrown into the upper arena. Next they raked, loaded and then dumped leaves and debris down into the north side ravine. They worked like bees cleaning up around the barn. Later, Stephen went into Valley Center to purchase a load of hay for the day worker to unload and stack in our barn.

A day or two later, we awoke to a rainy day so we had our usual morning session or wake-up call prior to feeding the animals and taking our Power Walk. After I returned from taking Naomi to school I suggested that we restructure our morning since it was raining cats and dogs. Nothing could be accomplished out in the downpour but there were activities we could do indoors, first in the bedroom, of course, and afterwards there was paperwork in the office to keep us busy. Stephen agreed. I moved the television and VCR from Lynx's room into our room. Stephen located an X-rated video that he currently favored and then, thank goodness, turned on the furnace as the house was a chilly fifty-four degrees and I was only wearing a purple lace teddy and fishnet stockings. We stayed under the covers until the room temperature was tolerable for me. I do not think Stephen ever felt cold unless he was feeling under the weather. Wish I could say the same. Once the bedcovers came off we had a wonderful time. After our session, we reluctantly emerged from the bedroom to fix and eat our lunch. We teamed up to pay the bills. First, I organized the bills and wrote the checks. Then he reviewed the bills and signed the checks while I dumped out the rain catching bowls and pans. Once the bills were done we started in on the fan mail. Later on Stephen moved over into the living room to do some reading while I finished the day's ironing. All in all a nice way to spend a rainy day at home.

One chilly weekend morning, Stephen went out to feed the horses with a promise to come back to bed for a second morning episode. The children were spending the weekend at friends' homes so we had the ranch to ourselves. When Stephen did not return quite as quickly as expected, I peeked out the windows to see where he was. I discovered him mucking out Monty's stall. I decided to be a bit impulsive, with the thought in the back of my mind of possibly rekindling some of the passion in our relationship, so I stripped naked, put on my red robe and waited in ambush for him. When Stephen approached the home I stood in front of the large picture window and gave him a very provocative flash. He stood there pretending to be in shock then grinned and gave me an elaborate bow. He met me in the bedroom for our second sensual session. I was hoping that this session would be mutually satisfying but it left me unfulfilled despite my best intentions. The numbness caused but the rift in our relationship pressed hard in the back of my mind and prevented me from having an orgasm.

I got up and kissed his big toe and got to work vacuuming the house. I started at the other end of the house so I would not disturb Stephen. I then waxed the woodwork in the living room, built a good fire and cleaned the master bathroom. When Stephen arose he requested I write five letters for him. He hated his own penmanship so pretty much any writing that needed doing was done by me while he dictated. I confess that I am not particularly fast taking dictation so I am sure there were times when I frustrated him. For dinner I prepared turkey slabs in gravy over mashed potatoes with steamed artichokes and a green salad. With the exception of cornbread Stephen never ate bread or rolls with dinner. Later, while watching *60 Minutes* on television, we each enjoyed a piece of apple pie with a chunk of cheddar cheese, Stephen's personal favorite.

CHAPTER 73
RESTORED PICTURES OF SANDRA; PEPPER TREE NEAR DISASTER

Our relationship had been stable and without incident for several days. I am not certain where Stephen's usual cloud had gone to but I sure did not miss it and I am convinced he felt the same. While cleaning and doing some organizing I discovered some black and white photo negatives in an old envelope. Upon closer inspection I ascertained the negatives were of Stephen's Sandra. On impulse I decided to have prints made from the negatives. The pictures turned out better than expected considering the age of the negatives and I knew my dearest Lord Tyrant would be very pleased. That evening, Lynx brought up two loads of wood and built the fire. Naomi made spaghetti with meat sauce, a garden salad and garlic bread for our dinner. Stephen's only comment was, "cooked the noodles too long." It was one of Naomi's earliest attempts at preparing dinner and our resident critic could not spare her. He did give the kids permission to invite a friend over the next day so we tried to focus on the positive. When Naomi and Lynx retired to their bedrooms for the evening I surprised Stephen with the photos I had made from the old negatives. My instincts were dead on - he was really amazed and pleased to have them after almost four decades.

Easter that year was a family affair at the ranch. We invited my brother, David, and his family in addition to my mother and Aunt Hilda. By this time Naomi's boyfriend, Tom Davis, was such a part of our lives and so thoroughly accepted that his presence was rather like one of the kids. My family and I always enjoyed each other's company so any excuse to gather together was appreciated. My family was delighted to discover that Stephen had arranged for my teeth to be fixed - my new braces were the talk of the event. David and Jo's young son, Zack, was delightful and such an important addition to our family. All of David and Joanne's children were adopted. Stephen was very gracious that day, sharing his home and table with this family who had embraced him as their own. I was always aware that we had altered his existence in many positive aspects. Before I entered his life, he had never experienced holidays where loving family members filled his home with laughter and witty discussions. He had told me so on many occasions. He prized each member of my extended family and found our brand of interaction refreshing.

On May 26, while Stephen and I were just sitting and talking, he shared that he had never experienced the storybook kind of love the movies show. He had difficulty relating to scenes in movies which showed some guy euphoric to be returning to his woman after being apart. He said he only felt that way once in his life. Although he did not admit it was with Sandra, when I asked he did not deny it either. No big surprise there. He then told me that the whole concept of putting his mate's wants or needs before his own was alien to him and was never going to happen. No wonder my feelings were always getting hurt, at least until I became conditioned to his attitude.

Every year we set aside a day for trimming the Pepper trees around the large arena. The process involved someone standing on a wide, wooden platform which was placed in the back of the pickup truck. One person drove the truck while another stood on the platform and trimmed the branches using a chainsaw. I had my once-a-month lunch appointment with my mother set for Wednesday so I assumed Stephen and I would be doing the trees on Thursday. My Lord Tyrant, however, decided he wanted to get started on the trees on Wednesday. Lynx had that day off so he offered to serve as driver of the pickup truck. They worked well together. Stephen stood on the platform and expertly trimmed the branches using the chainsaw. Lynx would gather the branches as they fell and toss them out of Stephen's way. At Stephen's direction, when each spot was finished and Stephen had stepped down from the platform, Lynx would jump back into the truck and drive to the next spot. While Lynx was standing at-the-ready and Stephen was up on the platform engaged in using the chainsaw, something went terribly wrong. The branch, Stephen and the chainsaw all came tumbling down together with the chainsaw fully engaged. Lynx somehow prevented Stephen from going over the edge of the truck and the chainsaw managed to fall harmlessly to the ground. Thanks to God.

CHAPTER 74
FIFTIETH ANNIVERSARY OF THE MR. UNIVERSE CONTEST

Steve Reeves had won the first Mr. Universe Contest back in 1948 so it was only appropriate for Stephen to be invited to appear at the Fiftieth Anniversary of the contest which was held in Birmingham, England in October of 1998. For some time Stephen had been turning down invitations for appearances and for most social events. The only time he made an exception was when the invitation was received from George and Tuesday or Roland and Virginia. During his long discussion with the organizers of the Mr. Universe Contest Stephen made it crystal clear he would only attend the event if it was to be a "steroid free contest" with legitimate testing of all contestants. Stephen understood that his presence gave his seal of approval on such an event. When the organizers agreed to his terms, he gave his word and agreed to make an appearance. Stephen shared with me not only the specifics of the duties required of him during the event but also his post event plans. He proposed to leave me in England once his event duties were completed so he could travel to Lausanne, Switzerland in order to handle certain bank business. He made sure that our travel schedule would allow him to be back in time to catch our return flight out of Heathrow.

By now, Lynx and Naomi were seasoned ranch caretakers so Stephen no longer lost sleep over whether or not they would do a good job managing things while we were gone. I still smile whenever I remember that his mantra used to be, "They'll probably burn the place to the ground!" So we finalized our preparations and then headed for England. We were looking forward to Stephen being able to reconnect with Bill Pearl, Reg Park and Mickey Hargitay. I had previously met Bill Pearl and liked the man quite well. The other two I would be meeting for the first time. Mickey lived in Southern California so it was no surprise when we ran into him and his now even more famous daughter, Mariska Hargitay, of the television series *Law and Order - Special Victims Unit*, at the LAX airport. Mickey and Mariska were warm, friendly and easy to like and talk to. Stephen was delighted to renew his relationship with Mickey. Later, at the event, Mickey really impressed me with his prepared speech.

During the question-and-answer phase of the public event, a man in the audience asked Stephen, "Mr. Reeves, now in your seventies, do you still have sex?" I was surprised to hear my dearest Lord Tyrant respond with, "Yes, three times a week." Later, when we were alone, I asked him about his answer to this man's question and Stephen said, "Wife, they would never believe it if I told them the truth!" At the main event that evening, Mariska and I sat side-by-side until the obvious steroid use by many of the contestants forced me to get up in protest. The audacity of the contest organizers to promise Stephen the event would be steroid free. My husband's reputation was being used to promote an international bodybuilding event that he could now see was definitely not all natural. Stephen was livid to say the least but felt conflicted as he had agreed to make an appearance. He could not break his word even if the organizers had broken theirs. The burden of protest was therefore placed on my shoulders so, at Stephen's behest, I stood up in the middle of the event and walked out. Public transportation required money which I did not have on me. I was not exactly certain where our hotel was located but I remembered the general direction we had come from after leaving our hotel and set off on foot. I was dressed in heels, a medium short cocktail dress and no panties.

No one knew about that last part except Stephen, of course. Remembering my psychology training, I focused on pretending I was confident and knew exactly where I was going. Other than that I just counted on God to help me. It was a really long, often dark walk in unknown territory. Fortunately the citizens of England speak a version of English so I could communicate if need be. Only once, however, did I open my mouth. I came around a blind corner and ran smack into a man with his penis out weeing on the wall. I bounced off his side and said, "I'm so sorry, excuse me." We were both startled and embarrassed so I just put my head down and kept going. It was taking me forever to walk back to our hotel. I felt more and more certain that Stephen would probably either beat me back or arrive very shortly thereafter. I was right. Stephen returned to our room only twenty minutes after I did. He was bursting with thoughts and irritations about the obvious use of steroids by many of the participants. To direct his thoughts away from the negative aspects of the evening's program I teased him about his comment that he only had sex three times a week. My ploy worked. He was surprised when he learned that I had walked all the way back to the hotel. He assumed that I had found a ride with someone at the event who was leaving early. He said it was remarkable that I had walked through so many dark back streets for that many miles without being mugged or challenged. I told him I had put myself in God's hands.

The next morning we enjoyed a quick interlude before Stephen departed for Switzerland. During his absence, I walked around parts of Birmingham, took pictures, absorbed the local history and found things to do that did not require spending money. We arranged to meet back at our hotel that evening then go out for dinner together. We spoke mostly of how his business in Switzerland had gone. Back at the hotel we relished an after-hours interlude but had obviously missed our regular afternoon session since during the day he was in Switzerland. We flew home the next morning.

CHAPTER 75
RETURN TO RANCH ROUTINE; TRAILRIDE; THIRD WARNING SIGN

Back home we quickly returned to our usual, but much loved, ranch routine. We were having good days together as Stephen was in a decent mood, mostly because his business went well in Switzerland but also because we enjoyed really good sex several times. Stephen rode Sugarfoot and then later Rocky on the trail. Sugar was our best single footing mare and Stephen always said she was really smooth. He had been using a special new saddle he bought that was supposed to give the rider better contact with the horse. He had also been doing a lot of ground work recently with Traveler. John Kendrick was not around to help Stephen much these days so I served as his main assistant again. Back in our early days, unless he was in a rotten mood, I was always thrilled to spend my hours in his company. The status of our current relationship was understandably calloused by our recent struggles. I did not feel the same excitement about being in his company even if he was in a decent mood. I was there for him, worked with him and looked after him but loved him at more of a distance. My guard tended to be up more often than not by then. Even our sexual interludes were different, at least for me. I had not been able to open up, relax and trust Stephen enough so as to be able to experience an orgasm. My body seemed to have a mind of its own and would no longer just let go.

On a totally unrelated subject, it finally dawned on me that Stephen just plain did not like straight hair on a woman. The cause of his preference was uncertain. It might have been a product of the styles prevalent in his youth and young adulthood or it might have simply been an innate inclination. Regardless, Stephen wanted my hair curling or at the very least wavy but never frizzy. In his opinion, if a woman had straight hair she curled it. If she had a straight haired daughter, she curled her daughter's hair whenever possible but always for any special occasions. I remembered that just about all women living during the 1940s and the 1950s eras spent considerable time with their hair up in rollers (curlers). Back then a woman was not really ready to go out unless her hair had curl. Unfortunately for Stephen, my hair is as straight as the proverbial straight stick. It may not be everyone's preference but I happen to like that part of how God decorated me. Regardless, whenever we went to any event I always curled my hair for Stephen. Truth be known, however, I have not curled it since the day of his funeral.

Since they both owned and loved Morgan horses, Stephen was friends with Gwen Tubach who owned what was known as the Couser Canyon Ranch in Valley Center. Gwen's ranch had a statue of a gorgeous black Morgan horse at the front gate nestled under huge old oaks. Each year Gwen held the Couser Canyon Ranch Horse Show and Brunch. The event was lovely and Gwen enjoyed showing her fabulous equines. One of the nicer aspects of horse people is they never pestered Stephen with photo or autograph requests. One of the reasons Stephen loved Valley Center was the simple fact that its citizens all treated him like just any other rancher. Stephen felt comfortable going into town wearing a dirty, torn, sweaty shirt, old jeans and his cowboy hat - a sweat and dirt stained misshapen version of its former self - because he knew no one would care. He was definitely not a gentleman rancher. After the event was over, Stephen surprised me by giving me an advance and the approval to go into town and purchase Lynx a new jacket for Christmas. I drove down the hill into Escondido hoping to find the jacket Lynx wanted still available. It was! Thank you God and thank you Stephen!

When Stephen and I went for a ride to Palma Valley one day I was doing better than normal and his mood was fair to middling. On the way back we rode up through the switchbacks of the avocado grove roads. Torrey and Rocky were feeling their oats so to speak due to the cooler, damp air that morning. As we started up the second sharp incline Stephen gave Rocky a stiff kick, bolted and disappeared into the avocado trees. I followed suit and gave Torrey a good kick. In an instant he charged up the dirt road through the trees, up past the leaning ladders awaiting pickers. I caught a glimpse of Rocky's hindquarters now and then as we galloped up the hill at an exhilarating pace. We reunited with Stephen when he slowed down at a clearing further up the long hill. Rocky was impatient to keep up his pace but Stephen had purposefully held him back so Torrey and I could catch up. I felt great about our whole ride and let Stephen know it when we returned to the ranch and began to unsaddle the horses. I was feeling sort of nauseated so it took me longer to remove Torrey's reins and bridle after slipping his halter around his neck which I then attached to the outdoor cross ties. When I attempted to lift Torrey's saddle off his back I felt a sudden dull pain in my left side and a tightening in my chest. I turned and put the saddle on the saddle rack then flexed my left arm and raised and lowered it to try and alleviate the tightness. I managed to reach up and remove the saddle blanket from Torrey and place it on top of the saddle. I tried breathing deeply and calmly to loosen the tightness and relieve the ongoing pain. I had the sensation of being squeezed coupled with lightheadedness. Just as I was about to turn and mention my condition to Stephen the pain began to subside. I assumed the pain was a delayed reaction to the wonderful but physically demanding trail ride. When Stephen returned from putting Rocky out to pasture I was just about midway finished with grooming Torrey. I told him about the nausea and pain in my left shoulder. He listened but shrugged it off as nothing more than a recurrence of the pinched nerve that he was convinced I had been plagued with off and on for quite a while. I said nothing but silently did not agree with his opinion.

A DAY IN THE LIFE

December 13, 1998
68 degrees
Fair Skies

Stephen said, "Why don't you wear your other shoes when we go up to Ranchita?" I replied, "Because I can't very well wear my good pair to go up to the desert and collect rocks." He said, "Wear the good pair and buy yourself a new pair," I responded with, "I can't afford to spend money on new shoes for myself this time of year," To which Stephen's reply was, "Buy yourself a new pair, you're married to a wealthy man!" I retorted, "Yes, well that doesn't mean a whole lot in my life, does it?"

Then Stephen said with a chuckle, "No, it doesn't."

The End.

CHAPTER 76
JACUMBA HOT SPRINGS; WORKING OUT

One day we decided to take time off from our regular routine. We did all of our morning required chores and exercises but afterwards packed our towels and bathing suits, jumped in the Jeep and took a leisurely drive to the mineral spa in Jacumba. We stopped off in Boulevard after checking out the land in Sierra Del Sol, as was our tradition. In Boulevard we bought our usual sandwiches at the deli and sat under a tree to enjoy them. Stephen drank his chocolate milk and I drank my Diet Squirt. When we arrived at the spa we shared the Jacuzzi pool with an older foreign woman, a full figured younger woman and a quiet forty year old man. After a while the other guests left and, finding ourselves alone, we decided to put the pool to a more provocative use. The mineral pool is quite lovely for sensual pursuits. Most spas have too many people coming and going, if not in the actual pool then in the surroundings, but not the mineral pool in Jacumba.

It rained the next day. Rainy weather always made Stephen's workout in the gym cozier as he moved from station to station with the sound of rain and the occasional stirring of the air as outdoor air pushed through the half open window on the west wall. We really liked the cooler days. Power Walking in cooler weather was so much nicer. Stephen was in a remarkably cheerful mood, laughing and teasing a lot like he did with his friends at social events. I liked that part of him as much as anyone else, probably more because I knew the depressed and angry side all too well.

I tried to understand the reason for his mood swings. Here he was, a remarkable, intelligent, self-educated man who had once been voted the most handsome man in the world. That title was not bestowed by People Magazine - it was the result of voting by movie-goers worldwide. He had won worldwide acclaim as the best of the bodybuilding world. His face and physique were startlingly perfect. Some said he was unreal, others referred to him as godlike. He was still in great physical shape and his mind sharp despite his advanced age but long gone was the perfection of his youth. He avoided looking in mirrors unless in the gym and then only to gauge his form as he did his repetitions. He found viewing his aging face and skin to be depressing. I loved every lump, scar and age spot on his entire body but he found those blemishes to be disheartening and the source of much of his melancholy. The problem with being the best of the best in looks is the distance one falls with advancing age. Keeping his muscles toned and his physique trim was never going to bring his youth and energy back. While he was a remarkable problem solver the ravages of time was something he could not fix.

After our Power Walk one morning in the middle of December Stephen went, as was his custom, to his gym to work out. It happened to be a day when he focused on doing more leg strengthening exercises than anything else. He had asked me to come and help him change the number of plates on the leg press. So after finishing my feeding routine I headed to the gym. When I stepped into the room I found Stephen lying naked on the bench press, hot to trot for me to suck his cock. I was somewhat surprised but obliged him. It was our third interlude already that day. We had enjoyed our standard wake up call. The next interlude occurred during our Power Walk as he decided he wanted an impromptu session down by the pond. Now, he enjoyed a blow job in the gym. Sometimes Stephen was outrageously randy!

CHAPTER 77
CHRISTMAS; YEAR END

The weather was bright and sunny and we had a house full of friends and family at the ranch for Christmas. Our dear friends George and Tuesday had joined our celebration. An eighty year old neighbor of my mother, a tiny little lady named Nell who was quite an accomplished artist and who had worked for Disney for a long time, was also there. My younger brother, Pete, and his wife, Lin, delighted everyone by coming down from Oregon. The rest of our guests included my cousin, Jack, and his wife, Sue, with their daughter, Amanda, my mother, my aunt Hilda, my older brother, David, and his wife, Joanne, with their son, Zack, and of course Lynx, Naomi and Tommy. Stephen enjoyed any occasion that included George and Tuesday Coates as they had become great friends and were never at a loss for words.

Our feast was wonderful and Stephen seemed quite happy and content. After we ate, he gave our guests a tour of our horses and the barn areas, sharing with them information about individual horses and their feed and care. My brothers were interested in everything from Stephen's horses to how his new truck was running and were always genuinely welcomed by him. While we were all outside, we seized the opportunity to take group photos. Although the best group photo of all of us was taken in bright daylight, it did not turn out as clear as I would have liked. Back then I was using 35mm film. There was no digital screen to confirm whether the photos were good enough. All things considered, it was a really good Christmas.

Stephen, Tuesday Coates, George Coates and Deborah

CHAPTER 78
1999 BEGINS;
THE HISTORY BEHIND THE RANCH

New Year's Day found Stephen sharing with me the details of how he had ended up purchasing and later living on this ranch in Valley Center, California. Stephen was born into a ranching family and was first and forever a rancher. He had owned and operated a 360 acre cattle ranch in Oregon but had it purchased out from under him via a legal process known as imminent domain. The government proposed building the Applegate Dam pretty much directly on top of his home. All of his ranchlands would disappear under the lake the dam would ultimately create. He had concentrated much of his hopes and dreams on building up his stock of prize winning Red Angus cattle, many of which he imported from England, Scotland and Ireland. If Stephen was going to raise Red Angus they were going to be among the world's best. His dream also included raising award-winning Morgan horses. He was breeding Morgans with considerable success on his Suncrest Cattle Ranch there in Oregon until the government moved in.

When he was informed that he had no choice but to give up his dream in Oregon he was forced to reevaluate and change his focus. Stephen had previously purchased fourteen acres in San Diego County's back country community of Valley Center. The property in Valley Center was not large enough to run cattle on but it was sufficient to raise Morgan horses. His mother, Goldie, and his stepfather, Earl, were caretaking his place in Valley Center which at the time featured a midsized two bedroom, two bath wood framed ranch house. Stephen offered to buy his mother and Earl a similar sized ranch up in Oregon now that they would have to vacate his Valley Center property. Aline was not happy with this offer and made her opinion abundantly clear. Upon inspecting the Valley Center property, Stephen decided to relocate the wood frame ranch house down to the bottom southwest corner of the property. This decision enabled him to build the adobe hacienda styled house he wanted, and had actually designed years before, on the location where the original ranch house had sat. The smaller ranch house was first used as his hired hand's residence and then later as a rental house. The adobe dream home was built in 1971. Once the ranch was ready, Stephen concentrated all his energies on raising Morgan horses.

During my time with Stephen, he traveled the Western United States looking at possible acquisitions. I was invited to join him on many of his trips. I went with him to help with the driving and to engage in intercourse, both verbal and sexual. Even on those trips he needed to slake his ever active sex drive. Once he selected a new horse, however, I was out of a job. There was no one Stephen wanted to accompany him on the trips to retrieve a horse except Dave Morris. I always felt a bit sorry for Dave when he served as Stephen's companion on those long, long drives in the truck hauling the horse trailer. I knew how tight Stephen could be with his money. When I was his companion, Stephen would buy a single Subway sandwich and split it with me. I later learned that he did the same with Dave. At least Dave did not have to share Steve's soda! Once, after they returned from retrieving a horse, I drove Dave back to his place. When I asked him how the trip went he smiled and said, "Good, but old Steve is tighter than the skin on a pearl!" That made us both laugh. Dave knew his friend very well and had the ability to overlook his quirks and foibles.

Whenever Stephen left on a trip, as mentioned a few times previously, I would always dream up a project to do on the ranch to surprise him when he came home. For one such project I painted WELCOME HOME SR on some of the trees we passed, and on the road surface we traveled on, during our Power Walks. For another I did similar signs on trees that he would pass during his trail rides. One of my favorite surprise projects was the mortar and rock work I did while creating Zorro's Garden in honor of his old Rottweiler. Another time I made him a special boot scrape with his brand on it which I conveniently placed in front of the laundry room door for his use when he would come in from work on the ranch. He liked that one so well he relocated it to the front door, "so company can see it". One time I planned to repaint the garage doors and the gym door but he returned early and I was only able to finish painting the gym door. There is an old cowboy saying about attitude: "If you work for a man, ride for his brand. Treat his cattle (and ranch) as if they were your own."

February arrived and it was time for me to clean out the henhouse and chicken coop. This job entailed mostly shovel and rake work followed by disinfecting it, inside and out. The final act in the process entailed catching and giving each hen an upside down dusting with lice powder. I hate this last part because I always feel little lice bites on my forearms which set off a general crawly feeling all over my body. Afterwards I always had to run to take a hot shower in order to rid myself of that awful sensation.

Picture taken in the Ranch House in 1999

CHAPTER 79
BROKEN DREAM

The next day there was a quiet lull on the ranch. Stephen announced that after finishing his routine morning chores he would load the horses, Ranger and Torrey, for an overnight trip to Ranchita. A few hours later found us loaded up and headed east about forty-five miles to his five acre parcel of land in Ranchita. We had to rough it whenever we stayed overnight on the property as all that was out there were horse corrals, feeders and water troughs. We slept in the horse trailer and dug an appropriate sized hole to use as a latrine. We parked the truck and trailer near the corrals and saddled the horses upon arrival. We discovered when we attempted to exit the property through the back gate that someone from the Warner Ranch had blocked our access to their lands. That was an unpleasant surprise. Stephen's primary reason for buying the land and wanting to build a weekend getaway there was to be able to have direct access to the wide open cattle range that was part of the Warner Ranch. He had been given permission by the Warner Ranch foreman to enter the ranch via his back gate. Finding the entrance into Warner Ranch blocked put a real damper on our Ranchita overnighter. We turned the horses around and headed out the northeast end of the property into the hills around Buck Canyon and beyond until we reached one of the largest of the old abandoned gold mines. It turned into a good ride but Stephen was really disturbed about losing access to all that open range. I promised him I would write to the owners of Warner Ranch and request a reinstatement of his permission to ride across their land. My assurance somewhat mollified him but he was not a happy camper.

Upon our return home, as promised I contacted the powers that be at the Warner Ranch and was informed that the ranch foreman who had given Stephen permission was no longer there. They were unwilling to reinstate permission for Stephen to ride the range from our back gate. As a consolation, they confirmed that Stephen could access and ride through the property by trailering his horses to a place some miles away where the Pacific Crest Trail entered their ranch. However, he would be expected, just like any other member of the public, to stay on that National Park trail as it moved through their ranch. They would not listen to reason that Hercules was not just any other member of the public. This situation was one of those changes Stephen had no control over. This particular development yanked one of his dreams forcefully out of his hands. The parcel of land had been purchased, a building pad created, corrals, feeders and shelters for the horses had been erected, and plans had even been drawn up for a small one bedroom, one bath cabin specifically for that property. Now his investment had pretty much become a moot point. His anger and depression flared every time he thought about it.

Although Stephen's dream was never realized, six years after his death I was able to put in a well, electricity, phone line and build a small weekend ranch house on the building pad Larry Herman had created for Stephen and me some eleven years before. Although it was the smallest, least expensive modular home I could find, a friend, David Beck, built a wonderful, full-length wooden porch across the front which made the little house distinctly Western in style. I know Stephen would love it.

CHAPTER 80
MORE WARNING SIGNS; SPRING CLEAN-UP

I still experienced recurring breathlessness after relatively minor exertion and the pain in my left shoulder and side refused to go away. I was not comfortable sharing these issues with Stephen as it was obvious that he thought I was some sort of hypochondriac. I was eating quite well and getting plenty of exercise but I stopped taking my diet pills out of fear that they could be part of the problem. My pulse continued to be way too fast and none of the pain or tightness went away. I would have dearly loved Stephen's counsel and concern regarding my physical issues but he was certain that I was faking it all just to elicit his attention. How do you convince someone who is always strong and always healthy that you are not? At twenty-five years his junior he expected me to be of sound body and, unfortunately, I was not.

We began sprucing up the ranch after the winter rains and usual road damage. It was our goal to have the ranch back in good order by the first of May each year. The nonstop weed growth on the fourteen acre ranch was a constant challenge. Debris was blown into the pool with each winter storm. Every hedge needed trimming and every window needed washing at the beginning of spring. Lynx handled the pool vacuuming and Naomi worked with me on trimming the hedges. We took turns trimming while the other one raked and loaded the branches and leaves into a wheelbarrow. We switched off wheeling the loads all the way down to the designated debris dump-off spots on the ranch. Stephen hired a day laborer to wield the weed whacker while he started the mower and headed for the larger arena. Later he took a break and did some shovel work on the small enclosure that held our breeding chute. As soon as the kids and I finished one project we would move to the next, sometimes working together sometimes apart.

After lunch Stephen checked Lynx's work on the pool and restarted the gas weed eater for our day worker as it had run dry. Next, he left to purchase more hay and feed from Terry's Hay N' Grain in town. He wanted to have the day worker there to stack it. We worked the mare Carmen and the stud colt Power Walker, each in their turn. Power Walker was Carmen's best foal and Stephen was well pleased with both horses. Belle Starr, the filly our Brendalee left us before she tragically died, was also in training. We had started training all three of the youngsters, Belle, Power Walker and Breezy, how to trailer by enticing them, one at a time, with a tray of grain and walking up into the trailer with the young horse on a lead. One of us acted as lead while the other would encourage the young horse with a polite tap on the rump if they shied away. In time the love of grain won over their fear of the trailer and the youngsters became at ease loading. Having every horse on the ranch loadable was a necessity. Loading horses is not always an easy task as many horse owners will attest. The annual spruce up efforts continued throughout the week. Naomi and Lynx would pitch in as soon as they came home from school or returned from work. We were an American ranching family after all.

In the middle of April we were out working with our stallion, Zee, but he was being something of a pain. He kicked out at me while I brushed his flank. Stephen decided that I must have somehow triggered the behavior. Perhaps I was at fault, I do not know. Anyway the attempted kick failed to make contact so no harm was done. Next we planned to comb out his tail, a task which could be a bit dicey if he was feeling his Cheerios like he was that morning. Stephen directed me to bind one of Zee's hind feet (a horse cannot kick if he is on three feet). I secured a rope loop on one of his hind feet and tried to raise Zee's hoof so Stephen could work on his tail. Well, Zee cooperated and raised his hoof only to stomp it back down the next instant despite my efforts. I was no match for Zee's strength. My Lord Tyrant took great exception to my lack of ability and swore under his breath that he would replace me with a real horsewoman. From that point on nothing I did with Zee met with his approval so I headed for the Memorial Garden to work out my resentment. The garden was receiving some neighborhood attention. One of our neighbors, George Speer, and his wife, who belonged to the local Garden Club, said they planned to take a picture of it for the club. To some passersby it may have looked like nothing more than a simple garden but it was much more to me and I appreciated their praise.

Stephen with Thunderhawk

71 year old Stephen showing off

CHAPTER 81
INSTRUCTIONS TO MY SUCCESSOR

In June I decided to prepare a detailed guide for the next woman in Stephen's life. He all too frequently reminded me just how easy I would be to replace. I was not entirely convinced that was the case but should something happen and I was no longer a part of his life I wanted him to be healthy, safe and happy. I had spent more than six years trying to figure out what Stephen needed and wanted. I now surmised, as an undisputed expert on both what not to do and on what he expected, that I could and should put pen to paper and shed light on these lessons learned. I hoped to forestall if not prevent the disintegration of his next relationship before it had a chance to develop. It also gave me an opportunity to summarize what went wrong in our relationship. My journals were more a recording of the what and where of our daily events. I had quit recording events in my journal on a regular basis when it became too depressing to write and Stephen found it too depressing to read. I found it therapeutic on some level to believe that I might be helping someone else to avoid the things that had caught me in a web of pain. I informed Stephen of my intentions and he seemed mildly amused.

I wrote pages full of Stephen's preferences and habits. If I had known half the information contained in those pages, and if I was a lot younger, and if I was naturally more muscular, and if I was willing to submit to that one personal sex act (I was not and did not), then maybe I might have been irreplaceable in his eyes. Stephen found my lists accurate and amusing. The following are excerpts from the guidebook for my replacement:

1. When Stephen seems angry or distant, try to remember all of his losses to soften your own reaction. Originally there was the obvious loss of his father, but think of the countless losses anyone his age has suffered. Family was gone when his mother Goldie died as he had no brothers or sisters and no close connection to aunts, uncles, or cousins. As time passed Stephen lost familiar places as the places changed or were obliterated. The music he knew is rarely heard now and has been replaced by loud, discordant, often hateful blasts which alienate him. Products change and the people and places that sell and service them change in a very unsettling way. The names of companies and businesses forever transform. Banks never used to shut down but our local bank has changed hands four times in five years, threatened to close entirely and the tellers keep disappearing.

2. Some of the products Stephen prefers include Prell, Pert or V05's Vanilla Blossom shampoos and Tone soap bars and he swears by Bullfrog sunblock. He prefers Barbosal for shaving and only uses an Atra shaver. He has trained his body to "eliminate" once a day after he has been up out of bed in the morning for five to ten minutes. He can hardly believe that some people go at different times or that they may go twice in a day or even skip a day. Unless your body is on a similar system expect his impatience at your imperfection.

3. His favorite candy is See's Chocolate Covered Ginger (A quarter pound nestled in the refrigerator makes him smile). He insists on 1% milk and Kellogg's Corn Flakes (but he rarely remembers to close the inner bag so the cereal usually gets stale if you don't remember to check it after he leaves the kitchen). He likes lemonade but prefers "pink" even if it is just coloring, but not with an added

bit of grape juice. If purchasing beer Stephen has decided he quite enjoys Red Wolf <u>not</u> Red Dog but keep in mind a six pack may be in the refrigerator a long time as he does not feel like drinking beer all that often. As for wine, he enjoys Pinot Noir and a good Merlot occasionally with his dinner or at the Holidays. Always keep on hand a bottle of 100% cranberry juice and fresh squeezed orange juice. Mix one third water, one third cranberry juice and one third orange juice. Do not add ice.

4. Stephen does not use drive-up windows: not for food, not for banking. He will not eat or drink in the vehicle and he actually looks down on people who do (that was one of the reasons he found me very hard to adjust to). While I acquiesced to his preference for no eating in the vehicle I was not always willing to go without liquid refreshment available while there. I was therefore declared to be low-class. Do not make the same mistake, because the damage spreads to other areas of the relationship.

5. He likes to threaten abandonment periodically while on a trip. He will take charge of the passports and the money then imply the possibility of not coming back for you when finished doing his business. Do not buy into it, he always comes back.

6. Speaking of trips away from home, if traveling by vehicle make sure you have packed a "pee bottle" under the front seat. Sometimes my Lord Tyrant needs to pee between official stops. Be cool with that. I swear if you make him feel bad or embarrassed I will come back from wherever I have gone and force-feed you cement!

7. He always sleeps on the right side of the bed as you lay on it face up. He starts out laying on his back without a pillow but later usually turns to lay on his right side and puts the pillow under his head. If he should decide to lie on his left side, his left arm, which has to extend out from his body (due to an injury, it doesn't bend upward at the shoulder), may come into contact with his bed partner. When he falls asleep in that position an involuntary muscle movement will cause him to swiftly raise the hand up and then slam it down. The result is very much like a karate chop so be ready for it. I have endured many karate chops, usually to my neck. I suggest that you keep your upper body and head at arm's length from his face and chest when sleeping.

8. Stephen cannot sleep or watch television with his watch on and he cannot pee with his glasses on.

9. Stephen hates today's technology and he abhors the phone. He believes a phone bill is too high if it is over $33 a month and he pours over the phone bill relentlessly. I really hope you have an independent source of funds because that way you probably will not need to worry about the phone bill. He will not allow cordless phones or computers of any sort in his home period! No exceptions.

Stephen was even more pleased with the extensive Help Wanted pages of a proposed classified advertisement I had prepared. It was all done somewhat tongue-in-cheek but even Stephen recognized the impossibility of his expectations. I entitled it "Classified Ad Job Description for my Replacement":

<u>Physical requirements</u>: Pretty horsewoman between 18 and 27 years of age, 5'5" to 5'6" height, 110 to 120 pounds. Curling long to longish hair in blonde, black or red. Blue eyes. Curvaceous, well muscled, athletic body with small waist, generous breasts and high firm derriere with great legs. Pretty hands with long polished nails. Must be non-smoker and non-drug user.

<u>Skills and abilities</u>: Good housekeeper, frugal spending habits coupled with independent income. Efficient, concise secretarial skills in conjunction with being articulate, punctual and a superior driver. Position will require that you act as agent/buffer regarding public events. Will need to echo conservative, Republican views, have geographical knowledge plus be skilled as a horsewoman. Must be handy indoors and out with a can-do attitude and follow through with all phases of ranch work plus

pool maintenance, lawn mowing, wood stacking etc. Will need to be skilled at building fires (in the fireplace and in bed), masseuse training a prerequisite and nursing background helpful.

Sexual requirements: Need to be giving in every particle of private life without thinking about or wishing to receive passion, affection, concern or compassion. Must be sexually available twenty-four hours a day. A large explicit vocabulary of sex talk would be a real bonus. Applicant for position must fully accept that giving oral satisfaction will usually be accompanied by his entertainment in the form of hard-core porn magazines and videos.

Attachments: No kids.

Pay: Room and chow plus $500 per month. No medical/dental. No vacation pay or vacation time off.

CHAPTER 82
DUNE AND THUNDER;
ABSCESS WARNING SIGN

I guess "marriage of convenience" would be the best description of our relationship even though we were never legally married. As far as he was concerned, I was there to service his desires and be a work partner. Years later my daughter, Naomi, would state a truth I had a hard time accepting, "Just because a man does not love the way we love does not mean he does not love us." I know that is true but it would have been easier for me to feel that Stephen loved me if he had not regularly brought up how easy it would be to replace me.

As time passed, my German Shepherd pup, Dune, became my constant outdoor companion. He was enthralled with our horses and developed a special bond with Thunder, one of our young geldings. Even Stephen, who never cared much for Dune, could not help but notice that, while his dogs Zorro and Rommel never looked twice at a horse, Dune loved horses and being with them. Thunder and Dune would play a game of keep-away with a horse ball (a large air-filled rubber ball with a handle on one side to enable the horse to pick it up). Dune would go into the paddock and Thunder would grab up his ball - knowing Dune would try to get it. Then Thunder would gallop around his paddock first shaking the ball left and right then up and down. Dune would give chase up and down and all around that paddock. If Thunder dropped the ball Dune would snatch it up and jet away with Thunder bucking and romping hot on his heels. Those two were best friends. I maintain a series of photos of their games.

In early June, I woke up with what I thought was a toothache, pretty much right up front and slightly to the left of center of my upper jaw. What started out a small, minor inconvenience soon blossomed into a full-blown, Excedrin defeating, throbbing pain in my head. Stephen finally agreed that I could make an appointment with Dr. Adair when the pain got so bad I felt like yanking the tooth out myself. As soon as Dr. Adair examined my mouth he discovered a huge, dark purple and red abscess up under my lip well above my front teeth. Once the abscess was lanced a significant amount of the pain was relieved. The good doctor put me on antibiotics and referred me to Dr. Tagge, an oral specialist in Escondido. I was grateful for the pain relief and antibiotics but never made an appointment to see Dr. Tagge. It was a bad decision. Some fourteen years later the problem resurfaced in exactly the same spot. The tooth had to be removed due to an infection in the bone. I recalled that my paternal grandmother, Katherine, at the age of forty-eight had died of complications from an abscessed tooth. In June of 1999, when the problem first exhibited itself, I was exactly forty-eight years old. I said a humble prayer of gratitude for the advances made in dental expertise and antibiotic medicines. Without such I might have suffered my grandmother's same fate.

Shortly after I recovered from the infection I wrote about a beautiful June day in my journal. Although the sky was clear on the ranch, a fog bank engulfed Cool Valley Road while we were on our Power Walk. The damp, fresh fog blanketed our ranch by the time Stephen was done with his workout. The sun though, not to be outdone, was able to burn away all the fog. We enjoyed a lovely, warm summer day until about 2 p.m. when thunder boomed over Palomar Mountain just east of us. It did not take long for the storm clouds to envelop the ranch followed by lightning, rolling thunder and a downpour. We had already enjoyed two personal interludes but the fury of the storm sent us scurrying back into the house for a third session. I laughed and teased Stephen that "we were rolling like thunder under the covers". Sure was a hot answer to the sudden chill of the stormy weather.

That day our little spring chicks announced that they were now Araucana chickens by laying for the first time their pretty pastel colored eggs. Although they would not lay eggs regularly for another couple of months it was exciting to discover that they had started. Zorro, Stephen's elderly Rottweiler, was content to sleep by the fire I built that evening. Lately he was inclined to lie on the front lawn snapping at "air bugs" (the floaters in his eyes caused him to think there were little bugs flying around his head). Poor old dog! He would bark at imaginary foes and intruders. Dune and Rommel would look up, assess that no danger was present and then go about their business. All three dogs were fed at or near noon and then at bedtime given one multivitamin and one Milk Bone dog biscuit (which Stephen called their cookie) as we locked up.

Naomi planned to be home the next night and volunteered to make dinner for the three of us. Her culinary expertise had grown as she sometimes practiced on Tommy's family. She made us Fettuccine Alfredo with steamed asparagus and a tossed green salad. Stephen was impressed and said so to Naomi. We all realized her dinner had to be exceptional for him to complement her on it.

The following morning after chores Dave came as scheduled to work with our horses. It took Dave longer to complete his services as the number of horses on the ranch had grown to fourteen. Our young horses were being expertly coaxed to cooperate by Dave who, like his friend Steve, could calm an anxious or frightened horse, regardless of age or demeanor. When Dave arrived, Stephen dismissed me so I could head out into our back country to gather a few plants and rocks for my Memorial Garden. Dune and I hiked into the hills east of the ranch. I was pleased to find two small enough native Lilacs for Dune to help me get out of the ground. I would just tap the ground at each plant's base and say, "Dig Dune!" He would dig a hole which helped me get a start on removing the small plants. I always carried a large heavy screwdriver to dig or pry rocks up and loosen small plants. That day I located a new source of my favorite quartz rocks too. It took me three trips to bring all my treasures down. For a person like me, a naturalist and a gardener, it was pretty close to heaven to be climbing up a ravine with my best friend, Dune, looking for rocks and plants to improve the landscaping of the ranch. It did not get much better than that! I relished every moment on those excursions into the hills.

CHAPTER 83
TRIP TO MONTANA

Stephen decided we would take another trip to Montana from June 12th to the 16th. The purpose of the trip was to find a summer home with horse property and access to trails, park land or BLM land. Stephen's new Featherlite three horse slant trailer coupled with his 1998 Dodge turbo diesel pickup truck meant that trailering three horses from Valley Center to a new place in Montana would be a breeze. We reviewed in detail the areas where we would be spending time looking for the right property. At one time this journey would have seemed like a dream to me. However, I now knew Stephen far too well and found it impossible to indulge in the rush of effervescent pleasure which normally occurred when discussing these plans. I was fully participating in Stephen's quest even though I was uncertain as to our future.

Stephen's favorite parts of Montana were becoming much more familiar to me. We spent some time checking out Hamilton, Montana but after visiting Stevensville's surrounding areas, we moved towards Seeley Lake. We found two properties there that we liked but both were too expensive. Stephen felt that we would find even better possibilities near Lincoln, Montana. We spent more time in and around Lincoln than anywhere else. A blind man could see that Stephen wanted to find his summer place somewhere there. I had known for a long time that part of Stephen's heart was there in Lincoln. It was easy to imagine loving summers spent riding through the incredible beauty of the mountains and valleys near Lincoln once my children were grown. Our Montana Man was trying to come home and I was one hundred percent behind his decision.

Although we enjoyed our time in Montana we failed to find a suitable summer place. Stephen made a verbal agreement with a real estate agent to return the following spring and see what was then on the market. In the meantime, if a picture perfect property was listed he agreed to give us a call so Stephen could catch a flight to Montana to check it out. We were content with that arrangement.

CHAPTER 84
LIFE ON THE RANCH CONTINUES; WALKER GETS HIS HEAD STUCK

We returned to the ranch as planned on June 16th with our relationship in decent shape. Stephen had managed to keep all of his negative opinions about me and my son to himself for a spell. Our newest foal, Shady Lady, was a fine little filly out of Carmen. Shortly after our return Power Walker caught his left foreleg on a wire that had worked itself loose along the bottom of one of his paddocks. His leg had a deep laceration which needed considerable tending. All such care we did as a team, there was still that much good will between us. Ranch life continued as we worked on projects most of our days. We worked on trimming the Pepper Trees between the house and the garage with Stephen using a chainsaw while standing on the platform in the back of the pickup. Fortunately, this year there were no serious mishaps. I stood by and helped by yanking the branches out of his way. We cut the larger branches into usable sections and I stacked them in the woodpile for use in a year or so once they had seasoned. He did the cutting, I did the cleanup. Then after lunch, a nap and a quickie we went down to the rental house to shovel some decomposed granite into the back of the pickup. We used the DG to fill potholes in our dirt driveway which ran from the Saddleback Road entrance to the garage's paved area.

August is always notoriously hot in Valley Center. Regardless, Stephen would work endless hours out in the hot sun. I tried to help prevent heat stroke by regularly delivering to him a glass of fresh fruit juice mixed with water. I decided to prepare his favorite Italian meal for dinner that evening. I purchased rolled slices of the best prosciutto at Lodico's meat market in Escondido and served it with fresh sliced cantaloupe, sliced tomatoes, sliced avocados and slices of mozzarella cheese all sprinkled with Italian seasonings and drizzled with extra virgin olive oil (see picture at end of chapter). He was really pleased. In the guidebook for my replacement I listed Stephen's favorite meals and this one was chief among them. At the end of August we went to my aunt Hilda's to celebrate her birthday. It was a family affair that included Naomi and Tom, George and Tuesday, my mother, Stephen and me. These people were always happy to spend time with each other. Stephen sincerely liked and even respected my aunt Hilda and my mother despite the fact that their political views were diametrically opposed to his.

Some days later, we went out to clean Walker's paddock early in the morning only to discover Stephen's pride and joy stuck with his head and neck shoved out and quite firmly stuck under the paddock fencing. Stephen dropped to his knees next to the poor colt's head so he could lift the tight fence wire. I placed my hands between Walker's eye and the wire as Stephen tried to pull the wire up with one hand and push the colt's head and neck back under the fence with the other. Stephen was straining with all of his considerable strength to shove his laid down colt back into his paddock. Stephen's soothing voice kept the understandably shaken colt calm as he pushed Walker inch by slow inch back under the wire. One of my hands protected his eye as my other hand tried to help pull the fencing wire up. It took all of my control not to scream, which would have really spooked the colt, when my hand was caught between the fencing and Walker's struggling head. Ever so slowly Stephen managed to scrape him through. I was certain my hand was broken. It was scraped raw and was black and blue but it held up long enough to keep Walker's eye safe. Stephen was so relieved that Walker survived he did not notice my hand was mangled. I have always been a big chicken when it comes to pain so once Walker was safe I started to cry.

Stephen's favorite meal: sliced cantaloupe, avocado, mozzarella and tomatoes sprinkled with Italian seasonings and drizzled with extra virgin olive oil flanking the best prosciutto (rolled).

CHAPTER 85
A MISUNDERSTANDING OF INTENTION

In September Stephen became angry with me for a new-to-me reason: he informed me that he was very upset at my work habits around the ranch. At first I really could not understand what more he could want from me. I had tried my best to learn and do everything he showed me. I tried to anticipate his next request of me. I even tried to start projects that were coming up on our agenda so that a part of the chore, or even all, was completed before he came out. I was rarely idle. In this case, however, I was missing the point. My Lord Tyrant interpreted my good intentions the wrong way. He said I was acting like the ranch was mine and that I did not need him. He was offended by my take charge attitude. He felt I was trying to show him up or demonstrate I was just fine without him. Since that was not my intention and he was misreading my purpose I wrote him a detailed letter in the hopes of helping him to understand the situation. I knew that he had read the letter because I saw him do so sitting in his recliner that evening. Apparently he did not feel the need to comment on or otherwise discuss what I wrote in the letter.

CHAPTER 86
CAPITOL REEF TRAIL RIDE

In September we attended a trail ride organized by people interested in single footing or gaited Morgan horses. The ride was held in beautiful Capitol Reef, Utah. Stephen surprised me by opting not to trailer our own horses despite having his truck and new Featherlite three-horse trailer which were ideal for the job. I just assumed he would want to take Torrey and maybe Ranger or Sugarfoot for us to ride. As uneasy as things were between us I did not dare question his decision. If we had flown to Utah I could understand his decision not to take our own mounts. However, we drove the Dodge pickup all the way there.

Along the way we stopped, as was our custom, and enjoyed McDonald's Egg McMuffins and orange juice for breakfast, and found an occasional Burger King for our ninety-nine cent Whoppers for lunch. We enjoyed the scenery and as we drove spoke of the ranch back home and the ride ahead. I was hoping that Jackie Farmer might attend the same ride so that Stephen could get a chance to meet her in person. It hovered in the back of my mind that she might turn out to be my replacement. We still did not know how old she was or much of anything about her other than she shared Stephen's passion for gaited Morgan horses. As we arrived at Capitol Reef he informed me that he planned to only borrow one horse from our friends, Mel and Mary Frandsen. I had been experiencing some pain in my knees after riding so I hoped his decision was a thoughtful gesture towards me rather than an indication that he would rather ride alone. In either case he did not ask for my opinion or input. He decided unilaterally that I was not going on this ride. Instead, I was relegated to waiting at the staging area with the trucks and empty horse trailers while this rather sizable group went off on an incredible trail ride. I was understandably not a happy camper. I satisfied my bruised ego by looking forward to finding rocks and bits of wood for my gardens back home while Stephen and the club of riders went on their ride. I inquired of Stephen if he approved of me gathering rocks to use back home and loading them in the bed of the truck since I was not going on the trail. He agreed. So that was the plan for this trip.

Our room at the motel was decent and the weather was perfect on the morning of the ride. I do not remember seeing Mary Frandsen but Mel's friendly face was a welcome sight there at the staging area. He provided a very nice chestnut gelding for Stephen to ride. Stephen had become less and less enamored about having photos taken of him (unless it was at George and Tuesday's get-togethers). So as a gesture of respect I asked permission to photograph him as part of the trail ride event. He consented without comment. After giving him a discrete assist in mounting the borrowed horse I took some photos. Riders on moving horses are difficult subjects for photographs so I also took a few from a distance of the whole group before they left. Once the group had departed I wandered around the nearby hills and ravines to my heart's content. I was content and just asked God to keep everyone safe on their ride. As far as I could tell Jackie Farmer did not attend the event but there was a big crowd.

I was surprised how long the riders were gone. When the first ones returned I was my usual excited self, waiting to see my Lord Tyrant. Eventually he appeared and I rendezvoused with him in order to render assistance as he unobtrusively dismounted behind a horse trailer. I grinned up at him and asked how the ride went. As he started his dismount I stood on the other side holding the one stirrup down as he put his weight into the other to ease to the ground. I heard a loud thud and quickly ran around the Chestnut. I found Stephen lying flat on his back! I moved to grab his outstretched hand, planted my feet and helped him to get back up. I glanced around and did not find anyone observing us. I told him so right away. He was having difficulty standing. I heard someone coming around the side of the horse trailer so I steadied Stephen by throwing my arms around him and giving him a welcoming kiss. The guy walking by said, "Wow, I wish someone would welcome me like that!" When the man was out of sight Stephen pushed me away and stiffly walked back to his borrowed mount. Although we did not discuss it openly we were both saddened by the knowledge that his days of horse riding were numbered. Despite my willingness to render assistance he knew there was a time coming when I would not be able to help enough to get him in and out of a saddle. The realization was depressing for Stephen and sad for me who loved him.

Later we did spend time talking of the trail ride and he expressed again a dislike for having to deal with and talk to other riders. If it had just been Mel with him on the ride he would have had a wonderful time. He considered the rest of the crowd an inconvenience and a hassle. Even though this riding club was full of warm, friendly, even like-minded horse people Stephen was beyond the age and stage of enjoying the company of a group of strangers when on a ride. He was too accustomed to picking his own way, riding at his own pace and enjoying solitude to be able ever again to enjoy anything like an organized ride. I had come to this realization a few years back so I had trouble understanding why he continued to join them. I think he liked the idea of going on new, unfamiliar trails and just hoped that the other riders would not ruin it for him. That evening, at the barbecue for this event, my conclusion was confirmed when he said to me, "Maybe you and I will load Torrey and Ranger next spring and come here on our own. I'll show you the trail without anyone falling off their horse or not being able to control their horse or having to wait for some idiot to find their sunglasses."

On the Capital Reef Trail Ride

CHAPTER 87
A NEW RENTER AT THE RANCH; THANKSGIVING

We returned home on a Monday in late September. We started the next morning with our Power Walk after which Stephen did his workout. While he headed for the gym I headed down to the empty rental house. I took Dune and my paint supplies with me. There was already a radio with cassette player there as I had been doing my level best to get the little house shipshape for new renters. Dune was the perfect companion. On this day I was painting the second bedroom a pale aqua. Stephen had already replaced two cracked windows on the back side of the house. We debated replacing the linoleum flooring in the kitchen. I felt it was severely dated and showed some minor gouges and small stains. Stephen's stand was, "If it ain't broke don't replace it." The Liquid Amber tree we planted in 1994 had grown nicely by the front gate of the small yard, so that part looked nice. In 1996 the renters had built a walkway from the gate to the porch steps out of two by fours. That walkway was damaged from use and inclement weather. On this issue we agreed. Stephen decided a concrete walkway from the gate to the bottom of the porch steps would last a long time and dress up the front yard a bit. I wanted to plant a bougainvillea where a water pipe was mounted on the front wall but Stephen said he did not think it was an eyesore and refused to pay for the plant. So I saved a bit out of my monthly allowance and bought a small bougainvillea. It filled the space in front of that ugly pipe just fine.

By late October the rental house was ready for Stephen to run an ad in two local newspapers. Forty-nine separate parties responded with interest in our little two bedroom two bath home with rustic atmosphere, a small fenced yard and large porch. As we made appointments to show the house it became apparent that it would not suit everyone. Some prospects considered the home far too outdated. We met a few very nice two-income families I felt would be just right and one or two couples that were not only enthusiastic but had a dog or cat as a pet and, of course, two separate incomes. On the second day of appointments, I was coming down the drive from the ranch house when a man pulled up to the parking area. He just sat there in his 1999 Suzuki Grand Vitara so I approached and asked him if he was there to see the rental. He seemed a bit embarrassed as he turned to me and admitted that he was fifteen minutes early and did not want to interfere with another party's appointment. I reassured him that Stephen was alone inside and that the previous appointment had finished viewing the house and was already gone. When he exited his car I surmised that he stood about 5'9" and weighed approximately 230 pounds. His eyes were a light blue in a face with high color and iron grey hair. There was something about his eyes that revealed past pain and compassion. My self-preservation instincts sounded a silent alarm. I knew better than to ignore my inner voice. It was warning me that I would be drawn to the gentleness I immediately sensed in this stranger. Before he even said a word to Stephen I made the decision to veto his occupancy. How hard would that be since we had a boatload of better applicants? He was a single man with only one income. Many of our applicants had a more legitimate need for a two bedroom, two bath, place to live.

Later that evening, when it was time to review the applications and compare our impressions of the individuals, I focused on promoting couples and small families. Stephen said abruptly, "I've already picked our renter." He caught me off guard as we had previously agreed that we would select the renters together since their presence affected both of us. I asked, "Who did you choose?" He replied, "Gene Stewart." I protested immediately by saying, "But the house is wasted on a single man. It's perfect for a couple or a small family." Catching my breath I continued, "Besides, Mr. Stewart's face is all red, he looks like an alcoholic! He's only one person with one income whereas several of these others have two incomes which better guarantees we'll get the rent." Capping my argument I declared, "I would really prefer not to have an unknown single man living here on the ranch." My Lord Tyrant merely shrugged his shoulders and said, "He's who I want. He's a maintenance man at Temecula Creek Inn and can fix anything that goes wrong on the rental and can help repair things here on the ranch. I've already decided. Now call all those others and tell them the place has been rented." I was not happy with his high-handed attitude or with his choice. I tried to reassure myself that my first impression was probably exaggerated. How on earth could I know he was compassionate or kind by just looking at his eyes? I tried to convince myself that this Gene person was probably just another guy looking for a place to rent. There was nothing special about him in reality, it was just my overactive imagination. Besides, with him living way down on the corner of the ranch I would almost never even see him. I reassured myself that I was being silly and that everything would be just fine.

Without informing me, Stephen had agreed that Mr. Stewart could start his move into the rental home on October 25th, even though his tenancy did not officially begin until November 1st. Of course, I was not finished with my painting of the cupboards and other details when Mr. Stewart showed up. Although my intent was to avoid our renter I was not going to be rude. When he came in toting some of his belongings he would pause briefly to visit with me. We spoke of such things as where he was currently living and how happy he was to be moving to Valley Center. I made it a point to stay away from the rental house when I knew he was coming back. Despite my best efforts, however, he showed up unexpectedly a few times as I was putting the finishing touches on the repairs to the rental home. On those instances, his manner was always polite and respectful. Dune was always present while I worked. Mr. Stewart spoke warmly of his own past dog, Josh. My normally overprotective Dune, who did not respond well to unknown men, liked him just fine. My first impression had not been wrong. Fortunately, Mr. Stewart was just happy to have found a place to live in Valley Center with a somewhat famous and interesting landlord and a landlady who was a fellow animal lover. From his perspective life was looking pretty good. Once I had finished with the inside I packed up my equipment and supplies and stayed away from the rental home. Stephen went down there periodically and seemed quite pleased with his choice of renter.

We had a delightful change in plans for our Thanksgiving holiday. George and Tuesday Coates invited us to their place for a holiday feast. Their kind invitation also included my mother, my aunt Hilda, my cousin's wife, Sue, and their daughter, Amanda, two visiting English ladies, and of course Naomi and Tom. Lynx enjoyed the holiday with his girlfriend and her family. We all had a great time. I was particularly pleased that my mother's guests from England experienced an American Thanksgiving in George and Tuesday's home. It was good to relinquish the Holiday hosting responsibilities that year as I was not feeling the genuine up-beat warmth inside which makes hosting a happy privilege.

Stephen's last Thanksgiving, November of 1999
Back Row (left to right): Aunt Hilda, Stephen, Deborah, George Coates and two guests
Front Row (left to right): Tom, Naomi, Audrey, Sue and Amanda

CHAPTER 88
STEVE REEVES SNEAKS OFF TO VISIT SANDRA

We spent most of our early winter days in our old routines. We began each morning with his wake-up call then he went out into the semi-dark to feed the horses. By January he would be feeding them in total dark. While he was out there I put my face on and pulled my hair back out of the way for my morning chores. I met him at the barn every weekday morning to begin our Power Walk. During each walk we discussed our plans for the rest of our day. I would outline my morning projects, everything I would take care of while he did his workout. We were long accustomed to each other's idiosyncrasies and habits. Stephen announced during one morning walk in late November that he was going to look at property in Arizona. He said he was hoping to find a small ranch he could afford, perhaps some sort of weekend sized home on acreage at an altitude high enough to allow us to escape the summer sweltering heat of the Valley Center ranch. Since we had actively been looking for such a place in Montana and California I was very surprised he now thought Arizona might be a viable option. It did not fit with all of our previous talks and the parameters he had always given me. After registering my surprise I asked when he thought he might like to leave. He said sometime in early December. I assumed he would drive so I discussed getting the oil changed in the truck and doing the usual pre-trip servicing. I was wrong but he did not correct me.

We had traveled together to Montana in search of our summer place that past summer. We had agreed to wait until next spring to return to Lincoln, Montana to continue our search unless something new came on the market before then. If Stephen wanted to expand his search into Arizona it was fine by me. While helping Stephen plan for his solo trip, I stumbled upon the true, underlying purpose behind the undertaking. The realization came to me in a rare, inexplicable epiphany that could not be supported at the time by logic. I discovered a tiny scrap of paper peeking out from under the large green mat just inside the front door. I picked it up and was about to toss it in the trash when the numbers scrawled on it peaked my curiosity. The numbers represented a phone number with an area code that arrested my breath. New Mexico. Sandra. I knew that Stephen's first love and first wife, Sandra, lived in New Mexico. The number on this tiny scrap of paper had to be Sandra's telephone number. I instinctively knew that he had been in contact with his beloved Sandra and was planning to be with her on this trip. Deep down I was certain that Stephen intended not to fly to Phoenix but to Albuquerque instead.

I had no proof and I was not insane so I understood the gaps in my reasoning. However, truth be known, I was not at the time thinking rationally - I was jumping to conclusions based on the information found on a tiny scrap of paper. Tons of people live in New Mexico. No matter how I chastised my lack of reason, my inner voice persisted in hammering its argument home: Stephen is flying to see his Sandra; you are the idiot that will lovingly help him pack and will listen to his directives all the way to the airport; you will send him off with a prayer that God will stay with him and then you will drive all the way back to the ranch to look after his domain like the good little doormat you are; when his friends or your family call, you will lie and say he has gone to Arizona to look at property for a summer home; you will not mention that your heart is now shattered that he would betray you by seeing the one woman, going to the one woman you could never forgive him for. On and on the little voice in my head pressed its point.

Before he left I did two things. First, I poured over our address book until I found an entry entitled "S something" but not Schakel which was her last name. The phone number next to the name was the one on the piece of paper but written backwards. Next, I dialed the phone number and, when a woman answered, all I said was, "Sandra?" The voice on the other end of the line answered, "Yes?" Then I hung up and waited for Stephen to say something about where he was really going. He continued talking about his trip to Arizona, nothing more. While I was packing his things for the trip I found his airline tickets and confirmed that his flight was to Albuquerque, not Phoenix as he had said. When it came time to drive to the airport I kept conversation light until we were there. I put my hand on Stephen's hand, looked him square in the eyes and asked, "Are you going to see Sandra?" He pulled his hand away and said with irritation, "Hell No!" I sighed and said, "Nonetheless, go with God." Years later George Helmer admitted to me during a telephone conversation that Stephen had gone to see his Sandra, just as I knew he did, then went on to Arizona in a rental vehicle. I suspected she went with him as he traveled because of two things. First, when he called to say he found a possible property in Strawberry, Arizona he said, "We found a possible property." I queried, "We?" He muttered and then said, "The real estate lady and I." In January, when he took me to see the property, the real estate lady looked totally confused when he introduced me as his wife. I suspected that she had met Sandra and assumed they were a couple. Meeting me caught her off guard.

Once I knew my Lord Tyrant had lied, betrayed my trust, all bets were off. While Stephen was gone on this trip I was largely alone at the ranch, both children were busy with their lives elsewhere. I had a lot of time to work out my feelings and try to come to terms with what was totally unexpected and unacceptable. I am not exactly sure why but somehow there was a big difference between Stephen finding a replacement "wife person" and him sneaking off to see Sandra. When Stephen called and informed me he would return the following evening, I sat down and wrote him one of my probably ill-advised but definitely heartfelt little pieces which I titled:

WAITING FOR MY LORD TYRANT

A plague casts into ruin the laughter of my spirit
So troubled is my sleep, I dread and fear it.

T'is the cursed erring of this woman's heart
Neither peace nor sweet relief does life impart.

Not so constant the rising moon nor the coming tides
As the longing, the hunger that within me abides.

Here, alone, in the silence of your great house, I await your return
My treacherous heart skips a beat and the heat of me begins its burn.

How unsweet the taste of truth as I sweep jubilant murmurs from my heart
An effort, however useless, to halt the pain before it starts.

Feeling the sharp stab I whirl to rake my despicable weakness into Hell's fire
Knowing a moment's reprieve as pain is usurped by ire.

It is said that after days gone, you return on the morrow
If only, if only, you would pull me to you and thereby end both sorrows.

Deborah Engelhorn Reeves
December 4, 1999

On December 5, I drove down to San Diego to meet Stephen at the airport. When he climbed into the Jeep I asked him how the flight was and he answered, "Good and short." Then I asked, "How's Sandra doing these days?" Focusing out the front windshield he said, "You're crazy!" I gave him one more chance and said, "You're saying you never saw Sandra on this trip?" And he replied, "I did not!" That still, small voice inside my head said, "Okay, have you had enough?" I waited until we arrived home and Stephen was rested before I gave him my little piece entitled, "Waiting for My Lord Tyrant." Once again he gave me absolutely no comment after he read it. As the days went by I found a particular song by the Carpenters kept playing over and over in my head:

> If I listened long enough to you
> I'd find a way to believe that it's all true
> Knowing you lied straight-faced while I cried
> Still I'd look to find a reason to believe
> If I listened long enough to you
> I'd soon believe the things you say are true

But I would not and I did not. I knew, and he knew that I knew, he had gone to see Sandra. He also sensed that it was the end of another part of my love for him. I believe he was either ashamed or sorry as he suddenly became particularly nice to me. I wondered what I should do now that our relationship was broken.

CHAPTER 89
YEAR END

In the meantime we did all our usual ranch maintenance and animal care. Many afternoons, when Stephen came in to take a nap I would lull him to relax with an intimate massage and then get up and go out and work on the Memorial Garden or gather rocks for basins. I did not stay and take a nap with him. Dune was my constant companion everywhere but in the house. He loved his sad mistress and found Valley Center life quite perfect.

During one conversation I mentioned my need for health insurance and suggested it as a possible Christmas gift. That year we were pleased to have George and Tuesday Coates at the ranch to add to our family gathering for Christmas. I came up with an idea to let them know just how much we loved them. I wrote a proclamation in which we adopted George and Tuesday into the family and had everyone sign it. The idea gave me just a small bit of Christmas cheer which I certainly needed during those bleak days. I was pretty good at pretending things had not changed in front of people When a loss or tragedy occurs it is not uncommon for your participation and memory of events surrounding the loss to become fogged. My memories of that Christmas are hazy at best. I do remember Stephen bought me athletic shoes rather than the health insurance I had hoped to receive. Everyone was there for Christmas but I never took photos so there is no official record. For me not to take any pictures was a first, totally out of character as anyone who has known me for the past forty years can attest. When I later reflected on what ended up being Stephen's last Christmas on this earth I was filled with regret about not taking photos.

A DAY IN THE LIFE

DECEMBER 30, 1999

Stephen made an interesting observation the other day. It was the day after Christmas and he was just about to roll on his side to go to sleep that night, when he suddenly spoke of (referred to) an incident that occurred on Christmas Day. David and Joanne's new youngster, Brittany (age 3) had quite decided she liked the looks of Steve and promptly invited herself up onto his lap. She nestled there for quite some time - seeming to note no unwelcome tone in Stephen's demeanor.

But at this time, more than twenty-four hours later, Stephen, thinking of the little three year old cuddling contentedly in his big arms, suddenly says, "You know, if I had ever had children, I would probably have been better off having daughters. With girls I wouldn't have had so many expectations. I mean if I had a son I would have wondered why he wasn't just like me, built like me, determined like me and so on."

The End.

That was the most introspective comment I had ever heard come from Stephen. I remember thinking, "Aha! He's making progress."

CHAPTER 90
2000 BEGINS

Life continued uninterrupted in January of 2000. On one early morning trail ride Stephen was on Sugarfoot and I rode Torrey. As we crested the top of the hill and started down toward Palma Valley I was attacked by four or five bees. One of the rascals stung me on the back of my neck - right at the base of my skull. The venom caused an ache that lingered for days. Torrey was afraid of the bees but he remained calm even when I hit the side of his face and neck as I slapped at the bees with my hat. He was really great. Stephen and Sugar were not bothered by the bees. After we returned to the barn I checked Torrey over and found no bee stings on him. I was the only unlucky one. It was our custom to give the horses a good grooming after a ride but this day I also treated Torrey to a little extra grain as a thank you for his understanding and efforts. Stephen had long since finished with Sugar and secured her in her paddock. I was always slower than Stephen at unsaddling, grooming and returning my mount to his pasture or paddock.

The area on the back of my neck that suffered the bee sting swelled and ached something awful. The stinger penetrated a lymph gland which then cascaded the pain and swelling to another lymph gland under my arm. I was in pure misery. After our lunch I gave Stephen a sweet little send off into nap time before leaving him to work on his family history. My head and neck ached too much to be able to actually sleep and I knew my tossing and turning would ruin his rest. Besides, I found ferreting out Stephen's past family relations and bits of their history to be quite fascinating, like putting a puzzle together. Mr. Harris of Rome, Georgia, one of Stephen's fans, was helping me on this project. He sent the best information and gave me great leads. I learned a lot from him.

When Stephen woke up he requested my help at the barn. He wanted to work first with Power Walker, then with my filly, Breezy. There was nothing on the Ranch I would rather do than work with my pretty Breezy. Power Walker, our young stallion was a handful but I could always see pride in Stephen's eyes when he looked at that colt.

CHAPTER 91
MORE MUSINGS;
MORE WARNING SIGNS

We had a blast during our sensual escapades and I was a damned good ranch hand by the time Stephen finished teaching me, but I wanted more. I was forty-eight years old when he first admitted to me, "You know, I just can't see myself with a woman who is fifty years old." Who would read my guidebook on his wants, needs and requirements and be willing to undertake the job? I was writing the book for my replacement while Stephen sat beside me in his recliner. He actually said he thought the guidebook might help smooth the way for the new recruit. At first I thought so too but later I realized no one would ever fill the bill. It was an exercise in futility. Well, I was not going to abandon him when the time came, that was for damned sure. He was frustrated by all the changes in the world. He was alienated by the unalterable fact that everywhere we turned something was lost forever. Favorite stores closing, cancelled television shows, changes in our town, transformations in our neighborhood and the march of technology all around us, it all grieved him deeply. Our access to riding areas was being cut off by the subdivision of open land and the building of houses. Watching friends and family age and die depressed Stephen. These were changes we had no control over. We prayed for suffering friends who were on death's door (Charlie Moss and George Eiferman) that God would take them home as soon as possible.

Stephen was having increasing difficulty climbing up into his saddle. He had to stand on a block of wood to get some height advantage while I steadied the saddle by putting pressure on the opposite stirrup or he could not raise himself into the saddle. It broke my heart and enraged him that he required assistance if he wanted to go for a horse ride. He worked his legs in the gym with ever increasing desperation but the leg press did not provide him with the strength required to mount his horse and he had no idea why. We never spoke of it but we both knew it was just a matter of time before riding horses would no longer be possible for Stephen.. When that day came I knew it would kill him. Obviously God knew it too. I decided to write a little prayer for him:

> "When I am not beside you to warn of uneven pavement, remove the spider from your bed, tighten the loose nuts on your old barn bench, run to get the jacket you forgot back at the house or the sunblock you left in the truck, when I sleep on the job and aren't out there to flip the tack when you've got it twisted, may Angels and God's eagle-eye keep you dry and safe and healthy. Amen."

I decided it was time for me to have a medical doctor check my various ailments including my high blood pressure, my racing pulse, the pain in my left arm and shoulder, and the sudden, irregular tightening in my chest. I also wanted to confirm that I suffered arthritis in several joints and find out if my serotonin levels were too low. So I raised the subject with Stephen again. He was only willing to cover the cost of a Pap smear and a mammogram (which I was years behind in having done). I was grateful and Stephen felt quite generous that late January of 2000 in paying for these medical tests. The mammogram found a very small lump in each breast and I was told to have another test done in six months to recheck them. The Pap smear was clean, which was good. However, the doctor was extremely concerned about my blood pressure. He warned me that if I had a massive stroke fifteen minutes after I left his office he would not be at all surprised. He wanted to run additional tests and prescribe medications to help get the problem under control but I knew I could not afford the cost. I also knew I could no longer ignore the situation. I thanked Stephen for covering the costs of the tests and informed him of what the doctor had said about my high blood pressure and the need for more tests. He did not actually verbally respond. He sort of scoffed at the whole idea and his body language communicated that he was quite annoyed as he stomped out. I knew that he was thinking, "I give her an inch and she wants to take a mile!"

CHAPTER 92
STEPHEN'S ERROR
IN JUDGMENT

Late that month, after Stephen had been down to inspect the rental house, he asked me to use my talents to fix up the yard and driveway area. I asked Stephen to find out when Gene would be at work so I would not disturb him. My desire to avoid our renter was never questioned. I could not very well admit, as desperately unfulfilled and unhappy as I was, that I was drawn to the compassion and kindness I sensed in Mr. Stewart. It never occurred to Stephen that I could find another man of any sort attractive for any reason. Besides, Mr. Gene Stewart was no Steve Reeves!

So I worked on the rental yard's landscaping as requested. Despite my best laid plans, Gene returned home while I was still toiling away and decided to stay and talk to me. He asked if he could help with the work. I knew if I accepted his offer it would keep him outside so I declined. I was hoping he would go inside but he just stood there chatting away. We talked about a feral cat that was living under the rental's porch which somehow led to a discussion of an animal sedative called ACE used by people to commit suicide. He admitted at one time in his life he had considered suicide. I found myself sharing with him my own occasional struggle to find a reason to live. I was amazed at how easy he was to talk to. While I had my hands in the dirt and he was sitting on the top step of his new home I realized that a bond of friendship had just been established. After that realization I personally confirmed his actual work schedule so I could avoid being at his place when he was home.

Life went on at the Ranch and we were dealing with the usual chores and responsibilities. Stephen announced one evening that he had gone ahead and purchased the place he had said he found of interest in Strawberry, Arizona. We drove to the real estate office in Strawberry to get the keys. When the real estate lady came to the door and Stephen introduced me as his wife she looked startled, sort of caught off guard. That was when I suspected Sandra had been with him when he looked for property back in early December. The agent recovered her composure and smiled brightly as she handed Stephen the keys. We drove the short distance to a nice small home constructed of milled, squared logs sitting on a large lot with neighbors on each side and a fire department across the street. There was a chain-link fence around the yard. I was stunned. Except for the scattered pines this home was nothing like what I thought we had been looking for. For one, the road was paved. Stephen refused to ride our horses on a paved road since we kept them shoeless most of the time. One of our main requirements for a summer place was the ability to stable our horses on site and have direct access to forest or wilderness lands for trail rides. This home was nice but it did not come close to meeting our primary requirement.

As we walked around I could sense Stephen was really distressed at his error in judgment. I tried to make him feel better by emphasizing the property's good points. The kitchen and master bedroom of the little house were very nice. We discussed what sort of furniture it would need and how we hoped the nearest neighbors dogs did not bark at night because they sure barked nonstop during the time we were there. It seemed like a very long drive back to our motel in Camp Verde as Stephen was so disappointed in himself.

Once back at our motel I found that I could not rest. I gave Stephen a light, sensual interlude, kissed his big toe and then went and sat at the table trying but finding it difficult to read. I was disturbed by his obvious blunder. Stephen never made mistakes of that magnitude.

The house in Strawberry, Arizona purchased by Stephen
but never used; sold after his death

CHAPTER 93
MY HEALTH ISSUES WORSEN

Not long after we returned from Strawberry I experienced more reminders of my high blood pressure and poor health condition. In addition to having nosebleeds that erupted without warning I discovered a large blood spot in the white of one of my eyes. Spontaneous blood spots in my eyes became a frequent event. I know beyond a shadow of a doubt that if Stephen truly believed I was in any danger he would not have hesitated to help me. Stephen thought I was perfectly healthy. He had difficulty believing that at twenty-five years his junior I could be sick. I think too that part of him suspected I was making it all up in order to manipulate him into obtaining health insurance for me. I knew the truth but had no idea how to convince him otherwise. In hindsight I suspect that the fast growing cancer inside Stephen may have adversely affected his decisions.

CHAPTER 94
A NEW ARRANGEMENT BETWEEN US

After seemingly endless thought and prayer I approached my Lord Tyrant and suggested we once again consider officially adopting a more business style relationship. I had previously proposed this arrangement but it was never adopted. He enjoyed and had long since come to depend on much of what he received from our relationship. I proposed to move into the groom's quarters, receive a reasonable salary for working for him five days a week, five hours a day and be on call there at the Ranch in case he needed me. I would provide every service I had always provided with the exception of sex. My job would be to provide: All cooking, cleaning, laundry and mending; All secretarial work (bills, tax prep, phones, letters, fan mail, writing out any new manuscript for any new books he wrote); All animal care and feeding that I usually did; All grounds keeping, landscaping and pool cleaning that I usually did; All ranch hand and horse training assistance I usually did; and all chauffeuring to markets, doctor's appointments and business appointments. I would buy my own health insurance

I included in the agreement the right for Naomi and Lynx to continue to have rooms at the far end of Stephen's home until they left the nest so to speak. Neither of my children spent very much time on the ranch by this time anyway. There was a cot out in the Groom's quarters that they could use to stay with me anytime they wanted. As with the first time I offered this business agreement to Stephen, he naturally objected to the lack of sexual contact. Since our relationship was going to be strictly business the sex part had to be removed from the deal. We would now be working together to keep the ranch going and the horses bred. I would have freedom to pursue my private life and obtain the medical help I knew I desperately needed.

CHAPTER 95
THE THORN
IN THE SIDE OF HERCULES

Just prior to moving into the groom's quarters, I wrote the following piece I entitled, "The Thorn in the Side of Hercules":

> Each dawn crouches low beyond the ridge to the east. As that stealthy brightening moves up to chase away the dark, the birds are first to mutter and fluff their feathered coats. And dawn's long bright fingers of light seek out the creatures of the night, to urge them to quicken their return to whatever shelter they left last evening. Sunflowers, whose faces are turned to the west where last they saw the disappearing sun, are now moving toward that eastern warmth to greet the new day's light.
>
> I am here, a witness to the new dawn, watching, listening and basking in that magic moment when the last cooling movement of the air hurries passed and the sun's light touches my cheek. I bid farewell to the retreating coolness and say Good Morn to the sleepy roadrunner sitting on the fence post.
>
> I am at peace with the world of God here in my back country home, but there is unease when I look over to where a man rumbles his hay cart as he feeds the horses. When his blue crystal eyes fall upon me they darken and anger flickers. I am left with the distinct feeling that he is not pleased to see me.
>
> For years I struggled to please him, to serve him as a wife, lover, partner and friend. For all of my unflagging effort and energies I am met with impatience and criticism. No matter how lovingly I attend his needs and seek out new ways to make a smile appear in those angry eyes of stern contempt, I fail.
>
> There are still long dark nights when I cannot slumber, cannot rest for there before me is the unquiet truth: I am nothing more than the thorn in the side of Hercules.

CHAPTER 96
GENE

I decided then, as I moved into the groom's quarters and the strictly business phase of our relationship began, that it was no longer inappropriate for me to become better acquainted with Gene Stewart. I had just been assigned by Stephen the job of installing curtains in the rental house. So I decided to make an appointment to start putting in the curtains when Gene would be home from work. I was suddenly nervous on some weird, different level about going down there knowing that he would be home. This was a time of general uncertainty on the ranch. Although he would not admit it, Stephen was not happy with the new business deal. He was sorely missing the intimate aspect of our somewhat long-term relationship. I understood that aspect of his frustration and that he was accustomed to being in control of almost everything I did. I knew that he was upset but I told him quite honestly, "Stephen if you actually wanted me I would never leave." A huge part of me was also accustomed to Stephen's and my relationship. After all our years together I was in tune to pleasing him. It was difficult knowing that he was unhappy because I had made a decision that benefited me more than him.

I headed down to the rental house with curtains and the necessary installation materials and tools piled on the backseat of my car. Dune tagged along when I called for him out the open car window. One embarrassing thing happened when I first got there that day. Dune spotted an almost a realistic statue of a reclining coyote sitting on the floor in the small library. He marched over, gave the coyote a quick sniff then, before I could stop him, hiked his leg and produced a graphic demonstration of his disdain. I was mortified. After Gene could contain his laughter he assured me no harm was done and I soon relaxed.

For the first time Gene and I conversed about our past lives without me being nervous. I shared my health concerns while putting up the curtains in the living room. He stepped out of the room and when he returned he produced his blood pressure equipment. Apparently we both suffered from high blood pressure. I gratefully placed the cuff on my arm and was not surprised to discover that my blood pressure was super high. I declined Gene's offer of one of his prescription pills. We talked about his health issues as well as the different jobs he had before he fell and broke his back some years ago. I briefly shared my life's work with juveniles. We discovered that we shared a similar love of animals, from crickets to horses. We laughed a little about the feral cat that lived underneath his porch. He named the mangy looking animal Porch and was trying to tame him.

CHAPTER 97
STEPHEN'S
MEDICAL CRISIS BEGINS

Some days later I scheduled a doctor appointment for Stephen to have a few pre-cancerous blemishes burned off his face. We were not particularly concerned; however, Stephen mentioned that he had a stomachache off and on for a few days. As we drove to his appointment I asked him to remember to mention his stomachache. Stephen asked me to run an errand for him while he met with his doctor. I was waiting for him when he came out and as he approached the car I could tell something was amiss. As soon as he climbed in and shut the door I asked him what was wrong. He said everything was routine until he remembered to mention his stomach ache. The doctor had him lay back on the exam table so he could examine Stephen's abdominal area. The doctor discovered a small mass under his rib cage.

The doctor informed Stephen that the mass could be something as serious as cancer and he referred him to an oncologist for further testing. We were both in a state of shocked alarm. I asked him how long he thought he might have to wait before his medical group, Family Health Plan (FHP), would clear him to see the specialist. He was certain, given the seriousness of the potential problem, that FHP would expedite the referral request. The doctor said that he would hear from FHP or the oncologist shortly. As soon as we returned home he had me feel the mass so I knew where and how it felt. We decided to pray together. We did not know exactly what we were praying for but we prayed and talked and then prayed some more. He tried not to show it but the unknown weighed heavily on him.

When two days passed and no one contacted us I called FHP offices to inquire as to the status of the referral request. They gave me the red tape bullshit bureaucracies are well known for. More days went by and I called again and again with no result. I also called and begged Stephen's doctor to put any pressure he could think of on FHP to expedite his request. I was sick with worry but Stephen was determined to work and take care of the ranch as if nothing was wrong. His steely, intense work ethic could not hide his anger and frustration though. At his request I was with him from morning until late afternoon. I had to stifle my urgent need to ask him how he was feeling. He did not want me fussing over him, naturally, as that would just boil his anger. He took over making the phone calls to FHP because he said I was not aggressive enough.

I shared the situation with Gene and we discussed how best to help Stephen. He offered to help care for the horses and ranch chores but I told him Stephen was determined to keep going as if nothing was wrong. I explained my need to spend more and more time with Stephen until he recovered. He understood totally. My own health concerns were sidelined until one morning when I woke up with both a nosebleed and a large blood spot in an eye. I needed advice so I went down to talk to Gene about obtaining health insurance. We discussed possible companies to contact and other options I might have.

I went into the ranch house in order to use the telephone to contact a few insurance companies and obtain price quotes on health insurance. Stephen came into the kitchen and seemed totally exasperated with me. After completing my calls I came to the realization that if you are not part of a group of some sort then health insurance is super expensive. With my pre-existing conditions, I could not obtain a health insurance policy that I could afford. I was dismayed to say the least at this realization. I spent my day with Stephen working out at the barn taking care of the horses. He did not suggest taking a trail ride. I could tell that he was in pain just by looking at his face and the way he moved. I gritted my teeth and carefully asked Stephen about the level of pain he was in. He tried to make light of it but he could not fool me. You do not live with someone for seven years and study their every nuance without knowing when they are not being honest about something as important as pain levels.

Feeling completely helpless and desperate, I broke Stephen's big rule of the moment to not tell anyone about his health problems. I called Dr. Roy Johnson of Valley Center even though I knew he was not affiliated with FHP. I knew if Stephen had been allowed to see any doctor he wanted he would have designated Dr. Roy Johnson as his attending physician. Roy was familiar with Stephen and a compassionate soul. I called and explained who I was and that Stephen would wring my neck but I needed him to come to the ranch as soon as possible. I explained about Stephen's probably cancerous mass and how much pain I was certain he was in. I asked him to bring pain medication with him. I did not know how else to help Stephen. He knew Stephen's pride was as strong as his body so he understood what I was saying perfectly. I prepared myself for the rage when Stephen learned that I had called in Roy. Stephen was relaxing in his favorite recliner and I was cleaning out the fireplace preparing to build a fire for him when I heard a vehicle approach. Only twenty minutes had passed since I made the call to Roy. Stephen did not seem to be aware that someone was approaching the house. As I opened the door I heard Stephen grumble his pained irritation at me for answering the knock at the door and letting someone in. As Roy entered the home I moved a little closer to Stephen and said urgently, "Stephen, I am so sorry but I did not know what else to do." Then I left them to their private discussion.

While Roy was conferring with Stephen and giving him some sort of medication to help with the pain I went down to the rental house to meet with Gene. He asked a lot of questions and one of them was, "Are you and Steve legally married?" Given the fact that Stephen and I had exchange private vows, and being aware that the common law in some places declares husband and wife status on those who have lived together for seven years, I was not certain how to answer him. All I could say was, "I better find out." I left Gene and went back to the ranch house uncertain how Stephen would treat me. Stephen made a comment that I seemed to be getting real chummy with Gene Stewart. I admitted that I liked Gene and found him easy to talk to. Stephen said, "Why don't you just move in with him if you like him so much?" I answered quite honestly, "We're just getting to know each other right now." Then I changed the subject saying, "Does the common law in California consider us husband and wife after seven years?" His reply was a curt, "No." Just to make sure I asked, "So I was never your wife and we don't need to file any divorce papers, right?" To which he replied, with a bit more vehemence, "Hell no!" His responses were given while he was in pain so I understood that it might be his anger speaking. The following day I called the attorney Stephen and I had used once before some years ago and asked his educated, unbiased opinion on the issue. He told me that there is no common law marriage in the state of California. So Stephen was right.

Every hour of every day seemed like an eternity while we were waiting for permission for Stephen to meet with the oncologist. I was absolutely livid with this damned FHP organization that would not clear my dearest Lord Tyrant for something as simple as an appointment with a specialist. I could not understand how any medical organization could ignore the potentially disastrous results caused by a delay in diagnosis. No one should have to experience this level of frustration and despair due to the incompetence of the medical industry. For the first time in my life I was having great difficulty in leaving someone I loved in God's hands.

On March 29, Stephen and I somehow managed to continue our normal schedule. I prepared his lunch the same as I had done one thousand times before. When he went to take his nap I mended the ripped pocket of his turquoise silk shirt. I worked quietly in the hushed ranch house as he slept.

CHAPTER 98
A MARRIAGE OF NECESSITY

The next day, once my chores and business with Stephen were finished, I was lost in a mixture of prayer and melancholy thoughts as I walked down to visit with Gene. Out of the goodness of his heart and with a sincere concern for my health, Gene offered to marry me so that I might be covered by his group health insurance plan. When he learned what the attorney had confirmed regarding my legal status with Stephen, Gene suggested we visit the County Courthouse in order to determine what paperwork needed to be completed and, most importantly, how long the process takes to be married by a Justice of the Peace. Just as soon as we were legally married he promised to contact his work's Human Resources office and add me as an additional insured on his plan. I was touched by his generosity to say the least.

I did not sleep much that night. All I could seem to do was toss and turn as chaotic thoughts swirled in my mind. I prayed on and off pretty much all night. I was feeling so guilty that I had ended my so-called marriage with Stephen just days before we found out he may be terminally ill. There is no way I could have predicted this situation but my timing, my decision to act when I did, would weigh heavily on my heart forever. Then my mind would return to prayers for Stephen that God would intervene on his behalf. Over and over again my mind pondered what I could do, how I could help, other than being there on the ranch to help whenever he would let me. Then my mind would think about the morrow and how strange it seemed that I was going with Gene to the courthouse to make arrangements to be legally married so I could have health insurance. Everything was complicated. So much was out of my control but I was determined to obtain the medical help I needed. I had to do that for me. I would continue to take care of Stephen as best I could. I would never abandon him no matter how much he liked to think he did not need me. I was no longer worried that he would replace me. Now I was terrified that he might actually die. Stephen always said he would live to be one hundred so he could not die yet - he was only seventy-four years old! Round and round my thoughts would go until I somehow passed-out from exhaustion.

On March 31, as planned, Gene and I went to the courthouse to start our application for a marriage license. We asked what the waiting period would be and were told there was no waiting period. I was stunned and at the same time excited when I realized that I could have health insurance this time tomorrow! We filled out the paperwork, paid a small fee and then went into a small room where a woman wearing a black robe asked us if we wanted the ceremony to be private or available on the public records. We had agreed to annul the marriage just as soon as I could afford my own health insurance policy so we told her we wanted the existence of the marriage to remain private. She then asked if we wanted a photo taken of the wedding. In unison we said, "No thanks." This was not that sort of wedding. Five or six minutes of official words later we signed one more piece of paper, thanked the justice of the peace and left. After the disasters and emotional wounds of his previous marriages, Gene had decided that he would live the rest of his life as a confirmed bachelor. I understood the magnitude of his sacrifice on my behalf. Gene went to work early the next morning so he could do whatever was required in order to add me to his health insurance plan. When the paperwork was completed he called and told me to contact his doctor, a Dr. Michael Barker, and make an appointment.

Dr. Barker's office scheduled me immediately and I felt an immeasurable level of pure relief. Suddenly doors were opening for me. First there was no wait to get married, then there was no wait to get on the insurance and then there was no wait to see the doctor. I was grateful to Gene and to God. I liked this Dr. Barker and he seemed really fond of Gene. He took really good care of me right away and I felt as if my life had just been saved. Now if only God would save Stephen everything would be right with my world.

CHAPTER 99
STEPHEN'S HEART SOFTENS

I continued working for Stephen every day. There seemed to be nothing noticeably different in those first few weeks. Stephen was short tempered pretty often but not always. One day in early April he called me over to where he sat resting in his recliner. He handed me two sheets of paper and said that he had written them for me. I was really surprised. He then apologized that only one of the pages was typewritten. He had used Phyllis, the same lady that typed up his Will a few years before, to type up the one sheet but he handwrote the other. I knew how much he hated his own penmanship. The first four lines are original to Stephen. The remainder is basically a copy of the old song entitled *I Wish You Love* which is all about bidding goodbye to a loved one. The typewritten note reads as follows:

Deborah,

This is where our story ends,
We once were lovers, can still be friends.

Let our hearts call it a day,
But before you walk away I sincerely want to say,

I wish you bluebirds in the spring,
To give your heart a song to sing.

And then a kiss, but more than this,
I wish you love.

And in July, a lemonade,
To cool you in some shady glade.

I wish you health
But more than wealth,

I wish you love.
My breaking heart and I agree

That you and I could never be
So with my best

My very best
I set you free

I wish you shelter from the storm
A cozy fire to keep you warm

But most of all when snowflakes fall
I wish you love.

Steve
March 2000

You can understand why I was sobbing while reading the sentiment expressed in this sweet note. I disagreed with the one line that says, "My breaking heart and I agree that you and I could never be." I always felt that he and I could have had it all but for his attitude and his cursed trip to see Sandra. I began to cry when I realized he had taken the time and made the effort to have it typed up so he could give it to me. The first one brought tears but the second one nearly did me in. It was a handwritten note, from the Stephen I loved and cherished, apologizing for hurting me during our years together and thanking me for loving him. It reads as follows (copy of actual letter in appendix):

> Deborah,
>
> I would like to thank you for bringing love, passion, excitement and adventure into my life when I needed it most. I will never be able to look at a full moon again without thinking of you and remembering all the loving special sessions we shared. I would also like to say that I am sorry and apologize for any hurt that I have caused you through neglect or inconsideration and for not being more sensitive to your needs.
>
> Via Con Dios Con Amor
>
> Steve
> March 2000

I told him how much it meant to me and then ran out to the groom's quarters so I could be alone to collect myself. Sometime later I noticed that he was preparing to clean the chicken coop. That had always been my job and he was not about to start doing my chores. I joined him at the chicken coup and told him I would clean the chicken coup if he would rake out the old dove enclosure which was full of dead weeds and tree bark. That way we could work near each other but not close enough to feel the need to talk much. I did not mention that my insurance problem had been solved by Gene marrying me. I did ask him for three hours off the next day to go to a doctor appointment. He agreed to the time off but questioned how Gene and I were getting along. I told him we were getting along fine. He grunted his response, finished cleaning out the dove enclosure and then went up toward the barn.

CHAPTER 100
STEPHEN'S PROGNOSIS

It seemed unforgivable that there was such a long period between the discovery of the small mass and when he was finally cleared to see the oncologist. He continued doggedly working on projects around the Ranch. He had me help with the groundwork for Ranger, Sugar, Power Walker and Zee. He could no longer ride by then due to an overall lack of energy and his ongoing pain. With a few exceptions he found food less and less attractive. Despite efforts to find food he could still enjoy he was losing weight, a lot of weight. Stephen still refused to let his condition be known outside of those on the Ranch and his doctor. One day when we were in the house he lifted his shirt to show me what had once been his muscled abdomen. My knees nearly buckled when I saw how large the yet to be diagnosed, unknown mass had become. All that came out of my mouth was an anguished, "Oh my God!"

On Easter Sunday, the 23rd of April, I was trying to dream up some way to help Stephen think about something other than his worsening condition or his responsibilities around the Ranch. I asked him if he would like to go see a movie and was really pleased when he agreed. So we took an easy drive in my comfortable car down to San Marcos's Edwards Cinemas to watch "*Where The Money Is*". I have no memory of the movie. I remember blindly listening to Stephen and thanking God each time Stephen laughed. All I could think about was that at least for the moment he was able to forget everything.

Stephen's referral was finally approved and I drove him immediately to Southwest Cancer Care on Grand Avenue in Escondido for a long-overdue consultation. He refused to allow me to go in with him. I had to sit in the waiting room while they did an exam and biopsy. No one other than God will ever know just how much I regretted my appalling timing in separating from him just days before the doctor discovered the mass. Until then Stephen always quipped that he would most likely outlive me. With everything that was going wrong with my body at the time I assumed he was probably right. Apparently God had other plans.

After the oncology appointment Stephen was feeling better for the moment and wanted to go to Burger King to have a ninety-nine cent Whopper. After picking up the hamburgers we were on our way to order his much loved chocolate shake at McDonald's when he suddenly said he felt ill and asked me to take him straight home. I did that of course and asked if he wanted me to stay with him. He said he was going to take a nap but he wanted me to stay in the house. Not wanting to disturb his nap I became as quiet as a church mouse as I washed windows and ironed his shirts. On the way back home he had not shared much about what the oncologist said, only that we now had to wait for the biopsy results. At least we were moving forward. I had been praying and praying for a miraculous change in his apparent cancer. With a man as strong and larger than life as Steve Reeves you do not expect he will ever die. He was so charismatic, so dynamic, it seemed like he should live forever. I left the ranch house a few hours later when he woke from his nap and dismissed me. I tried to think of something other than Stephen and his health. When Gene came home we discussed his day at work and my day with Stephen, as had become our habit. Gene's friend, Maddy (Madeline Beck), invited us to dinner at her house that evening but we declined. We felt we should stay on the ranch so I could check on Stephen during the evening hours.

A few days later we were told that the results of the biopsy were inconclusive. We were dumbfounded. How could they not find cancer in a mass growing at such an alarming rate? Why was Stephen suffering such horrible pain even though he was on heavy painkillers? Why was he continuing to lose weight if this evil mass was not cancerous? What the hell else could it be?! The doctors scheduled more tests. I cannot now remember the names of all the tests but I do remember that all the tests were as inconclusive as the first. By then I was hard-pressed not to cry all the time. I knew it would irritate Stephen so I did my best to behave. Stephen was constantly tense and in pain. He sat and racked his mind for a logical reason for this awful turn of events. The FHP powers that be finally agreed to allow exploratory surgery. There was some relief when we learned of this decision but I could tell Stephen was becoming more and more resigned to his fate as well. He was in touch with a lot of feelings that he chose not to share with me. He was beginning to shut me out again. After all we had been through together I was not allowed to comfort him and all because of my damned timing! If I had waited just a bit longer before placing my medical needs first I would have been by his side as his wife rather than his employee when he became ill. The "if onlys" whirling around in my mind were driving me nearly insane. When I spoke to Gene of my regrets, my guilt over deciding to separate from Stephen at such an unbelievably bad time, he disagreed and tried to ease my guilt by saying, "You didn't know what was going to happen, you were trying to save your own life, your own health. He told you he wasn't going to pay for your health insurance. He said he didn't love you, that he would replace you. This situation is not your fault." Unfortunately, I had trouble allowing enough logic in to snuff out all my festering regrets.

Sometime later, I came across a statement of wisdom penned by renowned author Mark Matousek. It spoke volumes to me about what my dearest Lord Tyrant must have been going through. Mr. Matousek says, "A dying person is grieving the loss of control over life, body image, of normal physical functions, mobility and strength, freedom and independence, security and the illusion of immortality. He is also grieving the loss of an earthly future and reorienting himself to an unknown destiny."

The next day Stephen and I filled fan orders and paid bills. When the secretarial duties were completed he told me that we were going out to repair a wooden fence post that broke when one or more of the horses rubbed against the fence. He gave me a look that communicated in no uncertain terms not to say a word of protest or concern about his health. I wisely kept my mouth shut. We left the house and headed for the barn. I grabbed two buckets of water and hoisted them into the back of the pickup truck while he went to bring the concrete mix and shovels. I knew the drill by heart but my stomach was in knots that Stephen was out working a labor-intensive chore when I could so clearly see his shoulder bones sticking through the fabric of his blue shirt. I volunteered to walk the wheelbarrow down to the lower northeast corner of the pasture so he would not see me cry. He nodded his approval as he finished loading the materials to fix the broken post.

I took off with the wheelbarrow purchased just last summer and repainted by Stephen a shiny solid black with a wide red enamel stripe around the top. I hated mixing concrete in a new wheelbarrow but it was the one he had indicated I was to use. I arrived at the gate just as he pulled up in the truck. Opening the gate wide I kept the geldings at bay as he drove the truck into the pasture, rolled the wheelbarrow in and then shut the gate behind me. We did not speak much; neither of us put voice to the distinct possibility of this being the last fence post we might ever replace together. We did not say how sad or how scared or how overwhelmed we were with the knowledge that in just over twenty-four hours he would be in surgery. He spoke of the treated post and how long he thought it might last. He spoke of taking an 8x10 photo he had signed to a new neighbor down Little Quail Run who had requested it. There were long silences as we worked side-by-side. A rancher to the core, Stephen needed to repair the weakened fence before going in for surgery. There was no way for us to know that he was never coming back. We refused to contemplate that possibility let alone speak of it.

Once the fence was repaired we returned to the house where he could not bear to look at food even though I offered it. I handed him an Ensure nutrition drink flavored with chocolate. I watered it down with milk because he abhorred how sweet the natural drink tasted He was in desperate need of nutrients and calories. He sat down at the small wood kitchen table and asked me to come close. Taking my hands in his he said with noticeable regret in his voice, "I should have married you, Deborah. I should have made you my wife years ago." All I could muster was, "Yes, Stephen, I needed that but I'm okay now so don't worry. Just know, as I've said many times before, I'll always love you." Then he told me not to worry because he would take care of me. I was not sure then what he meant exactly but I thanked him from the bottom of my heart. All that mattered to me, regardless of whatever he meant, was that he said it with nothing but love in his eyes.

Despite that tender moment, when my work day was finished Stephen stiffened and said I was excused for the day and that he would not need me again until the next morning. I hesitated then told him Gene's niece and her husband had invited us to dinner at their place in Oceanside. I said if he was sure he did not need me, Gene and I would accept the invitation. I asked him to try and consume one of the Ensure protein and vitamin drinks that I had prepared and put in the refrigerator for him. Stephen told me to quit bothering him but to be back to cut his toenails in the morning.

A renewed yet somehow different bond existed between us ever since he had handed me the written apology and the typewritten song lyrics. However, all our energies at that point were focused on his recovery from the disease plaguing his body. If I could have saved him by love or prayers he would never have died. I had read that statement somewhere and knew that I was not alone in this feeling of helplessness. At least I still lived on the ranch and was close enough to respond should Stephen need or want something. He only ever called me to come back up to the ranch once. He had been trying to take a nap but a wasp somehow found a way into the bedroom and was buzzing against the window. Stephen called and asked me to catch and escort it out of the house, which I did in a flash.

While I was out with Gene to have dinner with his niece in Oceanside Troy Bertelsen showed up at the ranch. I do not know if it was one of his more impromptu visits or if Stephen had called him. Stephen's illness was supposed to be kept secret so I am not sure. The next morning when I arrived for work, Troy's attitude towards me seemed quite changed. He was distinctly aggressive and unpleasant as I went in to see Stephen. Troy gave off the aura of being in charge of Stephen's care and needs. At first I was offended by his new arrogant demeanor but then I wondered what exactly Stephen had said to make Troy act so territorial. Regardless, Troy made it clear he wanted me out of the house. I was not about to abandon Stephen without a fight but then I saw a glint in Stephen's eye and knew that he had been up to some mischief even if he was terribly ill. So I turned and asked Stephen what he wanted me to do. He initially told me to work on the hospital's admittance paperwork but then changed his mind and had me wash his feet and trim his toenails. "So they don't look so ragged while I'm in surgery," he said.

Our plan had been for me to drive Stephen to the hospital at the appointed time. I would deal with the administrative requirements and hold onto the bag of his belongings after he changed out of his street clothes. I was going to be there for and with my dearest Lord Tyrant. That was the original plan. However, after I finished trimming his toes I stood up and he told me, "I won't need you anymore today, go away." I was caught off guard and started to inquire but he abruptly interrupted me, announcing with an air of satisfaction, "Troy will take me." The sudden coldness of the dismissal, rather than his actual words, was the cause of great pain. I could feel my hands shaking but kept my chin high until I walked out to the driveway. Then and only then did I allow the tears to pour down my cheeks.

CHAPTER 101
STEPHEN'S SURGERY

The day of Stephen's surgery was unbelievably difficult to wait through. I had work at the Ranch that Stephen would, despite his abrupt dismissal of me the previous afternoon, expect to be completed. I found myself entreating God with disorganized, desperate prayers while I worked. Later I went to the ranch house and called the hospital to check on Stephen. The hospital would only tell me his surgery was expected to start on time that evening and that he was resting comfortably in his room. After cleaning the kitchen and bathrooms I returned outside to groom our mares. Finished with that assignment I decided to hand water all the garden areas that were not serviced by the sprinkler system. All chores completed, I showered, dressed, joined Gene in offering another prayer for the successful outcome of Stephen's surgery and then left for the hospital.

Once at the hospital I waited outside the operating room. I think Troy was there part of the time. I was in such an emotional and mental state I had trouble remembering who was there. I do know that when Stephen's medical team came out to talk to me I was alone. They informed me that when they opened Stephen's midsection they found lymphoma had invaded his entire abdominal cavity. They admitted that once they saw the extent of the lymphoma only chemotherapy could address the complicated spread, which they recommended commencing after three days. His body needed time to stabilize from the surgery. They also admitted there was a real concern about his liver function. I acknowledged that I had noticed a yellow cast to his facial skin during the past few days. They said they had never seen such an aggressive case of Lymphoma. I mentioned my surprise that this cancer could take him down so quickly given Stephen's lifestyle of vigorous exercise and healthy living. One of them announced that Stephen's superior health was probably the reason the disease advanced so quickly! Apparently Stephen's superior blood flow and circulation was causing the lymphoma to spread at an accelerated rate. I was trying to keep it together so I could understand what they were saying but I could not hold back my tears and there was a strange roaring noise in my head. Out of concern they asked if I was going to be okay. I somehow found the energy to assure them that I would and asked what exactly was next. They said they would keep Stephen comfortable and have vitamins and key minerals started intravenously. I think they tried to give me hope by saying, "The more aggressive the Lymphoma the better it responds to chemo." Maybe that is true. I was informed that Stephen would come out of the operating room once the staff had him cleaned up and bandaged. I asked when he might be conscious and was told that he was already awake and had been told the outcome and the plan.

I felt so sick inside that I could not sit so I paced for a while. Eventually Stephen was wheeled out to where I was standing. As he was brought near, the hospital staff paused and moved back to let us speak. As soon as he saw me his eyes averted. He grabbed my hand and kept it held tight but would not look at me! His abdomen was covered in heated white hospital blankets. He looked so pale and gaunt but I managed not to wince in case he did glance at me.

I told him, "Stephen your doctors came and told me everything. I know you're angry and upset but they said that the chemo they have you scheduled for is very successful with this type of lymphoma. You aren't alone in this, God is right here with you every minute!" He said, "I know. They told me about the chemo. I start it in three days." I think he said, "I'm glad you're here." but maybe I just wanted him to say that. I told him, "The orderlies are going to take you to your room now but I'll come find you tomorrow morning." He responded with, "Yes, come find me in the morning." Then I said, "I love you, go with God." and they whisked him away through the doors. As soon as he was out of sight I felt my legs buckling so I grabbed a nearby counter, managed to catch my breath and then collapsed on a chair. Everything the doctors shared with me kept tumbling over and over in my mind. I do not have any memory of finding my car in the parking lot or of how I ended up back at the Ranch. Some sort of automatic mindless behavior took control of my body while my mind endlessly replayed all the events that had just occurred in the hospital.

I returned to Palomar Hospital the next morning and located Stephen's room. I brought with me his latest favorite book, *Montana: The Last Best Place*. Stephen did not behave as if he was pleased to see me but he answered my queries about pain levels and food intake. I showed him his book and he said he wanted me to read stories out loud. I noted that his skin seemed tight on his cheekbones and forehead but was slightly less yellow. I did not say to him anything about the tightness but did mention the somewhat improved coloring. Then I read aloud. He interrupted me after a while to say he wanted me to go find him some broth and lime Jell-O. I went out, found someone at the nurse's station and put in his request. When I returned to his room, Stephen asked me to continue reading for another half hour, so I did. As I closed the book Stephen looked at me and said, "Deborah, you really let me down." I knew he was referring to our separation. I looked him straight in the eyes and repeated the same words I had spoken to him before his illness had been discovered, "If you had actually wanted me, I never would have left." He nodded and sighed then assigned me a laundry list of duties to perform at the ranch, "See to the horses when you get home, put Traveler and Ranger in the large arena to graze for four hours, no more. Scrub down the pool walls and clean the filter then run the pump for about two hours. Irrigate the persimmons, figs and blood oranges for the same two hours then clean the paddocks until 1:30 p.m. I want you to shed-out (remove loose winter coat) Sugar, Carmen and Monty first and if you have time, do Torrey as well." I had already shed out all of our mares but realized it was best not to interrupt him. I answered, "Consider it done. God be with you every minute, I love you." I then kissed his closest big toe and left. Over the years I had developed the custom of kissing his big toe as a sign of affection, especially when he was in a grumpy mood.

A dark gloom fell over me as I left for the ranch. It did not feel right leaving Stephen behind in the hospital. The ranch was quiet and peaceful when I returned home which pleased me. I stopped and let Dune out of the rental's yard and he loped up the dirt road to the ranch to keep me company. As promised, I systematically took care of each chore and was just finished returning Torrey to the pasture when I heard someone driving into the ranch from the Little Quail Run front gateway. Dune went on alert and growled low. It was Troy returning so I put my hand on Dune to settle him and walked back down to the rental. Gem and Isis, my two cats, were sunning themselves on the front porch so I knew the feral cat Gene named Porch must not be around. Mr. Shivers, my cockatiel, issued his wolf whistle from his cage at one end of the porch. That particular whistle normally brought a smile to my face. Mr. Shivers had developed the habit of using it to announce to the world that Stephen had his magnificent manhood out as he relieved himself next to the lime tree. This routine always tickled my dearest Lord Tyrant and made him laugh. Today it triggered a near breakdown as I suddenly realized that this simple observance in all probability would never happen again. I collapsed there on the porch as the tears began to fall.

CHAPTER 102
THE PASSING OF A LEGEND

The first day of May had a benign beginning but ended up being the most incredibly heart-wrenching day of my adult life. By 7:20 a.m., I was on my way to Palomar Hospital in Escondido. On the Valley Center Grade, which connects Valley Center with Escondido, there was a fender bender of some sort which briefly held up traffic heading downhill. I reached the hospital and then Stephen's room a few minutes after 8 a.m. where I found him lying in his bed with some of his breakfast still in evidence. I greeted him with my usual cheerfulness but it was obvious that he was not feeling all that well. We spoke of the chemotherapy treatment that was scheduled to start the next morning. He told me he wanted a cup of hot tea so I left briefly to put in the request. Then he asked me to begin reading his book out loud so I started where we left off the morning before. After about thirty-five minutes he told me to go check on his tea, which I did, and ended up bringing it back with me. Then I continued reading. About 9:50 a.m. Stephen complained that his legs hurt and were not getting any circulation. He told me, "I'm not used to lying around all day doing nothing - come over here and rub my legs first up, then down, then back up." I worked each leg as I had innumerable times through our years together. When he said they felt a lot better I went back to reading. He interrupted me at one point and, looking out his hospital window toward Valley Center and home, he said, "When I get out of here you're going to take me to Carrow's for prime rib." I answered, "Absolutely guaranteed!" and then I resumed reading.

After a little while someone came into Stephen's room. I think it must have been Troy but I am vague on this matter as I was not internally recording anyone except Stephen. Whoever it was caused Stephen to say it was time for me to leave. His dismissal stung but I put away his book as he gave me his orders for chores on the ranch. As his first order he said, "I want you to repaint all the barn doors - use the paint I bought last February." I stood up to leave and said, "God be with you every minute, I love you." As I headed out the door, just as I was exiting, he said in that strong masculine voice I knew and loved so well, "And don't be late tomorrow, you were five minutes late today!" I was smiling as I found my way to the elevators and thinking to myself, "He's getting stronger; he must be getting better because he's grumping at me just like always." I headed for the parking lot and clearly remember seeing our friend, George Helmer, walking toward the hospital. I knew he lived in Rancho Cucamonga which is a good two hour drive north of us. Maybe my surprise at seeing him there instilled that piece of memory in my mind. Back on the ranch, I let Dune out so he could roam free then headed for work at the barn. Dune went to play horse ball "keep away" with Thunder Hawk, his favorite gelding, while I started to paint the large double barn doors leading from the cross tie area to the small walled arena.

I was still there quite a while later when I heard vehicles enter the ranch. Dune had worn himself out playing with Thunder and was laying in the shade of the barn. I went to see who was arriving and recognized both George Helmer and Troy as they parked their vehicles out in front of the ranch house. I told Dune to relax and I went back to painting. Troy and George were in the house for some time. Dune growled a warning as they later approached the barn. I do not remember who spoke or exactly what words they used but the general idea was they had come out to where I was working to let me know that my brother David had called and said he was coming to talk to me. I asked them, "About what?" They said they did not know. So I asked them, "When?" Sometime pretty soon they seemed to think. I believe I said, "Well, when he arrives, tell him I am at the barn." I remember one of them said something like, "No, he wants to talk with you at your place." The whole conversation felt weird but all I said was, "Thanks for the message." I chalked up their ill at ease to them considering me to be some sort of enemy now that Stephen and I were separated. All too often friends think they are supposed to take sides when couples split up so I assumed the whole cold shoulder routine from these men had something to do with that. I also wondered if Stephen had said something to make his friends act this way.

Dune led the way as we went inside Gene's rental house. I waited on the porch after washing up a little. Then David arrived. As David mounted the front steps Dune went ballistic inside the house. He was barking and snarling and baring his teeth through the windows. I was really surprised as my brothers are both dog lovers and are generally received well by strange dogs. I can only surmise that Dune somehow sensed high tension in my brother since David certainly did not intend me any harm. I thought we could sit and talk on the porch but in spite of Dune's aggressive behavior David said he wanted us to go inside to talk. I put Dune in one of the bedrooms and reassured him that I would be fine as I shut the door. David said he wanted me to sit down on the couch which seemed odd but I complied. Then he said, "I'm really sorry to have to tell you but Steve died this morning in the hospital." He said it slow with a very gentle, kind voice. My response was the age-old denial, "No, he can't be dead. I was just with him and he was getting stronger." David explained that after I left the hospital George and Troy had a meeting with Stephen during which Stephen said he needed to use the restroom. They helped him shuffle with his intravenous bottles to and from the bathroom. As Stephen turned to sit down on the bed he suddenly collapsed. They caught him as he fell. David said George and Troy called immediately for medical assistance but that Stephen was already gone.

I do not know how many times David had to repeat the circumstances behind Stephen's death because I kept saying, "No, no, he can't be gone, Oh God, he can't be dead! We weren't through!" By through I did not mean as a couple I meant we had not worked through the kinks in our new relationship - we were still at odds, still uneasy in our new roles. I knew we just needed more time. I planned to work for him and with him for years to come. If I thought I had regrets before, I could not have ever imagined the pain and remorse brought on by such finality. No chance to make things work out. I was totally stunned, totally unprepared for David's pronouncement. I should have been for heaven's sake as my dearest Lord Tyrant was seventy-four years old and riddled with an aggressive cancer. What the heck did I expect? I must have been the absolute definition of denial. All this notwithstanding, reality was so hard to bear that I fell apart. For the first time in my life I became hysterical. David wisely called Gene at work. Then he called Naomi and Lynx, both of whom had been praying for some miracle and were now blown away that Stephen was gone. Gene came home immediately and I found solace in his words of comfort and concern. David waited to see Gene calm me before he left. I remember the concerned faces of my children as I tried to reassure them I would be alright when all I wanted was to curl up and die. Gene gave me two Valium pills and I finally drifted into sweet release.

CHAPTER 103
MEMORIAL SERVICE

The next few days are nothing but a big blur. I was wallowing in so much sorrow it hurt to breathe. There was a meeting at George and Tuesday's to plan Stephen's memorial. I know I told them Stephen wanted to be buried in the Riverview Cemetery in Stevensville, Montana but George Helmer or Troy said, "No, he wanted to be cremated." That was news to me. I was informed that I was at the planning meeting only as a courtesy and that there were those who did not want me to attend the memorial. It appears that not only was my legal status non-existent but my social position as well. I remember thinking, "Now that Stephen is in heaven and is no longer angry at me I bet he is flipping raging at how I am being treated by his friends. He knows no one ever loved him more or took better care of him than I did." Still, these people felt they were doing right by Steve Reeves in ostracizing me. In their way they only thought to honor him. While the loss of their respect and friendship felt very much like a hard kick to my knotted-up stomach, I tried to keep in mind that it was their love and respect for Stephen that was the source of their coldness towards me.

On the morning of Stephen's memorial service I arose early and hiked out into the back country to find native flowers to make a bouquet for the occasion. I did not know what flowers others had ordered from florists but I knew which flowers he cherished from the backcountry where we loved to trail ride. I drove by myself to the service. None of it seemed real. I was feeling abandoned and under intense scrutiny by people who had been dear friends. Before the service started I mingled with some of the people in attendance. Dave Morris was there and I knew how pained he was at having lost his best friend. I offered him my condolences. Seeing some other friendly faces from Valley Center, I moved to speak with and welcome them. Dr. Ronald Adair was there talking to someone else and sharing funny stories about Stephen. Dr. Adair told the story about what happened after he had removed one of Stephen's teeth. Dr. Adair said Stephen insisted that he be allowed to take the tooth home. When Dr. Adair inquired why Stephen was so insistent he replied, "That way I can honestly say I still have all my own teeth!" The story was so typically Stephen and one that I had not heard before. In my emotionally charged state I overreacted a little and laughed out loud. I noticed some old friends of ours (who were now lost to me) turn and look with disapproval at what they perceived to be a lack of respect towards Stephen. I meant no discourtesy. I just could not help but laugh at Dr. Adair's shared memory. It was absolutely perfect. No one, not one person in whole world, was more impacted by the death of Stephen Lester Reeves than me. I almost stepped forward to apologize but then realized it was their problem. I was tired of apologizing for having decided to separate from my dearest Lord Tyrant. Before he died, Stephen knew and understood the reasons behind what I had done. My actions were nobody else's business. No one knew better than me that my timing turned out to be appalling. When I saw Stephen's cousin, Gordon, in the front row I asked if I could sit with him. He kindly said, "Of course."

There were those who stood up and shared stories about Stephen as is common at memorial services. My brother, David, spoke about having Stephen as a brother-in-law and how Stephen took David's newest adopted children out to see the horses and allowed them to ride them on the hot walker. I found myself afraid I was going to have a complete breakdown so I tried not to focus too closely on what people were sharing. All of these wonderful memories and stories being shared were causing my tenuous hold on my emotions to start to give way. I could not make a scene at Stephen's Memorial and found the strength I needed from the comforting presence of Naomi, Lynx and my brother, David. You know how they say there is nothing more important than family when things get rough. During this time period I was really appreciating family.

After the service a Memorial dinner was held at the Lawrence Welk Country Club. Gene had once worked there and was a great source of information, like who to call and how to arrange everything. My Mother fronted the deposit for the dinner but was later repaid by Stephen's estate. The dinner itself went off really well. The food was good and I believe everyone enjoyed interacting with others who had known and would miss Stephen. I was in no state of mind to take pictures that day. A few of the attendees later shared a handful of their photos with me. Stressors being so high there is much I do not remember.

CHAPTER 104
THE BATTLE
OVER THE ESTATE BEGINS

Sometime after Stephen's memorial, I was advised that I would need legal representation. Remembering the kind offers of aid I received from various friends and neighbors, I called our neighbors, Jerry and Carolyn Snowden. They recommended Earl Husted, an attorney friend of theirs from church. Earl started out as my attorney but quickly became a good friend to Gene and me. Whenever an issue arose regarding Stephen's estate Earl was there to offer his counsel and help me understand the legal process involved in a probate administration. At one point, since he was not a trial attorney, he recommended that I engage the services of Greg Lievers to represent me at court hearings. I am profoundly grateful for Earl and Greg's counsel, advice and advocacy on my behalf during this very difficult time.

On May 10, I drove up to Pacific Family Funeral on Crane Street in Lake Elsinore, approximately forty miles north of the ranch. George Helmer and Troy had agreed to meet me there as it was time for Stephen's cremation. It was quite obvious how unwelcome the two men considered me to be but I was not about to let them stop me from saying goodbye to my dearest Lord Tyrant. I cannot remember why Troy and George even had to be there, some sort of witnesses to the cremation I would imagine. I knew why I was there. At the appointed time we were escorted into the room where the cremation occurs. Lying there on a gurney was Stephen's body covered from the neck down by a white sheet-like fabric. I had not seen him since I left the hospital just before he died. Now here he was laying on a gurney silent, cold and gaunt. I said a prayer, leaned down and kissed his cold, smooth forehead and then said, for the last time, "Go with God my love." We all watched as the employee for the crematorium pushed Stephen's body into the waiting furnace. Shaking like a freaking leaf I managed to exit the furnace room. The men suggested we wait at a nearby Denny's restaurant until the cremation and cooling period were completed and then return together to retrieve Stephen's cremains. I have no memory of what we talked about there in the diner. All I remember is that some hours later we returned to the crematorium and that I was not allowed to keep Stephen's cremains. I believe George arranged for Troy to have them. All that remained of Stephen was placed in a plain chocolate brown plastic box. What a bizarre end. The Stevensville, Riverview Cemetery certainly seemed much more appropriate for my dearest Lord Tyrant than this funky little plastic box.

As directed by Stephen's last will and testament George Helmer was appointed by the Probate judge as the administrator of the estate. George selected someone other than me to manage the ranch during the administration process. I was deeply offended that management of what had been Stephen's and my home (and was to be a major part of my inheritance) was placed into someone else's hands. Working at and continuing to manage the ranch would have been the best balm for my aching heart. It hurt even more when the ranch manager treated the property as his personal party place. I would smell barbecue and Gene would say he saw a group of strangers up at the barn saddling horses. When I went outside I could hear people laughing and loud music playing by the pool. Cars and trucks were coming and going before and after all the parties. The peace and quiet of the ranch was gone. One afternoon, the ranch manager rode my favorite horse, Torrey, down to the little rental house and demanded that I give him Stephen's tooth. That was one of the strangest requests I ever heard. I had been told by friends in town that the ranch manager was now claiming to be Stephen's illegitimate son. So his peculiar request for Stephen's extracted tooth made my antenna go on alert. What would he want with a tooth? There was no way in Hell that was I giving anyone my Lord Tyrant's tooth!

Some days later, the ranch manager stole Stephen's 1998 Dodge Ram turbo diesel pickup truck, the Featherlite three-horse trailer and two horses. He also absconded with, for unknown reasons, an assortment of Stephen's mother's linens and miscellaneous other items. When I entered the ranch house it was a complete mess. There were moving boxes along several walls. Someone had been packing Stephen's and my things. When I went down to the master bedroom I found the plastic box of Stephen's cremains sitting in the middle of the bed. As soon as I confirmed the ranch manager had skipped town with the truck and trailer that was designated in Stephen's will to go to Dave Morris, plus the horses, I called the sheriff to report the theft. Our neighbor Jim McClain, who as you may remember was a retired sheriff, assisted me there at the ranch in filing a report with the local sheriff. Two days later we checked with the local sheriff's office to see what was happening. We were informed that no report had ever been filed. There was no theft reported on the books. That made zero sense as we had completed, signed and handed the complaint to the sheriff's deputy who had responded to the call. So no one was even looking for the ranch manager and the stolen items. Monty and Torrey were gone and I had no idea where to find them.

Some weeks later we were told that the ranch manager's sister had convinced him to return all the stolen property. He was supposed to drive back from out of state and deliver the horses, truck, trailer and other stolen items to the ranch. However, the ranch manager apparently did not want to face me or Gene (or maybe the law) because we were told that he had abandoned the stolen property in Norco, California. I needed another driver so Jim McClain volunteered to accompany me to Norco so that we could retrieve what had been stolen. When I started the engine of my car I realized I had almost no gas. I also had no money. Jim likewise did not have any cash on him. As I headed through town I tried to think of a money source since I had no bank account to access. I received a sudden inspiration and turned quickly into the parking lot of Dr. Adair, our dentist. Feeling more than a bit foolish I nonetheless dashed into the office and explained the situation to the office staff. Without another word the receptionist, Sue, and everyone else that worked in the office offered their assistance. They contributed even more money than I had requested and then sent me off with their prayers. I love Valley Center people.

Jim and I found the place in Norco (which is about 75 miles north of the ranch) where the ranch manager had supposedly left all the stolen goods. The trailer and truck were there as was one horse but the eldest Morgan, Monty, was missing. Monty was the first horse born on the ranch back when Stephen and Aline first started it so he had to be about twenty-nine years old. I was heartbroken. Where was poor Monty? Realizing we were not going to find any answers in Norco, Jim hopped in and drove the truck and the trailer back to the ranch. I kept looking up at heaven and saying, "Stephen, where's Monty? What do you want me to do now? Stephen, Monty is missing and I don't know how to find him and bring him home!"

CHAPTER 105
THE WHEREABOUTS
OF STEPHEN'S ASHES AND MONTY

A few weeks later I received a letter from one of Stephen's cousins, Colleen Raty, who lives in Chinook, Montana. The letter said that the ranch manager had informed Stephen's cousins that he was planning a memorial service for Stephen on one of the family ranches in Montana. Several members of the family attended the service and reported that the ranch manager had scattered Stephen's ashes as a part of the service. At the conclusion of the memorial service the ranch manager announced that he planned to walk one of Stephen's old horses (Monty!) to the crest of the nearby hillside and shoot the horse as his version of some sort of American Indian style memorial. The family did not want any part of that ceremony. Stephen, I was thinking, would be appalled. Who the Hell did the ranch manager think he was and how could he have Stephen's ashes? The container from the crematorium had been left in the ranch house. I had taken the container home with me after the ranch manager and all his buddies had vacated the ranch.

So next on my to-do-list was to ascertain whether the box contained Stephen's cremains. I first drove down the hill to the funeral home in Escondido where the memorial service for Stephen had been held. I reassured the staff that I was not there to accuse or alarm anyone. I just needed to know if the contents of the brown box were human cremains. I explained my suspicions that the cremains had been stolen and replaced after the container had been delivered to the administrator of the estate. I added that I needed a professional's help in confirming my hunch. They were not very cooperative. They told me that they were prohibited by law from opening the container. So I drove to the crematorium, Pacific Family Funeral, on Crane Street in Lake Elsinore. Upon entering the facility I asked to speak in private with the manager. I assured the manager that I was not questioning the integrity of their business, repeated my suspicions of what had happened and then explained that I just needed help verifying whether the contents of the container were indeed human ashes.

The manager flat refused to help and asked me to leave. That of course was definitely not going to happen. I stood up and informed him I was not going anywhere until I had verification if my Stephen was in the box or not. When he picked up his phone and called for assistance in expelling me, I opened his office door and, raising my voice, said unless he helped me right then and there I would announce to everyone in their damned building that something was wrong with my beloved's ashes. I demanded that he find someone in their facility to open the container and confirm my suspicions. In that somber, hushed environment the last thing management wanted was some irate woman making a scene. He picked up the phone and asked someone to come to his office. The man who responded to the request was the same man who had performed Stephen's cremation. I repeated my request to him. Without hesitation he opened the container, unsealed the inner plastic bag, peered inside while shaking the contents this way and that and then announced, "These are fireplace ashes. Look, here's a bit of wood and a bent nail." I thanked him profusely and then took my leave.

I was lost in thought as I slowly drove home. At Temecula I pulled off the freeway and drove straight to the Temecula Creek Inn to find my rock. He was, as always, delighted to see me and full of warmth and concern. He took a break from his labors so he could listen to me. I was important to him. I related all that had transpired since breakfast at the ranch. He was outraged at the fraud that was perpetrated and the blatant, uncalled for execution of Monty. He could not comprehend why the ranch manager thought Stephen would approve of his actions. I felt much better after my Gene-o fix.

CHAPTER 106
POST DEATH GRIEF AND AN EPIPHANY

For the first several months, when I would talk to someone about the day Stephen died, I often made a Freudian slip and referred to "the day we died." For a long time after the service I was not sure how I could live through the loss of Stephen and I even struggled somewhat with the temptation of suicide. Living any sort of life while Stephen was dead felt like I was somehow being disloyal. I do not expect anybody to understand but I carried guilt for not dying with him. My guilt was not tied to logic. The only time I obtained some relief was when I fell asleep at night and dreamed that Stephen was alive, healthy and, as usual, upset at me for one thing or another. No matter how angry he seemed to be I cherished his presence in my dreams so much that I could hardly wait to fall back asleep. Very much like the old song says, "I was living in the memory of a love that never was, 'cause I've done everything I know to try to make you mine, and I think I'm going to love you for a long, long time." I was ultimately moved to seek professional help sorting out my feelings and emotions. I went to a Christian psychologist for advice. I opened up and laid out my concerns and what I thought was plaguing my peace of mind. I went several times although I realized during my first session that for me the counselor in question was entirely too lenient in his belief system. I eventually terminated our relationship after giving his version of what God requires considerable thought and prayer.

I wrote several poems to Stephen and about Stephen that helped me sort through my feelings and still feel close to him. I found that this exercise in writing helped me navigate my own personal losses. The following is a message I penned to Stephen as a part of the grieving process:

> Most everywhere I go, I see you or hear you or remember you or just plain miss you. All of which is really a bittersweet irony since you loved and liked me so little. I guess you never asked me to love you but you certainly needed it. And I know you knew you needed me, even when you did not want me. I guess that must have been hard on you. The excessively handsome, extra intelligent, marvelously strong, extraordinarily independent, man among men known as Steve Reeves, who never leaned on anyone much, needed this somewhat ordinary, flawed, left brained, mother nature's child? Yes, that must have amazed and dismayed you.
>
> I wish you could have helped me bypass all the years of fruitless aching for some real affection. But we do not always reap what we sow. My leaving you was the ultimate statement of my despair over unrequited love for you and my very delayed determination to live in spite of your inability to love me. My physical health was warning me to notice my precarious hold on life. Gene could hear me, You could not.
>
> Your Wildflower
> December 21, 2000

Another one of my pieces, written after Stephen died, is entitled, "If There are Tractors in Heaven," and reads as follows:

In your current existence, wherever you are, I wish you all the dreams I could never make come true - could never realize for you. I pray you have the important needs and comforts of course but I also hope you have (or there is) a tractor like the one you always wanted, the earth mover you always hoped to get to use someday. So you can "play in the dirt" in the way of men, shaping, contouring, smoothing or mounding, just as you always hoped to be able to do. I could not give you that, but I wanted to.

I wish you a little ATV to carry you when those oak-like legs get tired or too heavy. I pray you are allowed to raise your voice to God's ears and sing the most beautiful opera imaginable, because you always wished you had trained as an opera singer. I pray the thunder of horse's hooves still quickens your pulse and that your hands still run along the horseflesh you admire. May you always sit a fine horse and breed even better. I pray there are horses and tractors in heaven.

Your Palomino
January 2001

About a year after Stephen died I met Sherrie Ellsworth, a friend of Maddy Beck. Our conversation shifted to my ongoing feelings of distress and guilt over separating from Stephen at such a terrible point just prior to his death. She wiped the whole burden right out of my soul with a simple, very Deborah-like analogy. Sherrie, who had never met me before, said, "You know when you get in the shower and you see a little spider in the corner?" I cocked my head to one side, wondering what she was getting at, and then replied, "Yes." Sherrie continued, "So you get a cup, scoop the spider up and place him somewhere safe, right?" I nodded and wondered how she could know that is exactly what I would have done, what I have always done, whenever I stumbled upon one of God's creatures, no matter how small, in distress. She went on, "You scoop up that spider because he cannot see or understand the disaster that is about to occur in his world." I smiled and agreed. She then applied her analogy directly to me by stating, "God knew what was going to happen in your world so He scooped you up out of harm's way. You were in God's cup - you just did not know it."

In a sudden flash, everything that had occurred since October of 1999 made perfect sense. Nothing I did prevented Gene Stewart from renting our little house. Over my concerns and objections Stephen selected Gene as his renter. God understood that my will to live was inseparably entwined with my life with Stephen. God knew I was heading for a cliff if and when my dearest Lord Tyrant died. I was the spider and Gene the cup in God's gentle hand. Sherrie Ellsworth's little analogy set me free to thank God and enjoy having Gene in my life. What a wonderful a gift. Throughout all of my emotional upheaval, every last tear and all of my regrets, Gene stood beside me allowing me the space and the time I needed to grieve. He was kind, honest and I grew to love him with all my heart. People talk about someone being their rock. Well, my Gene-o was the rock I rebuilt my life on.

CHAPTER 107
EPILOGUE

The Probate judge surprised everyone by deciding that the language in Stephen's will was somewhat vague and ambiguous in so far as his desire that I only receive $50,000 per year for life was concerned. So, after the specific bequests were given out and all the debts, taxes and administration costs were paid, the remaining balance of Stephen's estate was given to me outright and free of trust. I had to sell the ranch because, as I had suspected all those years ago, I could not afford to keep it and cover the higher property taxes, monthly expenses and maintenance costs. Besides, George Helmer, the administrator of the estate, elected to sell all the horses so I really had no use for a horse ranch anymore. George did allow me to participate in the selection of a new owner for my own special filly, Breezy. She was purchased by a Texas ranch owner, Debbie Strong, who loved Breezy the way I loved her.

More than half of Stephen's estate went to the government in the form of estate taxes because we were not legally married and he did not have a well thought out estate plan, just as friends had tried to warn him. I am mentioning this fact in the hopes that it will motivate someone else, who feels no need for estate planning, from losing a large chunk of their estate to the government. It also required more than eighteen months to probate Stephen's estate. A living trust would have been a much easier, less expensive and less time-consuming option.

For those who wonder or are curious, I did not blow the estate of Stephen Lester Reeves within a year as Stephen used to predict. Unfortunately, the collapse of the stock market eight years later did some damage.

I would turn fifty-one years old before I suffered the first of five minor strokes. My doctors later told me that but for my being on a regiment of blood pressure medication at the time any one of the strokes would have caused substantial, permanent disability or even death. I now take Plavix so I avoid even those minor strokes that can take away the use of my hand for a day or two, or make one side of my face sag for a while, or can mess with my speech and memory. I do suffer from expressive aphasia (trouble finding nouns when speaking) which can really be a pain the neck. I am not complaining, I am thanking God for my life.

Naomi currently resides in San Juan Capistrano, California with her longtime boyfriend, Bret Shotwell. She was the closest thing to a daughter that Stephen ever had. He preferred calling her Sky and found her absolutely delightful. He was a gruff sort of stepfather but it was easy for me to see how much he loved her. Lynx lives in Temecula, California and has two beautiful daughters. His daughter, Trinity, was born in 2005 and Savina followed two years later. I have often thought if Stephen had lived, and we were still together, that Trinity and Savina would be the light of his days as they have been for Gene and me. My children have developed into warm, responsible, hard-working adults that any parent would be proud of.

What started out on March 31, 2000, as a marriage of convenience so I could obtain health insurance and save my life, turned out to be the best relationship either Gene or I had experienced. Until his death on January 20, 2014, Gene put my wants and needs before his own and I put his before mine. That arrangement worked like a charm for us.

I will never forget Stephen or the years we spent together. I will love him forever. My life is much simpler now. I used some of the proceeds of sale of the ranch to purchase a smaller home sitting on just under four acres on the western side of Valley Center. With Gene gone, I tend my gardens, care for my animals and keep an eye on my eighty-five year old mother. Although she suffers with dementia she is able to carry on a quite independent life while residing in a small cottage located on my property in Valley Center. I look forward to visits from Lynx, Naomi and my granddaughters, Trinity and Savina. What happens and where we go when death occurs, I do not know. I just hope and pray that there will be horses and tractors in heaven.

VIA CON DIOS MI AMOR

The last picture taken of my dearest Lord Tyrant. We were on our way to his eventful appointment with the doctor. I had a strong urge to take this picture - somehow I knew he would never allow me to take another.

The End

Thank you for reading Steve Reeves - Legends Never Die. If you enjoyed reading my book, would you please take a moment to let me know? I would love to hear from you.

Deborah Reeves Stewart

stevereeveslnd@gmail.com

APPENDIX

Deborah   March 2000

I would like to thank you for bringing love, passion, excitement and adventure into my life when I needed it most.

I will never be able to look at a full moon again without thinking of you and remembering all the loving special sessions that we shared.

I would also like to say that I am sorry and apologize for any hurt that I have caused you through neglect or inconsideration and for not being more sensitive to your needs.

Via Con Dios Con Amor

Steve

The Ranch

The Ranch House

Front view of the Ranch House

The Barn/Horse Stables

Stephen with Torrey at the Barn

One of Stephen's creations

Arrival Interview in Battapaglia, Italy
November 8, 1996

Paparazzi held at bay by Bodyguard Phillipe at the
World Bodybuilding Championship held in Italy December 1996

Accepting a lifetime achievement award for leadership in bodybuilding, health and nutrition

Stephen showing land he once owned in Garner Valley, California, April 1998

Mr. and Mrs. Reeves
Summer of 1994

At David and Jo's home for Thanksgiving 1994

Back Row (left to right): Glen Sunbe, Eddie Sylvestre, John Grimeck, Stephen, George Coates and Charlie Moss
Middle Row (left to right): Angela Grimeck, Millie Dawson, Naomi, Deborah, Jean Warner and Eddie's wife
Front Row (left to right): Russ Warner and Ken Dawson

George Coates, Stephen and Roland Essmaker

Gordon Scott, unknown cowboy, and Stephen
at a Hollywood Collectors Show during the summer of 1993

Picture of Stephen on Torrey taken by professional photographer

Printed in Dunstable, United Kingdom